FREE DVD  FREE DVD

Essential Test Tips DVD from Trivium Test Prep

Dear Customer,

Thank you for purchasing from Cirrus Test Prep! Whether you're looking to join the military, get into college, or advance your career, we're honored to be a part of your journey.

To show our appreciation (and to help you relieve a little of that test-prep stress), we're offering a **FREE *Praxis Essential Test Tips DVD*** by Cirrus Test Prep. Our DVD includes 35 test preparation strategies that will help keep you calm and collected before and during your big exam. All we ask is that you email us your feedback and describe your experience with our product. Amazing, awful, or just so-so: we want to hear what you have to say!

To receive your **FREE *Praxis Essential Test Tips DVD***, please email us at 5star@cirrustestprep.com. Include "Free 5 Star" in the subject line and the following information in your email:

1. The title of the product you purchased.
2. Your rating from 1 – 5 (with 5 being the best).
3. Your feedback about the product, including how our materials helped you meet your goals and ways in which we can improve our products.
4. Your full name and shipping address so we can send your **FREE *Praxis Essential Test Tips DVD***.

If you have any questions or concerns please feel free to contact us directly at 5star@cirrustestprep.com.

Thank you, and good luck with your studies!

---

* Please note that the free DVD is <u>not included</u> with this book. To receive the free DVD, please follow the instructions above.

TExES History 7–12 Study Guide (233):
Test Prep with Practice Questions for the Texas Examinations of Educator Standards

J.G. Cox

Copyright © 2023 by Cirrus Test Prep

ISBN-13: 9781637984185

ALL RIGHTS RESERVED. By purchase of this book, you have been licensed one copy for personal use only. No part of this work may be reproduced, redistributed, or used in any form or by any means without prior written permission of the publisher and copyright owner. Cirrus Test Prep, Trivium Test Prep, Accepted, and Ascencia Test Prep are all imprints of Trivium Test Prep, LLC.

Pearson was not involved in the creation or production of this product, is not in any way affiliated with Cirrus Test Prep, and does not sponsor or endorse this product.

Image(s) used under license from Shutterstock.com and Library of Congress

About the Authors

Alicia Chipman has taught history and social sciences in Chicago, Illinois, since 2003. Having worked with both high school and junior high school students, Alicia has developed curricula to prepare students for AP exams and entrance into the International Baccalaureate diploma program. She is now Student Teacher Supervisor at the Chicago Center for Urban Life and Culture. She obtained her master's degree in Educational Policy at the University of Illinois Urbana-Champaign in 2013.

Caroline Brennan spent several years on the front lines of multilateral diplomacy at the United Nations, working with the International Committee of the Red Cross (ICRC) in humanitarian affairs from 2007 – 2012. Previously, she studied international development, postcolonial theory, and history in Canada, Europe, and North Africa; she obtained her master's degree from the University of Pennsylvania in 2007, specializing in Middle Eastern history.

Sandy Thomson is currently an instructor at Wright Career College and at Park University. She previously worked as a social studies teacher in Tulsa, Oklahoma, in the Union Public Schools from 1997 – 2014, both online and in the traditional education program. She served as the Department Chair from 2009 – 2011.

Tom Brennan is adjunct faculty at Drexel University's Antoinette Westphal College of Media Arts and Design in Philadelphia, Pennsylvania, and an educator with 826NYC, a nonprofit writing center in Brooklyn, New York. He has a decade of editorial experience for print, digital, and web content.

Table of Contents

ONLINE RESOURCES I

INTRODUCTION III

ONE: WORLD HISTORY   **1**

Early Civilizations and the Great Empires 1
World Religions 18
Feudalism through the Era of Expansion 20
Armed Conflicts 49
Global Conflicts 74
Post-Cold War World 103
Practice Questions Answer Key 111
Check Your Understanding Answer Key 113

TWO: UNITED STATES HISTORY   **115**

North America Before European Contact 115
Colonial North America 121
Revolution and the Early United States 131
Civil War, Expansion, and Industry 144
The Gilded Age and the Progressive Era 153

The United States Becomes a Global Power 160
The United States and World War II 166
Postwar and Contemporary United States 169
Political Conservatism, Social Liberalism, and the Twenty-First Century 175
Practice Questions Answer Key 182
Check Your Understanding Answer Key 185

THREE: TEXAS HISTORY   **187**

Precolonial to Texas Revolution 188
Revolution to Statehood 193
Civil War and Reconstruction 201
Early Twentieth Century 210
Modern Texas 213
Answer Key 220

FOUR: FOUNDATIONS, SKILLS, RESEARCH, AND INSTRUCTION   **221**

Historical Perspectives 221
Historical Sources of Information and Perspectives 226

Social Science Inquiry and
Interdisciplinary Perspectives 231
Public Discourse and
Democratic Values 239
Answer Key 244

FIVE: PRACTICE TEST 1   245
Answer Key 271

Online Resources

Cirrus includes online resources with the purchase of this study guide to help you fully prepare for your Texas Examination of Educational Standards (TExES) History 7–12 (233) exam.

Practice Test
In addition to the practice test included in this book, we also offer an online exam. Since many exams today are computer based, practicing your test-taking skills on the computer is a great way to prepare.

Flash Cards
Cirrus's flash cards allow you to review important terms easily on your computer or smartphone.

From Stress to Success
Watch "From Stress to Success," a brief but insightful YouTube video that offers the tips, tricks, and secrets experts use to score higher on the exam.

Reviews
Leave a review, send us helpful feedback, or sign up for Cirrus promotions—including free books!

Access these materials at:
www.cirrustestprep.com/texes-history-online-resources

Introduction

Congratulations on choosing to take the Texas Examination of Educational Standards (TExES) History 7–12 (233) Exam! By purchasing this book, you've taken a vital step toward becoming a history teacher.

This guide will provide you with a detailed overview of the TExES history, so you know exactly what to expect on test day. We'll take you through all the concepts covered on the test and give you the opportunity to test your knowledge with practice questions. Even if it's been a while since you last took a major test, don't worry; we'll make sure you're more than ready!

What is the TExES History?

TExES tests are a part of teaching certification in Texas. In conjunction with completion of an educator preparation program, TExES exam scores are used to complete a state application for teacher certification. The history exam ensures that the examinee has the skills and knowledge necessary to become an educator of history in Texas public schools.

What's on the TExES History?

The TExES is a 100-question, multiple-choice test designed to assess whether you possess the knowledge and skills necessary to become a history educator in the state of Texas. The test's content covers four domains, or concepts, that are illustrated in the following table. The number of questions specific to each domain is approximate. You have a maximum of five hours to complete the test.

What's on the TExES History 7–12 (233)?

Domain	Approximate Number of Questions per Subject	Percentage
World History	30	30%
US History	36	36%
Texas History	20	20%
Social Studies Foundations, Skills, Research, and Instruction	14	14%
Total	**Always 100**	**5 hours**

How is the TExES Scored?

On the TExES, the number of correctly answered questions are used to create your scaled score. Scores are scaled to a number in the range 100 – 300, a passing score being 240. The score shows your performance on the test as a whole and is scaled to allow comparison across various versions of the tests. There is no penalty for guessing on TExES tests, so be sure to eliminate answer choices and answer every question. If you still do not know the answer, guess; you may get it right! Keep in mind that about twenty multiple-choice questions are experimental questions for the purpose of the TExES test-makers and will not count toward your overall score. However, as those questions are not indicated on the test, you must respond to every question.

Your score report will be available online through your ETS account two to three weeks after your testing date. Scores are automatically made available to TEA and EPP, so you do not have to manually report your scores.

How is the TExES Administered?

TExES exams are administered at testing centers throughout Texas and the United States. Check http://cms.texes-ets.org/cat/testcenters/ for a testing center near you. The TExES history exam is a computerized test offered continuously throughout the year. After you set up an account at http://cms.texes-ets.org/youraccount/, you can locate testing centers, register for a test, or find instructions for registering via mail or phone.

On the day of your test, be sure to bring your admission ticket (which is available on your ETS account) and valid photo ID. You are allowed no personal effects in the testing area. Cell phones and other electronic, photographic, recording, or listening devices are not permitted in the testing center at all, and bringing those items may be cause for dismissal, forfeiture of your testing fees, and cancellation of your scores. For details on to expect at your testing center, refer to http://cms.texes-ets.org/texes/dayofthetest/day-test-general-guidelines/.

About Cirrus Test Prep

Cirrus Test Prep study guides are designed by current and former educators and are tailored to meet your needs as an incoming educator. Our guides offer all of the resources necessary to help you pass teacher certification tests across the nation.

Cirrus clouds are graceful, wispy clouds characterized by their high altitude. Just like cirrus clouds, Cirrus Test Prep's goal is to help educators "aim high" when it comes to obtaining their teacher certification and entering the classroom.

About This Guide

This guide will help you master the most important test topics and also develop critical test-taking skills. We have built features into our books to prepare you for your tests and increase your score. Along with a detailed summary of the test's format, content, and scoring, we offer an in-depth overview of the content knowledge required to pass the test. Our sidebars provide interesting information, highlight key concepts, and review content so that you can solidify your understanding of the exam's concepts. Test your knowledge with sample questions and detailed answer explanations in the text that help you think through the problems on the exam, and with two full-length practice tests that reflect the content and format of the Praxis. We're pleased you've chosen Cirrus to be a part of your professional journey!

World History

EARLY CIVILIZATIONS AND THE GREAT EMPIRES

PALEOLITHIC AND NEOLITHIC ERAS

The earliest humans were hunter-gatherers until the development of agriculture in about 11,000 BCE. They began migrating from Africa 60,000 – 70,000 years ago, gradually spreading out across the continents in several waves of migration throughout Europe and Asia and eventually into Australia, the Pacific Islands, and the Americas.

Human history begins with the **Paleolithic Era** followed by the **Neolithic period**.

Early **hominids** of the Paleolithic Era:

- *Australopithecus*
- *Homo habilis* (descended from *Australopithecus*)
- *Homo erectus* (descended from *Australopithecus*)
- *Homo neanderthalensis* (descended from *Australopithecus*)
- *Homo sapiens sapiens* (descended from *Australopithecus*; the modern-day human)

All are now extinct, save for us, *Homo sapiens*.

Figure 1.1. Early Hominids

DID YOU KNOW?

Evidence suggests that *Homo sapiens sapiens* and *Homo neanderthalensis* coexisted.

Table 1.1. The Paleolithic and Neolithic Eras

Paleolithic Era	Neolithic Era
▶ before agricultural development and settled communities ▶ the use of tools exhibited by hominids (up to and including our ancestors) ▶ rudimentary human technology based on stone; referred to as the **Old Stone Age**. ▶ took place before 11,000 BCE	▶ humans began settling communities, developing agricultural practices, and domesticating animals ▶ notable technological advancements (tools, weapons, and other metal objects) made by working with copper and tin; the start of the **Bronze Age** ▶ also referred to as the *New Stone Age* ▶ all species of humans extinct except *Homo sapiens sapiens* ▶ behavioral and technological changes, such as the invention of the wheel ▶ began approximately 11,000 – 10,500 BCE

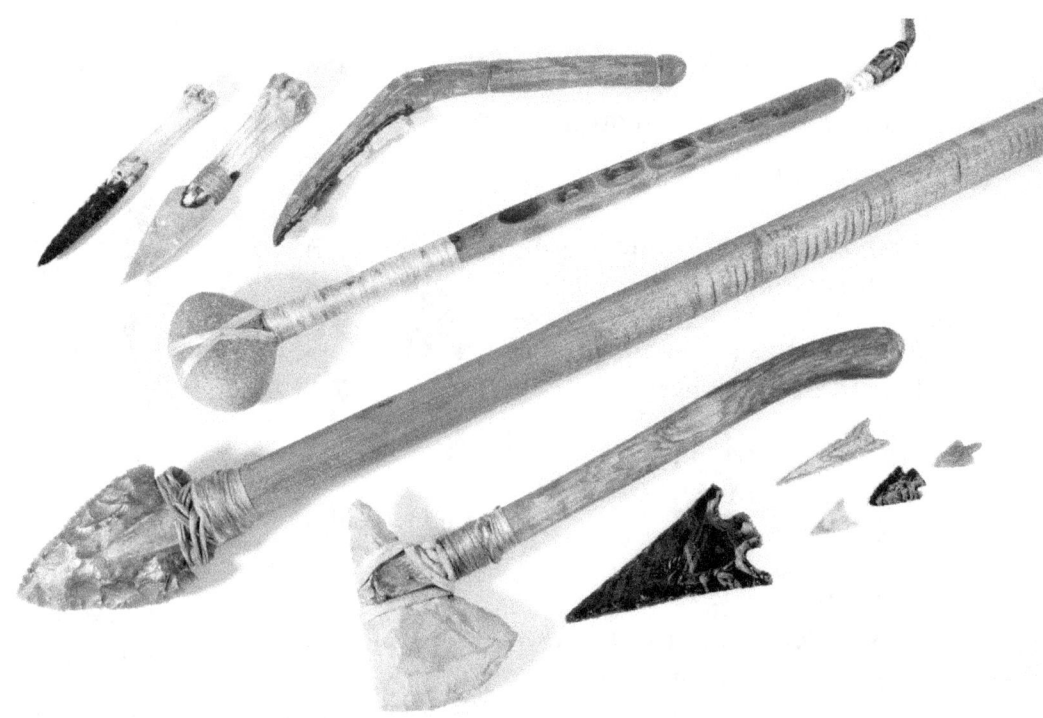

Figure 1.2. Early Tools

Middle East and Egypt

Beginning in the Near East, settled societies organized into larger centralized communities. These were characterized by early social stratification and rule of law. The earliest known examples of these were in the **Fertile Crescent**, the area in North Africa and Southwest Asia stretching from Egypt through the Levant and into Mesopotamia.

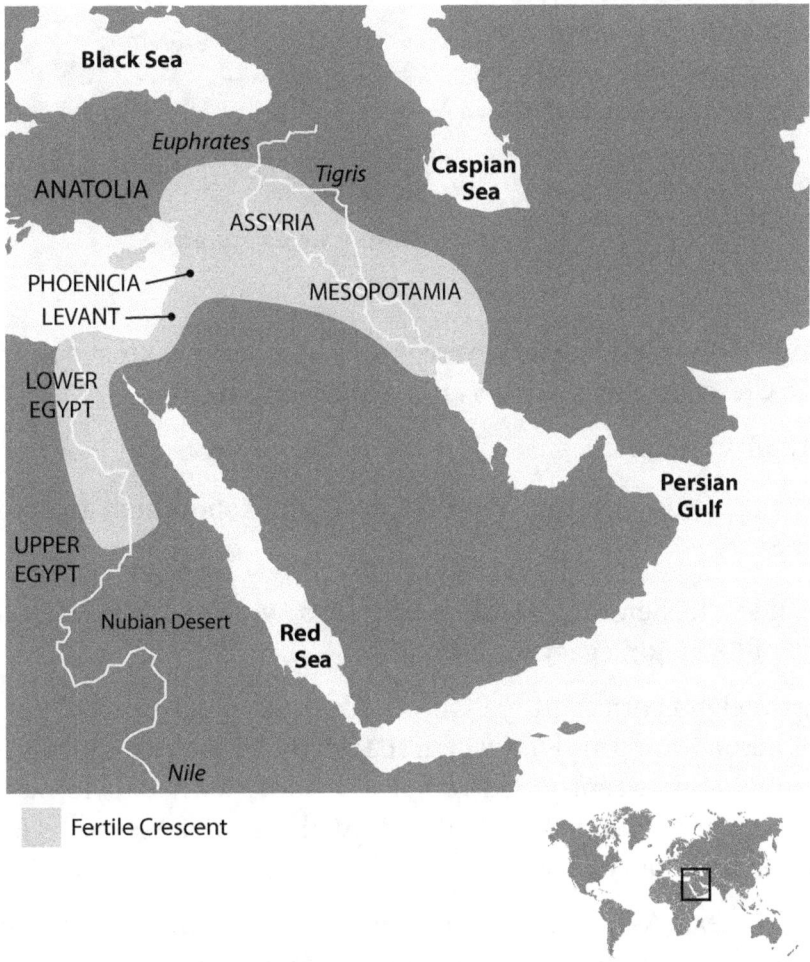

Figure 1.3. Fertile Crescent

Around 2500 BCE (or possibly earlier) the **Sumerians** emerged in the Near East (eventually expanding into parts of Mesopotamia). By developing irrigation and advanced agriculture, they were able to support settled areas that developed into city-states and eventually major cities like Uruk.

The Sumerians are known especially for the following:

- cuneiform: the earliest known example of writing to use characters to form words

- early education, literary, and artistic developments (the *Epic of Gilgamesh*, for example); made possible by the Sumerian's development of cuneiform
- architectural achievements (ziggurats, for example)
- the creation of city-states and advanced governance and administration; also facilitated by cuneiform as a written language
- the potter's wheel, early astronomy, mathematics, religious thought

Figure 1.4. Ziggurats

Eventually the Sumerians were overcome by Semitic-speaking, nomadic peoples in the Fertile Crescent: the result was the **Akkadian Empire**.

The Akkadian Empire:

- grew to encompass much of the Levant, Mesopotamia, and parts of Persia;
- includes the Semitic Akkadian language, which adopted cuneiform, as one of its major legacies.

Around the eighteenth century BCE, the Akkadians had given way to **Babylonia** in southern Mesopotamia and **Assyria** in the north. These two civilizations would develop roughly concurrently and remain at odds, with Babylonia eventually coming under Assyrian domination until the final defeat of Assyria by Babylonia in 612 BCE in the battle of Nineveh, the Assyrian capital.

Before its defeat, Assyria had developed as a powerful city-state in northern Mesopotamia. The Assyrians had based much of their culture on the Sumerian and Akkadian legacies, contributing unique sculpture and jewelry, establishing military dominance, and playing an important role in regional trade.

> **HELPFUL HINT**
>
> Settled communities needed the reliable sources of food and fresh water a temperate climate could provide. Surpluses of food enabled civilization and culture, not just survival.

At odds with Babylonia over the centuries, the Assyrian Empire had grown to encompass most of the Fertile Crescent. The Assyrian identity persists to this day among the (widely persecuted) Assyrian people in Iraq, Syria, Turkey, and Iran.

Around 1200 BCE, during a time of instability in Mesopotamia, the region became vulnerable to the **Hittites** from Anatolia.

The Hittites are especially known for the following:

- developing in the Bronze Age but flourishing in the **Iron Age**
- developing expertise in metallurgy to create strong weapons
- mastering horsemanship
- inventing chariots
- becoming a strong military power (due to their advancements in the Iron Age)

As a result, the Hittites became a threat to both the Assyrians and, later, the Egyptians (see below). Not only did these empires risk losing land, they also lost control of trade routes throughout the Fertile Crescent. Eventually, however, Assyria grew strong enough to overcome the Hittites.

Like Assyria, Babylonia inherited the Akkadian language and used the Sumerian language in religious settings; it also inherited other elements of Sumerian civilization and developed them further.

Major achievements in Babylonia included:

- the development of courts in the eighteenth century BCE by King Hammurabi
- the development of an early codified rule of law—**the Code of Hammurabi**—which meted out justice on an equal basis: "an eye for an eye, a tooth for a tooth"
- the continuation of settled urban development supported by organized agriculture, warfare, administration, and justice
- the creation of Babylon as a major ancient city
- the development of more advanced astronomy, medicine, mathematics, philosophy, and art (particularly in working with clay, building bricks, and bas relief)
- literature, including developing the Sumerian poetry that was the basis for the *Epic of Gilgamesh* into the extended work we know today

After the fall of Nineveh, Babylonia would control Mesopotamia until the fall of Babylon to the Persian Achaemenid Empire in Persia in 539 BCE (see below).

> **DID YOU KNOW?**
>
> According to the Smithsonian, more lines from the *Epic of Gilgamesh* have been discovered in stone fragments in Iraq as recently as 2011.

Meanwhile, development had been under way in the **Nile Valley** in ancient **Egypt**. Despite the surrounding Sahara Desert, the fertile land on the banks of the

Nile River lent itself to agriculture. The early Egyptians were able to develop settled communities thanks to agriculture and irrigation.

The ancient Egyptians:

- emerged as early as 5000 BCE
- are known for their pyramids, art, and pictorial writing (**hieroglyphs**)
- were united under one monarch, or **pharaoh**, dating to the First Dynasty, around 3000 BCE

Civilizations developed on the Upper and Lower Nile, unifying under the early dynasties, which established the Egyptian capital at **Memphis**.

By the Fourth Dynasty, Egypt's civilizational institutions, written language, art, and architecture were well developed. It was during this period that the famous **pyramids** were erected at Giza. These structures were actually burial tombs for the Pharaohs Khufu, Khafre, and Menkaure circa 2400 – 2500 BCE. In addition, the religious framework of ancient Egypt had become established, with a complex mythology of various gods.

> **CHECK YOUR UNDERSTANDING #1**
>
> What were the contributions of the early Middle Eastern civilizations? List several.

Following this period, around 2200 BCE, Egypt became increasingly unstable. Eventually fighters from the city of Thebes took over, establishing the Eleventh Dynasty. The subsequent Twelfth Dynasty took control of Nubia (now Sudan), an area rich in gold and other materials. Egypt grew in power and reached its apex during the Eighteenth Dynasty, between 1550 and 1290 BCE. Led by the powerful Pharaoh **Thutmose III**, Egypt expanded into the Levant.

Later, **King Akhenaten (Amenhotep IV)** abolished the Egyptian religion, establishing a cult of the sun—Aten—linked to himself. During this period Egypt saw a surge of iconoclastic art and sculpture. However, Akhenaten's successors, particularly Ramesses I and Ramesses II, founded the Nineteenth Dynasty and returned to traditional values.

Figure 1.5. Egyptian Hieroglyphs

Under **Ramesses II**, Egypt battled the aggressive Hittites in the Levant, reaching a stalemate. Egypt eventually fell into decline, losing control of the Levant and ultimately falling to Assyria.

ASIA

Meanwhile, early civilizations also developed farther east. The **Indus Valley Civilization** flourished in the Indian subcontinent and the Indus and Ganges river basins. The **Harappan** civilization was based in Punjab from around 3000 BCE.

The Harappan civilization is known for the following:

- creating the major cities of **Harappa** and **Mohenjo-daro**, which may be the earliest planned cities in the world and featured grid systems indicative of detailed urban planning

- trade links between the civilizations, as evidenced by Harappan objects found in Mesopotamia

Centuries later, concurrent with the Roman Empire, the **Gupta Empire** emerged in India. The Gupta Empire introduced the Golden Age of India, characterized by its strong economy due to active trade by sea with China, East Africa, and the Middle East.

- Traded goods included spices, ivory, silk, cotton, and iron, which was highly profitable as an export.

- The Guptas encouraged music, art, architecture, and Sanskrit literature and philosophy.

- The empire, practitioners of Hinduism, was tolerant of Buddhists and Jains.

Organized administration and rule of law made it possible for **Chandragupta II** to govern a large territory throughout the Subcontinent. However, by 550 CE, invasions from the north by the Huns and internal conflicts within the Subcontinent led to imperial decline.

> **DID YOU KNOW?**
>
> Chandragupta II was considered a benevolent ruler and earned admiration for providing free hospitals and rest houses.

In China, the **Shang Dynasty**, the first known dynasty, ruled the **Huang He** or **Yellow River** area around the second millennium BCE.

Achievements of the Shang Dynasty include:

- developing the earliest known Chinese writing, which helped unite Chinese-speaking people throughout the region

- the use of bronze technology, horses, wheeled technology, walled cities, and other advances beyond those of the Neolithic societies

Around 1056 BCE the Zhou Dynasty emerged. It succeeded the Shang and expanded Chinese civilization to the **Chiang Jiang (Yangtze River)** region.

The Zhou Dynasty is known for:

- developing a social and political infrastructure in China in which family aristocracies controlled the country, with the capital at Hao (near Xi'an)

- tracts of land throughout the country controlled by ancestral cults in a hierarchy similar to later European feudalism

- setting the foundation for hierarchical rule and social stratification

DID YOU KNOW?

Shared customs like the use of silkworms, jade, chopsticks, and the practice of Confucianism are also indications of early Chinese unity.

The unstable period toward the end of the Zhou Dynasty is known as the **Spring and Autumn Period**. During this time **Confucius** (c. 551 – 479 BCE) lived. His teachings would be the basis for Confucianism, the foundational Chinese philosophy emphasizing harmony and respect for hierarchy.

Figure 1.6. Confucius

DID YOU KNOW?

The concept of the **Mandate of Heaven**, in which the emperor had a divine mandate to rule, emerged from the understanding that land was divinely inherited.

Following the chaotic **Warring States Period** (c. 475 – 221 BCE) the short-lived but influential **Qin Dynasty** emerged, unifying disparate Chinese civilizations and regions under the first Emperor, **Qin Shi Huang** (also known as **Shihuangdi**).

The Qin dynasty (221 – 206 BCE) was characterized by:

- a centralized administration
- expanded infrastructure
- standardized weights and measures
- standardized writing
- standardized currency
- strict imperial control

The administrative bureaucracy established by the emperor was the foundation of Chinese administration until the twentieth century.

During the Qin Dynasty, China expanded as far south as Vietnam. In addition, Emperor Qin Shi Huang constructed the **Great Wall of China**. His tomb is guarded by the famous **terracotta figurines**.

Figure 1.7. Great Wall of China

Despite the short length of the Qin Dynasty, it had a lasting impact on Chinese organization. The **Han Dynasty** took over in 206 for the next 300 years (206 BCE – 220 CE), retaining Qin administrative organization and adding Confucian ideals of hierarchy and harmony.

The Han prized education in the Confucian tradition. The idea that educated men should control administrative government began to take root in China. Women were not included in politics or administration.

The Americas

Prehistoric peoples migrated to the Americas from Asia during the Paleolithic period, and evidence of their presence dates to 13,000 years ago. Remnants of the **Clovis** people from this time have been found in New Mexico; however, recent findings in Canada suggest that prehistoric peoples may have come to North America even earlier—about 13,300 years ago.

- Migration from Asia was gradual, probably occurring over hundreds or thousands of years.

- Early humans likely crossed by land from Siberia to Alaska, while some may even have had naval capabilities and arrived by boat.

- Gradually, humans spread throughout the hemisphere.

From around 1200 BCE, the **Olmec** civilization developed on the Mexican Gulf Coast. Its massive sculptures reflect complex religious and spiritual beliefs. Later civilizations in Mexico included the **Zapotecs**, **Mixtecs**, **Toltecs**, and **Mayas** in the Yucatán peninsula. Throughout Mesoamerica, civilizations had developed irrigation to expand and enrich agriculture, similar to developments in the Fertile Crescent.

Meanwhile, in South America, artistic evidence remains of the Chavin, Moche, and Nazca peoples, who preceded the later Inca civilization and Empire.

The art produced by the Chavin, Moche, and Nazca peoples each had distinct features:

- The **Chavin** style, which was complex, focused on animals and went on to influence Andean art.

- The **Moche** people left behind complicated ceramics that are comparable to Hellenic artifacts.

- Enormous sketches in the ground, known as the famous Nazca lines, are visible only from the air. How they were constructed by the **Nazca** peoples remains a mystery.

Figure 1.8. Nazca Lines

In North America, the remains of mounds in the Mississippi Valley region may be evidence of ancient spiritual structures. For more discussion of precolonial North American peoples, please see Chapter One, "United States History."

PERSIA AND GREECE

The Persian Emperor **Cyrus**, founder of the **Achaemenid Empire**, conquered the Babylonians in the sixth century BCE. His son **Darius** extended Persian rule from the Indus Valley to Egypt, and north to Anatolia by about 400 BCE, where the Persians encountered the ancient Greeks.

Known for its fundamental impact on Western civilization to this day, the neighboring Greek, or **Hellenic civilization**, included political, philosophical, and mathematical thought; art and architecture; and poetry and theater.

> **CHECK YOUR UNDERSTANDING #2**
>
> How is Greek philosophy and its focus on reason important in modern culture?

Greece was comprised of city-states like Athens, the first known democracy, and the military state Sparta. Historically these city-states had been rivals; however, they temporarily united to come to the aid of Ionian Greeks in Anatolia under Persian rule and drive Persia from Greece.

In Anatolia, the Persian king Xerxes led two campaigns against Greek forces. The Greeks held the Persians at bay, and much of Greece became unified under Athens following the war. The Persians had been decisively defeated at the battles of **Marathon** (490 BCE) and Salamis (480 BCE) around 460 BCE. It was during this period, the **Golden Age** of Greek civilization, that much of the Hellenic art, architecture, and philosophy known today emerged.

Democracy in the Hellenic civilization was participatory rather than representative: instead of being elected, officials were chosen by groups. Of the many small political bodies, Athens was the strongest. Under the Athenian leaders Pericles and Ephialtes, Athens became a revolutionary democracy controlled by the poor and working classes.

> **DID YOU KNOW?**
>
> The word political comes from the Greek word **polis** meaning "city-state" or "community." The term democracy comes from the Greek word **demokratia**—"people power."

During the Golden Age and into the fourth century BCE, numerous achievements took place. Many of these would go on to influence western society:

- The **Parthenon** was built, as were other masterpieces of ancient Greek sculpture and architecture.

- **Socrates** began teaching philosophy, influencing later philosophers, like **Plato**, who founded the Academy where figures such as **Aristotle** emerged. This established the basis for modern western philosophical and political thought.

▶ Playwrights like Sophocles, Euripides, and Aeschylus emerged; their work influenced later western literature.

Figure 1.9. The Parthenon

Despite its status as a democracy, Athens was not fully democratic: women did not have a place in politics, and Athenians practiced slavery. Furthermore, those men eligible to participate in political life had to prove that both of their parents were Athenian (the criterion of double descent).

Toward the end of the fifth century BCE, Athens and Sparta were at odds once again during the **Peloponnesian War** (431 – 404 BCE), which involved most of the Hellenic world and ultimately crippled the Athenian democracy permanently.

Instability permitted the rise of the northern state of Macedon, and in the fourth century BCE, Philip II of Macedonia was able to take over most of Greece. His son **Alexander** (later known as Alexander the Great) would go on to conquer Persia, spreading Greek civilization throughout much of western and central Asia.

ROME

Meanwhile, in Italy, the ancient Romans had begun consolidating their power. The city of **Rome** was founded as early as the eighth century BCE and became strong thanks to its importance as a trade route for the Greeks and other Mediterranean peoples. Early Roman culture drew from the **Etruscans**, Indigenous inhabitants of the Italian peninsula, and the Greeks, from whom it borrowed elements of architecture, art, language, and even religion.

Originally a kingdom, Rome became a republic under Lucius Junius Brutus in 509 BCE. As a **republic**, Rome elected lawmakers (senators) to the **Senate**. Economically powerful Rome began conquering areas around the Mediterranean with its increasingly powerful military, expanding westward to North Africa in the **Punic Wars** (264 – 146 BCE) against its rival Carthage (in present-day Tunisia).

With the conquest of territory and expansion of trade came increased slavery and the displacement of Rome's working class (**Plebeians**). At the same time, the wealthy ruling class (**Patricians**) became more powerful and corrupt. Resulting protest movements led by the tribunes Gaius and Tiberius led to legislative reform and republican stabilization, strengthening the republic by the first century BCE.

> **DID YOU KNOW?**
>
> The Romans developed highly advanced infrastructure, including aqueducts and roads. Some remain in use to this day!

The increasingly diversified republic, while militarily and economically strong, was still divided:

- the wealthy ruling class (the **Optimates**, or "the best")
- the working, the poor, and the military (the **Populare**, "the people"), who favored more democratization

As the Senate weakened due to its own corruption, the First Triumvirate of the military leaders **Gaius Julius Caesar** and Gnaeus Pompeius Magnus (Pompey the Great), and the wealthy citizen Marcus Licinius Crassus consolidated their rule of the republic. Pompey and Crassus belonged to the Optimate class, while Julius Caesar, a popular military leader, was firmly of the Populare.

Caesar had proven himself in the widely chronicled conquest of Gaul (today, France), and was respected and beloved by the military for his personal devotion to his troops. Meanwhile, Crassus was the wealthiest man in Rome, controlling most of the political class. Despite his wealth and though he had played a role in the defeat of the widespread slave rebellion led by the gladiator **Spartacus**, Crassus was unpopular among the Populare and was not regarded as a military leader on the level of Caesar.

Pompey had led successful missions conquering territory for Rome in Syria and elsewhere in the Levant. He also took credit for defeating Spartacus, though he played less of a role than Crassus, which caused a rift between the two.

With resentment between Crassus and Pompey over credit for the defeat of Spartacus, Crassus's insecurity over his perception as a military leader, and Caesar's popularity among the Populare, the Triumvirate was short-lived. Crassus was killed fighting the Parthians in Turkey in 53 BCE, at which point Pompey and Caesar declared war upon each other. The two fought in Greece where Pompey was defeated, fled to Egypt, and assassinated.

Forcing the corrupt Senate to give him control, Caesar began to transition Rome from a republic (if, at that point, in name only) to what would become an empire. Caesar was assassinated by a group of senators led by Brutus and Cassius in 44 BCE. However, in that short time he had been able to consolidate and centralize imperial control.

His cousin, **Marcus Antonius (Mark Antony)**, his friend Marcus Aemilius Lepidus, and his nephew **Gaius Octavius Thurinus (Octavian)** defeated Brutus and Cassius two years later at the Battle of Philippi, forming the Second Triumvirate.

Lepidus was sent from Rome to Hispania (Spain) and Africa while Mark Antony and Octavian split control of Rome between east and west, respectively. However, the two went to war after Antony became involved with the Egyptian queen Cleopatra, upsetting the balance of power. Octavian defeated Antony and Cleopatra, taking control of Rome in 31 BCE. He took the name **Augustus Caesar** when the Senate gave him supreme power in 27 BCE, becoming the first Roman emperor and effectively starting the Roman Empire.

At this time, Rome reached the height of its power, and the Mediterranean region enjoyed a period of stability known as the **Pax Romana**. Rome controlled the entire Mediterranean region and lands stretching as far north as Germany and Britain, territory into the Balkans, far into the Middle East, Egypt, North Africa, and Iberia.

> **CHECK YOUR UNDERSTANDING #3**
>
> How did social divisions emerge in the republic of Rome and ultimately lead to the creation of the Roman Empire?

In this time of relative peace and prosperity, Latin literature flourished, as did art, architecture, philosophy, mathematics, science, and international trade throughout Rome and beyond into Asia and Africa.

A series of emperors would follow and Rome remained a major world power, but it would never again reach the height of prosperity and stability that it did under Augustus.

It was during the time of Augustus that a Jewish carpenter in Palestine, named Jesus, began teaching that he was the son of the Jewish God and that his death would provide salvation for all of humanity. Jesus was eventually crucified. Followers of **Jesus Christ**, called Christians, preached his teachings throughout Rome. Despite the persecution of Christians, the concept of forgiveness of sin became popular and **Christianity** would eventually become the official religion of Rome. Christianity's universal appeal and applicability to people of diverse backgrounds would allow it to spread quickly.

By 300 CE, Rome was in decline. Following a series of unstable administrations, **Diocletian** (284 – 305 CE) took over as emperor, effectively dividing the empire into two: the Western Roman Empire and the Eastern Roman Empire.

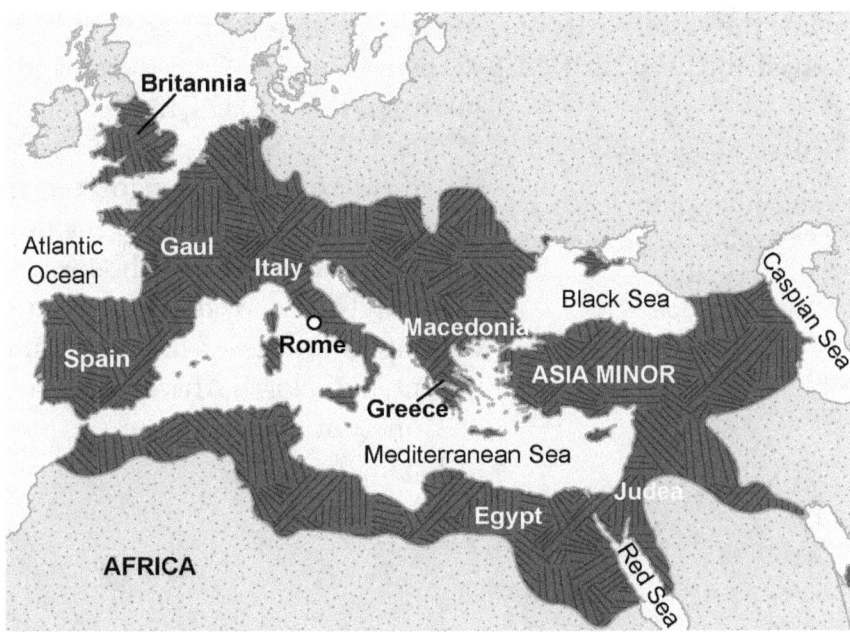

Figure 1.10. Pax Romana

Diocletian reestablished some stability and more effective administration, creating a loose power-sharing agreement throughout the empire. The Christian **Constantine** took over the eastern half of the empire, establishing a new capital at **Constantinople** and Christianity as an official religion. The ambitious Constantine reconquered the Western Roman Empire and reunited the empire in 324 CE. The capital remained at Constantinople, and the balance of power and stability shifted to the east.

This political shift enabled the western (later, Catholic) Church to gain power in Rome. One of Jesus Christ's followers, Peter, was considered to be the first **pope**, or leader of Christian ministry. He had been executed in Rome in 67 CE after a lifetime of spreading the religion. Since then, the city has been a base of Christianity and home to the **Vatican**, the seat of the Catholic Church. Over time, the Catholic Church would become one of the most powerful political entities in the world. Even today, following several schisms in Christianity, there are around one billion Catholics worldwide.

The western part of the Roman Empire gradually fell into disarray. A weakening Rome had created security agreements with different European clans like the **Anglo-Saxons**, the **Franks**, the **Visigoths**, the **Ostrogoths**, and the **Slavs**, among others, to protect its western and northern borders.

Eventually, these groups rebelled against the government and what was left of the Roman Empire in the west finally fell. In Western Europe, the last Roman emperor was killed in 476 CE, marking the end of the empire. The west dissolved into territories controlled by these and other tribes.

Meanwhile the eastern part of the Roman Empire, with its capital at Constantinople, evolved into the unified **Byzantine Empire**. The Byzantine Emperor **Justinian** (527 – 565 CE) re-conquered parts of North Africa, Egypt, and Greece, established rule of law, reinvigorated trade with China, and built the Hagia Sophia, the cathedral and center of orthodox Christianity. Ultimately, the Byzantines would control varying amounts of land in Anatolia, the Levant, and North Africa until the conquest of Constantinople by the Ottoman Turks in 1453.

> **DID YOU KNOW?**
>
> These clans and others from Central Asia were able to defeat the Romans in the north and settle in Europe, thanks to their equestrian skills, superior wheels, and iron technology.

Figure 1.11. Hagia Sophia

Justinian also continued the establishment of Christianity, rebuilding the Hagia Sophia and eliminating the last vestiges of the Greco-Roman religion and competing Christian sects. However, over time, differences in doctrine between the church in Rome and Christians in Constantinople would give way to a schism, creating the Roman Catholic Church and the Greek Orthodox Church.

During the early Middle Ages in Europe and the Byzantine Empire, the roots of another civilization were developing in the Arabian Peninsula. In the seventh century, the Prophet Muhammad began teaching **Islam**. Based on the teachings of Judaism and Christianity, Islam presented as the final version of these two religions, evolving its own set of laws and philosophical teachings. Like Christianity, it held universal appeal.

The process of converting to Islam and practicing the faith was (and is) considered easy. The religion transcends national and ethnic differences and offers the possibility of redemption, forgiveness of sins, and a pleasant afterlife. Furthermore, due to ideological similarities, Muslims were willing to accept Jews and Christians as **People of the Book** rather than forcing their conversion, enabling their later conquest of Southwest Asia and facilitating relationships in the region.

Leading a small group of followers out of the desert to conquer the Arabian cities of Mecca and Medina, where they would establish the beginnings of the **Caliphate**, Muhammad's followers would later come to control Southwest Asia and North Africa.

> **DID YOU KNOW?**
>
> The Caliphate is the political embodiment of the society envisioned in Islam.

PRACTICE QUESTIONS

1) **What is required for a settled community?**

   A. domesticated animals

   B. a source of fresh water

   C. technology

   D. weapons

2) **What is the earliest known form of writing to use characters to create words?**

   A. cuneiform, developed by the Egyptians

   B. cuneiform, developed by the Sumerians

   C. hieroglyphs, developed by the Egyptians

   D. hieroglyphs, developed by the Sumerians

3) **The Shang and Zhou Dynasties are particularly relevant in Chinese history for their contributions in**

   A. developing Chinese administration.

   B. centralizing Chinese imperial power as symbolized through the terracotta figurines in the imperial tombs.

   C. forming a Chinese identity through the development of written language, the emperor's Mandate of Heaven, and fostering Confucianism.

   D. ensuring China's safety by building the Great Wall of China.

4) Which of the following did the Athenian concept of democracy embrace?
   A. participatory democracy, permitting the poor to dominate the process rather than the elites
   B. an anonymous electoral process similar to that of the United States in which officials were elected
   C. people of all backgrounds, so that all residents of Athens had a stake in the political process
   D. an educated electorate in order to ensure the best possible decision-making

5) How did Julius Caesar rise to and retain power?
   A. He invaded Rome with his armies from Gaul and used his military resources to control the empire.
   B. He was elected president of the Senate by the people thanks to political support throughout the Republic.
   C. He took control of the Senate and maintained control of Rome thanks to his charisma and widespread popularity among the people.
   D. As part of the Triumvirate, he was guaranteed a leadership position and the support of Crassus and Pompey.

WORLD RELIGIONS

JUDAISM

Judaism was the first **monotheistic** religion. Its adherents believe in only *one* god, Yahweh. It is believed that God came to the Hebrew Abraham and that the Hebrews—the Jews—were to be God's *chosen people*, to serve as an example to the world.

Later, Moses would lead the Jews out of slavery in Egypt, and God gave him **Ten Commandments**, or laws, which would become the basis of Judeo-Christian and Islamic moral codes. Notably, these moral codes applied to all people, including slaves. In addition to confirming the singular nature of God, the Ten Commandments laid out social rules for an organized society under that one god: to refrain from theft and murder and to honor one's parents, among others.

Judaism's holy texts are the **Torah** and the **Talmud** (religious and civil law, respectively). There are different branches of Judaism with varying teachings, including Orthodox, Conservative, and Reform Judaism, among others.

CHRISTIANITY

In Roman Palestine, the Jewish carpenter Jesus taught that he was the son of the singular, Jewish God and gained many followers. According to Christian belief:

▶ Jesus was crucified and died so that all mankind may be forgiven for their sins.

- Jesus rose from the dead three days after his crucifixion (the **Resurrection**) and ascended to heaven
  ▷ Christians celebrate the Resurrection on Easter Sunday.
- Jesus was miraculously born from a virgin mother (the **Virgin Mary**)
- God is made up of the Father, the Son, and the Holy Spirit—the **Holy Trinity.**

The **Catholic Church** is led by the pope and descended from the early western Church that followed the Schism of 1054, when theological disagreement divided the Church into the western Catholic Church and **Eastern Orthodox** Christianity.

Later in Western Europe, the **Protestant Reformation** gave rise to other forms of Protestant, or non-Catholic, Christianity.

ISLAM

Islam is rooted in the Arabian Peninsula. Its faithful—Muslims—believe that the angel Gabriel spoke to the **Prophet Muhammad**, transmitting the literal word of **Allah** (God), which was later written down as the **Qur'an**.

Muhammad is considered by Muslims to be the final prophet of the god of the Jews and Christians, and Islam shares similar moral teachings. Islam recognizes leaders like Abraham, Moses, and Jesus, but unlike Christianity, views Jesus as a prophet, not as the son of God.

The Prophet Muhammad was a religious, military, and political leader. By conquering the Arabian Peninsula and eventually other parts of the Middle East, he protected the **People of the Book**—Jews and Christians. After his death, discord among his followers resulted in the **Sunni-Shi'a Schism** over his succession and some teachings. To this day, deep divisions remain between many Sunnis and Shi'ites. Like Judaism, Islam also has a book of legal teachings called the Hadith.

> **CHECK YOUR UNDERSTANDING #4**
>
> Explain monotheism. What are the major monotheistic religions and who are their main figures?

HINDUISM

Major tenets of Hindu belief include:

- reincarnation, the belief that the universe and its beings undergo endless cycles of rebirth
- karma, the idea that people create their own destiny

The soul is reincarnated until it has resolved all karmas, at which point it attains moksha, or liberation from the cycle.

Hindus believe in multiple divine beings. Religion is based in the **Vedic scriptures**; other important texts include the Upanishads, the Mahabharata, and the Bhagavad Gita. Hinduism is the primary religion in India and is intertwined with the **caste system**, a hierarchical societal structure.

Buddhism

In Buddhism, the Prince **Siddhartha Gautama** is said to have sought **enlightenment** around the third century BCE, renouncing worldly goods and living as an ascetic in what is today northern India. Buddhism teaches that desire—the ego, or self—is the root of suffering, and that giving up or **transcending** material obsessions will lead to freedom, or nirvana—enlightenment. While Buddhism originated in India, it is practiced throughout Asia and the world.

The main Buddhist schools of theology include:

- Mahayana, prevalent in northern and eastern Asia (Korea, parts of China, Mongolia)
- Theravada, dominant in Southeast Asia and Indian Ocean regions
- Vajrayana, central to Tibetan Buddhism

Confucianism

Confucianism teaches obedience and adherence to tradition in order to maintain a harmonious society. Ideally, practicing integrity and respecting wisdom would ensure that authority would be used for beneficial purposes.

Confucius himself was a Chinese scholar in the sixth century BCE. His philosophy would go on to inform Chinese culture for centuries.

Feudalism through the Era of Expansion

The Middle Ages in Europe

The Byzantine Empire remained a strong civilization and a place of learning. Constantinople was a commercial center, strategically located at the Dardanelles, connecting Asian trade routes with Europe. Later, missionaries traveled north to Slav-controlled Russia, spreading Christianity and literacy.

The ninth-century missionaries Saints Cyril and Methodius are credited with developing what would become the **Cyrillic** alphabet used in many Slavic languages. In 988 CE, the Russian Grand Prince of Kiev, **Vladimir I**, converted to Christianity and ordered his subjects to do so as well. Russian Christianity was influenced by the Byzantine doctrine, what would become Greek Orthodox Christianity.

Despite the chaos in Western Europe, the Church in Rome remained strong and became a stabilizing influence. However, differences in doctrine between Rome and Constantinople became too wide to overcome.

Beginning in 1054, a series of **schisms** developed in the now-widespread Christian religion between the **Roman Catholic Church** and the **Greek Orthodox Church** over matters of doctrine:

- the role of the pope and papal authority
- the use of leavened versus unleavened bread in religious services
- other theological concepts

Eventually the two would become entirely separate churches.

In Europe, the early Middle Ages (or **Dark Ages**) from the fall of Rome to about the tenth century, were a chaotic, unstable, and unsafe time. The protection and stability that did exist were represented and maintained by the Catholic Church and the feudal system.

Society and economics were characterized by decentralized, local governance, or **feudalism**, a hierarchy where land and protection were offered in exchange for loyalty. Feudalism was the dominant social, economic, and political hierarchy of the European Middle Ages from the time of Charlemagne (discussed further below).

Economic and social organization consisted of:

- vassals, freemen who would pledge **fealty**, or pay homage to lords
- lords, landowners who would reward their vassals' loyalty with land, or **fiefs**
- manors, self-sustaining areas possessed by lords but worked by peasants
- serfs, peasants who were tied to the land and worked for the lord in exchange for protection

While not exactly enslaved, serfs were effectively controlled by the lord, though they were not required to fight. They were also usually granted some land for their own use.

Warriors who fought for lords were called **knights**. They were rewarded with land and could become minor lords in their own right. Lords

Figure 1.12. Depiction of a Medieval Knight

themselves could be vassals of other lords; that hierarchy extended upward to kings or the Catholic Church.

The Catholic Church itself was a major landowner and political power. In a Europe not yet dominated by sovereign states, the pope was not only a religious leader, but also a military and political one.

Small kingdoms and alliances extended throughout Europe, and stable trade was difficult to maintain. The **Celts** controlled Britain and Ireland until the invasion of the Saxons. Around 600 CE, the Saxons conquered Britain while the Celts were pushed to Ireland, Scotland, and Brittany in northwest France.

Though the Church was gaining power, it was insecure in Italy as the Germanic tribes vied for control in Germany and France. Monasteries in Ireland and England retained and protected classical documentation in the wake of the fall of Rome and insecurity in Italy. The Germanic tribes themselves were threatened by Asian invaders like the Huns. This caused further instability in central and eastern parts of Europe, where Slavs also fought for supremacy north of Byzantium.

One exception to the chaos was the Scandinavian **Viking** civilization. From the end of the eighth century until around 1100, the Vikings expanded their influence from Scandinavia.

Thanks to their extraordinary seafaring skills and technology, their influence ranged from the Baltic Sea to the east to the North Sea through the North Atlantic. The Vikings traded with the Byzantine Empire and European powers and were known to travel to—and sometimes raid—parts of Britain, Ireland, France, and Russia. The Icelandic Erik the Red established a settlement in Greenland, and his son **Leif Erikson** may have traveled as far as North America.

> **DID YOU KNOW?**
>
> Byzantine and Middle Eastern artifacts have been found among Viking excavations in Scandinavia.

In addition to military prowess and advanced shipbuilding technology, the Vikings had a complex religion with a pantheon of gods and well-developed mythology. They also developed a literary canon of sagas in Old Norse, the basis of some Scandinavian languages today. Viking achievements have been documented in literature from other European cultures like the Anglo-Saxons, as well as the Arab historian Ibn Fadlan.

Meanwhile, by the eighth century, the North African **Moors**, part of the expanding Islamic civilization, had penetrated Iberia and were a threat to Christian Europe. Charles Martel, leader of the Franks in what is today France, defeated the Moors at the **Battle of Tours (or Poitiers)** in 732 CE, effectively stopping any further Islamic incursion into Europe.

Martel, a Christian, had previously consolidated his control of France, leading the Franks in victory over the Bavarians, Frisians, and other tribes and supporting their conversion to Christianity. But instability followed Charles Martel's death. **Charlemagne**, the son of a court official, eventually took over the Merovingian kingdom following disputes over succession.

Charlemagne was able to maintain Frankish unity and consolidate his rule, extending Frankish control into Central Europe and defending the Papal States in central Italy. In what is considered the reemergence of centralized power in Europe, parts of Western and Central Europe were organized under Charlemagne, who was crowned emperor of the Roman Empire by Pope Leo III in 800 CE. While in retrospect this seems long after the end of Rome, at the time many Europeans still perceived themselves as somehow still part of a Roman Empire.

> **DID YOU KNOW?**
>
> Today, Charlemagne's rule is referred to as the Carolingian Empire.

Several notable achievements occurred under Charlemagne's rule:

- Charlemagne brought stability to Western and Central Europe during a period when two powerful, non-Christian, organized civilizations (the Vikings in the north and the Islamic powers in the south) threatened what was left of western Christendom.

- Charlemagne brought stability to Western and Central Europe at a time when insecurity was growing to the east with the decline of the Byzantines and the emergence of the Umayyad Caliphate based in Damascus.

- During Charlemagne's reign, the Roman Catholic Church was strengthened, enabling the reemergence of Roman and Christian scholarship that had been hidden in English and Irish monasteries.

- The feudal system became truly organized, resulting in increased stability in Western Europe.

The Catholic Church would dominate Europe from Ireland toward Eastern Europe, an area of locally controlled duchies, kingdoms, and alliances. In 962 CE, Otto I became emperor of the **Holy Roman Empire** in Central Europe, a confederation of small states which remained an important European power until its dissolution in 1806.

While the Holy Roman Empire remained intact, the Carolingian Empire did not. Spain and Portugal remained under Muslim control, and France dissolved into small fiefdoms and territories. Meanwhile, England and Scotland were controlled by Norsemen (Vikings), especially Danish settlers and various local Anglo-Saxon rulers, the remnants of the Germanic tribes that had come to rule Europe and led to the fall of Rome.

In 1066, **William the Conqueror** left Normandy in northwest France. The **Normans** established organization in England, including a more consolidated economy and kingdom supported by feudalism. They also consolidated Christianity as the local religion.

> **DID YOU KNOW?**
>
> There were limits on sovereign power. In 1215, long before the revolution, English barons forced King John to sign the **Magna Carta**, which protected their property and rights from the king and was the basis for today's parliamentary system in that country.

English possessions included parts of France, nominally a kingdom but consisting of smaller territories with some level of independence. Intermarriage and conquest resulted in English control of Anjou and Bordeaux in France; William had brought control of French Brittany with him when he arrived on the island of Britain. Conflict between Britain and France would continue for several centuries, while rulers in Scandinavia and Northwest Europe consolidated power.

THE ISLAMIC WORLD

Meanwhile, in the wake of the decline of the Byzantine Empire, **Arab-Islamic Empires**, characterized by brisk commerce, advancements in technology and learning, and urban development, arose in the Middle East.

Before the rise of Islam in the seventh century, the Arabian Peninsula was located at the intersection of the Byzantine Empire—a diverse collection of ethnicities ruled by Greek Orthodox Christians and the Sasanians (Persians), who practiced Zoroastrianism. Both of these empires sought to control trade with central and eastern Asia along the Silk Road. They also sought to establish trade ties with Christian Axum (Ethiopia).

In Arabia itself, Judaism, Christianity, and animist religions were practiced by the Arab majority. The Prophet Muhammad was born in Mecca around 570 CE. He began receiving messages from God (Allah), preaching them around 613 CE as the last affirmations of the monotheistic religions, and writing them as the Qur'an, the Islamic holy book. Driven from **Mecca** to Medina in 622 CE, Muhammad and his followers were able to recapture the city and other major Arabian towns by the time of his death, establishing Islam and Arab rule in the region.

After Muhammad's death in 632 CE, his followers were led by a Caliph, who was considered both a political and religious leader. The first Caliph was Abu Bakr who, along with his followers, went on to conquer land beyond Arabia north into the weakening Byzantine Empire. The well-organized Muslim Arabs, based in Arabia, led incursions into Syria, the Levant, and Mesopotamia, taking over these territories.

Thanks to military, bureaucratic, and organizational skills, as well as their ability to win over dissatisfied minorities, the Arabs eventually isolated the Byzantines to parts of Anatolia and Constantinople and crushed the Persian Sasanians.

Muhammad's cousin and son-in-law **Ali**, his wife, **Fatima** (Muhammad's eldest daughter), and their followers believed the leader of the Muslim Arabs should be a blood relative of Muhammad. Muhammad had no sons, so the logical choice was Ali. Meccan elites felt differently, and the popular Abu Bakr was chosen as the first caliph. The first four caliphs are known as the *Rashidun*, or "rightly guided ones":

> DID YOU KNOW?
>
> Ali's followers called themselves the Party of Ali or, in Arabic, the Shiat Ali, which is the origin of the word Shia or Shi'ite Muslims.

- Abu Bakr was succeeded by the second caliph, Umar.

- The third caliph, Uthman, took over when Umar died. Widely accused of corruption, Uthman was murdered in 656 CE.

- The Islamic leadership finally settled on Ali to take over as the fourth caliph.

Others in power felt differently. Muawiya, based in Damascus, led the opposition to Ali; this conflict is at the heart of the **Sunni-Shi'a Schism**.

Ali and Fatima established their base in Kufa, in Mesopotamia. Unable to come to an agreement over leadership, the Arabs became embroiled in the First Civil War (656 – 661 CE). The conflict ended when Ali was murdered in 661 CE. Unrest continued, and the bloody massacre of Ali's son Hussein and his family in Karbala (680 CE) triggered the Second Civil War (680 – 692 CE).

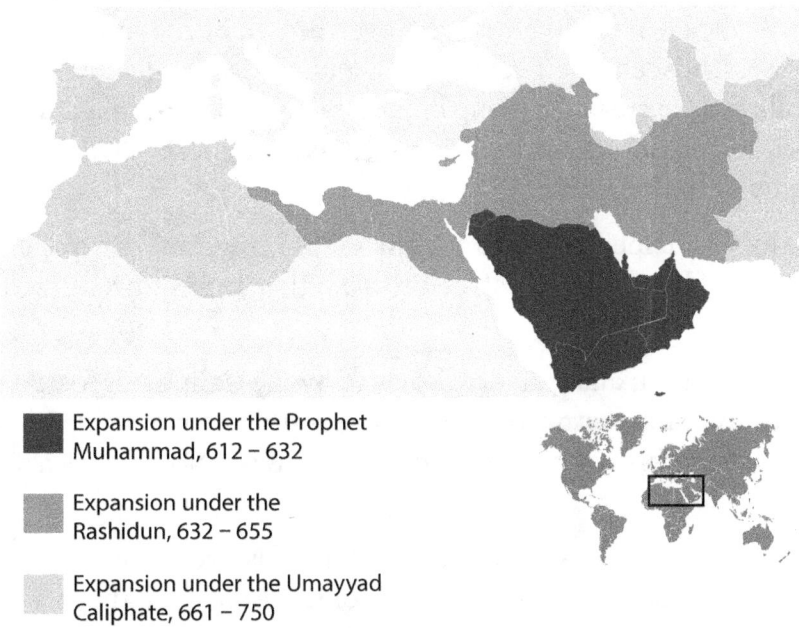

■ Expansion under the Prophet Muhammad, 612 – 632

■ Expansion under the Rashidun, 632 – 655

■ Expansion under the Umayyad Caliphate, 661 – 750

Figure 1.13. Islamic Expansion

The violence of these years cemented divisions in Islam, and **Shi'ite Islam** emerged in Mesopotamia. The Shi'ites believed that Ali was the rightful heir to Muhammad's early Islamic Empire, and maintained a focus on martyrdom, especially that of Ali and Hussein.

The followers of the Meccan elites became known as **Sunnis**, "orthodox" Muslims with a focus on community rather than genealogy. Over the centuries, other differences in theology and history would develop.

Muawiya is considered the first caliph of the **Umayyad Caliphate** (empire), named for the leading Meccan tribe that had supported Muhammad from the beginning. The Arabs already controlled Arabia; Spain (al-Andalus) was settled as early as 711 CE. By 750 CE, they would control parts of the following:

- Iberia
- North Africa
- Egypt
- the Levant
- Mesopotamia
- Persia
- Armenia
- Central Asia into Transoxiana (Uzbekistan)
- the Indus River Valley (areas of Pakistan)

Ongoing conflict among Arab elites resulted in the **Abbasid Caliphate** in 750 CE, based in Baghdad. The Umayyad were overthrown by the Arab-Muslim Abbasid family, which established a new capital in Baghdad. Caliph al-Mutasim professionalized the military. He created a group of professional soldiers called **mamluks**, who were freed slaves usually of Turkish origin. It was thought they would be more loyal with no family or national ties.

The mamluks helped the caliph consolidate imperial control and improve tax collection. Abbasid administration was also highly organized, allowing efficient taxation.

The administration and stability provided by the Caliphates fostered an Arabic literary culture. Stability permitted open trade routes, economic development, and cultural interaction throughout Asia, the Middle East, North Africa, and parts of Europe.

Furthermore, the Abbasid ruler al-Ma'mun fostered cultural and scientific study. This, combined with the universality of the Arabic language, lent itself to a number of cultural and scholastic contributions:

- Scientific and medical texts from varying civilizations—Greek, Persian, Indian—could be translated into Arabic and shared throughout the Islamic world.

- Arab thinkers studied Greek and Persian astronomy and engaged in further research.

- Arabs studied mathematics from around the world and developed algebra, which enabled engineering, technological, and architectural achievements.

- Islamic art, well known for its geometric designs, gained recognition during this time.

Around this time, the **Song Dynasty** (960 – 1276) controlled most of China. Under the Song, China experienced tremendous development and economic growth. The Song Dynasty is most notably characterized by the following:

- increased urbanization

- complex administrative rule, including the difficult competitive written examinations required to obtain prestigious bureaucratic positions in government

- the emergence of traditions now recognized as Chinese, such as the consumption of tea and rice and common Chinese architecture

- overland trade along the Silk Road with exports of silk, tea, ceramics, jade, and other goods

- sea trade with Korea, Japan, Southeast Asia, India, Arabia, and East Africa

CONFLICT AND CULTURAL EXCHANGE

Cultural exchange was not limited to interactions between Christian Europeans, Egyptians, and Levantine Muslims. Indeed, international commerce was vigorous along the **Silk Road**, trading routes which stretched from the Arab-controlled Eastern Mediterranean to Song Dynasty China, where science and learning also blossomed.

The Silk Road reflected the transnational nature of Central Asia:

- The nomadic culture of Central Asia lent itself to trade between the major civilizations of China, Persia, the Near East, and Europe.

- Buddhism and Islam spread into China.

- Chinese, Islamic, and European art, pottery, and goods were interchanged between the three civilizations, an example of early globalization.

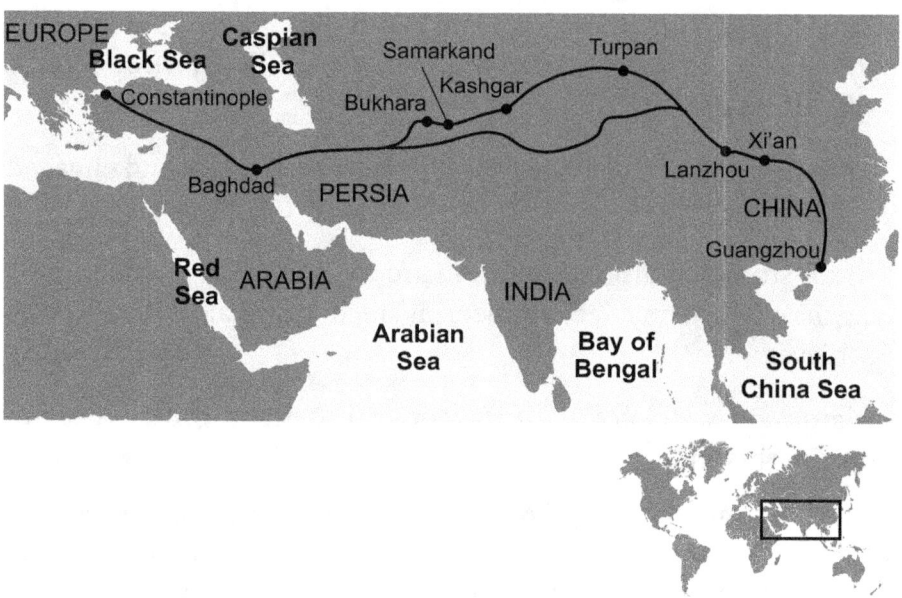

Figure 1.14. The Silk Road

The Islamic tradition of the **hajj**, or the pilgrimage to Mecca, also spurred cultural interaction. Islam had spread from Spain throughout North Africa, the Sahel, the Middle East, Persia, Central Asia, India, and China. Peoples from all these regions traveled and met in Arabia as part of their religious pilgrimage.

Islam also spread along trans-Saharan trade routes into West Africa and the Sahel. Brisk trade between the gold-rich **Kingdom of Ghana** and Muslim traders based in Morocco brought Islam to the region around the eleventh century. The Islamic **Mali Empire** (1235 – 1500), based farther south in **Timbuktu**, eventually extended beyond the original Ghanaian boundaries all the way to the West African coast and controlled the valuable gold and salt trades. It became a center of learning and commerce. At the empire's peak, the ruler **Mansa Musa** made a pilgrimage to Mecca in 1324. However, by 1500, the **Songhai Empire** had overcome Mali and eventually dominated the Niger River area.

> **CHECK YOUR UNDERSTANDING #5**
>
> How did the Silk Road and Islam both contribute to global cultural exchange?

Loss of Byzantine territory to the Islamic Empires meant loss of Christian lands in the Levant—including Jerusalem and Bethlehem—to Muslims. In 1095, the Byzantine emperor asked Pope Urban II for help defending Jerusalem and protecting Christians.

With a history of Muslim incursions into Spain and France, anti-Muslim sentiment was strong in Europe, and Christians there were easily inspired to fight them in the Levant (Holy Land). The pope offered lords and knights the chance to keep lands and bounty they won from conquered Muslims (and Jews) in this

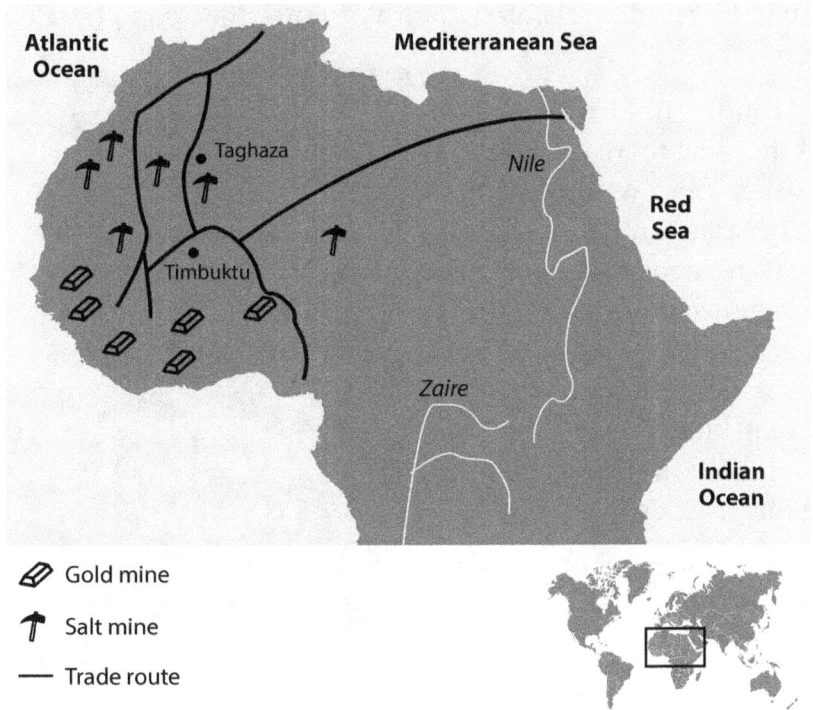

Figure 1.15. Trans-Saharan Trade Routes

crusade. He also offered Crusaders **indulgences**—forgiveness for sins committed in war and guarantees they would enter heaven.

Meanwhile, toward the end of the tenth century, the Abbasid Caliphate was in decline. The Shi'ite **Fatimids** took control of Syria and Egypt, addressing the Shi'ite claim to the Caliphate. Other groups took control of provinces in Mesopotamia, Arabia, and Central Asia.

In Spain, Abd al-Rahman III (891 – 961 CE) had defied the Abbasids and the Fatimids, taking over al-Andalus (Spain) himself and fostering a unique Hispano-Arabic culture where intellectual pursuits bloomed:

▸ Rahman was responsible for the Great Mosque of Cordoba.

▸ The Muslim philosopher Averroes developed his commentary on Aristotle.

▸ The Jewish philosopher Maimonides developed religious and philosophical thought.

Still, conflict persisted with the Carolingians and with smaller Christian kingdoms in northern Spain.

In Western Europe, instability had been ongoing as control over continental territories passed between England and France. France never regained the strength it had under Charlemagne. While the French monarchy existed, smaller states remained powerful, and power was decentralized. Despite internal divisions, organization in England accelerated upon William's 1066 conquest. The two civilizations were at odds.

Despite conflict in Europe, Christians found they had more in common with each other than with Muslims. European Christians united to follow the pope's call to arms to fight in the Middle East. The decline of the Abbasids had left the Levant vulnerable, and Christian Crusaders established settlements and small kingdoms in Syria and on the Eastern Mediterranean coast, conquering major cities.

The Crusades continued over several centuries:

Figure 1.16. Great Mosque of Cordoba

- By 1099, Jerusalem was captured by Christian Crusaders in the First Crusade as called for by Pope Urban II (see above).

- In 1171, the Kurdish military leader Salah al-Din (Saladin) abolished the Fatimid Caliphate. Following his death and a succession of rulers, elite slave troops took power.

- In 1187, Salah al-Din reconquered Jerusalem, driving European Christians out for good.

- The **Mamluks** (1250 – 1517) controlled Egypt and would later defeat the Mongols in 1260, protecting Egypt and North Africa from the Mongol invasions.

DID YOU KNOW?

The Egyptian rulers, the Mamluks, descended from Abbasid Caliph al-Mutasim's fighting force.

While the ongoing Crusades never resulted in permanent European control over the Holy Land, they did open up trade routes between Europe and the Middle East, stretching all the way along the Silk Road to China. This increasing interdependence led to the European Renaissance.

Ongoing interactions between Europeans and Muslims also had other societal effects as well:

- Europeans were exposed to improved education and goods, which they could now afford thanks to international trade.

- The **Bubonic (Black) Plague** spread to Europe as a result of global exchange, killing off a third of its population from 1347 – 1351, and having a worldwide impact, with empires falling in its wake.

Back in Europe, conflict reached its height throughout the thirteenth and fourteenth centuries, known as the **Hundred Years' War** (1337 – 1453):

- France was in political chaos during the mid-fourteenth century, decentralized and at times without a king.

- The region was suffering the effects of the Black Plague.

- France remained vulnerable to English attack and periodically found itself under English rule.

- After ongoing conflict, England lost its last territory, Bordeaux, France, in 1453 to the French King Charles VII.

> **DID YOU KNOW?**
>
> During the Hundred Years' War, Joan of Arc led the French in the 1429 Battle of Orléans, reinvigorating French resistance to English incursions.

In al-Andalus (Spain), despite some coexistence between Christians and Muslims under Muslim rule, raids and conflict were ongoing during the lengthy period of the **Reconquista**:

- From the zenith of Muslim rule under Abd al-Rahman, Christian raids continued, as did shifting alliances between the small kingdoms of Christian Spain and Portugal.

- By the second half of the thirteenth century, the only remaining Muslim power in Iberia was Grenada.

- By the fifteenth century, small Christian Spanish kingdoms were vying for dominance.

- The marriage of Ferdinand of Castilla and Isabella of Aragon in 1479 connected those two kingdoms, and the monarchs were able to complete the Reconquista by taking Grenada and uniting Spain.

- The period of the Reconquista ended in 1492 when Christian powers took Grenada.

Ferdinand and Isabella also launched the Inquisition, an extended persecution of Jews and Jewish converts to Christianity who continued to practice Judaism in secret. Jewish people were tortured, killed, and exiled; their belongings and property were confiscated. Muslims were also persecuted and forced to convert to Christianity or be exiled.

Empires in Transition

Beyond Egypt and the Levant, the collapse of the Abbasid Caliphate led to instability and decentralization of power in Mesopotamia, Persia, and Central Asia:

- Smaller sultanates (territories ruled by regional leaders, or sultans) emerged, and production and economic development declined.

- Tang Dynasty China closed its borders, resulting in a decline in trade on the Silk Road.

- The nomadic **Seljuks**, Turks from Central Asia, nominally took over the region from Central Asia through parts of the Levant in the eleventh century, though they lacked effective administration or central authority.

- Political decentralization ultimately left the region vulnerable to the Mongol invasions of the twelfth and thirteenth centuries.

> **DID YOU KNOW?**
>
> During this period, Persian-influenced Sufi (mystical) Islam and poetry developed. Shi'ite theology and jurisprudence also developed as part of a strengthening independent Shi'ite identity.

Despite the lack of political cohesion, Islam remained a unifying force throughout the region, and political instability and decentralization paradoxically allowed local culture to develop, particularly Persian art and literature. Islam was also able to thrive during this period: local religious leaders (*ulama*) had taken up community leadership positions following the loss of any powerful central authority, and Islam became a guiding force in law, justice, and social organization throughout the region.

In the Near East, the **Mongol invasions** destroyed agriculture, city life and planning, economic patterns and trade routes, and social stability. After some time, new patterns of trade emerged, new cities rose to prominence, and stability allowed for prosperity, but the Mongol invasions dealt a blow to the concept that Islam was inherently favored by God.

Despite the rich history of transnational activity across Asia, the continent was vulnerable. Central Asia lacked one dominant culture or imperial power, and Southwest Asia was fragmented following the decline of the Abbasids. Combined with the disorganization of the Seljuks and the remnants of the Byzantines, these weaknesses allowed the Mongols to take over much of Eurasia.

Important facts about the **Mongol Empire** include:

- It was based in Central Asia.

- It was led by **Genghis Khan**.

- It expanded throughout Asia thanks to abilities in horsemanship and archery.
- It ultimately controlled Pannonia (Hungary) through the Middle East, Persia, Central Asia, Northern and Western China, and Southeast Asia.

The impact of the Mongol invasions was not limited to Eurasia. In China, the Mongols destroyed local infrastructure, including the foundation of Chinese society and administration—the civil service examinations.

In order to govern the vast territory effectively, the Mongols in China took a different approach. Genghis Khan's grandson Kublai Khan conquered China and founded the Mongol Yuan Dynasty in 1271.

> **CHECK YOUR UNDERSTANDING #6**
>
> What were the vulnerabilities on the continent of Asia that facilitated the Mongol invasions? How did these vulnerabilities come about?

The Yuan Dynasty:

- abolished the civil service examinations until 1315
- maintained most of the administrative policy of the preceding Song Dynasty
  - the Six Ministries
  - the Secretariat
  - provincial administrative structure
- upended Chinese social hierarchy, placing Mongols at the top, followed by non-ethnic Han Chinese, and then Han Chinese

Mongol attempts at imperial expansion in China into Japan and Southeast Asia, coupled with threats from the Black Plague, financial problems, and flooding, led to the decline of the Yuan Dynasty and the rise of the native Chinese **Ming Dynasty** in 1368:

> **DID YOU KNOW?**
>
> Despite Mongol distrust of Confucianism and Confucian administrator-scholars, Kublai Khan educated his son in the Confucian tradition.

- Zhu Yuanzhang led the Chinese to victory and ruled as the first Ming emperor from Nanjing.
- The capital later moved to Beijing in 1421.
- Ming China controlled land throughout Asia, accepting tribute from rulers in Burma, Siam (Thailand), Annam (Vietnam), Mongolia, Korea, and Central Asia.

- ▶ The Ming reasserted Chinese control and continued traditional methods of administration; however the construction of the **Forbidden City**, the home of the emperor in Beijing, helped consolidate imperial rule.

- ▶ The Ming emphasized international trade: demand for ceramics in particular, in addition to silk and tea, was high abroad, and contact with seafaring traders like the Portuguese and Dutch in the sixteenth century was strong.

- ▶ The Ming also encouraged trade and exploration by sea; the Chinese explorer Zheng He traveled to India, Sri Lanka, and Asia.

Despite some decline in Mongol hegemony throughout Asia, the military leader **Timur (Tamerlane)** began conquering land in the area around 1364. By 1383, he occupied Moscow and turned toward Persia. Up to the turn of the century he would go on to conquer numerous areas:

- ▶ Persia
- ▶ Mesopotamia
- ▶ much of the Caucasus
- ▶ parts of India (Delhi)

His conquests continued into the early fifteenth century:

- ▶ Syria was taken.
- ▶ Anatolia was invaded.
- ▶ Tribute was exacted from Egypt.

> **DID YOU KNOW?**
>
> Tamerlane was a Mongol descendant from Transoxania, present-day Uzbekistan.

While rarely spending too much time in one place, Timur had contributed to the development of the capital of his empire, Samarkand, enriching Central Asia culturally. Timur died in 1405 on an expedition to China.

Mongol decline was not only isolated to China. In Russia, **Ivan the Great** brought Moscow from Mongol to Slavic Russian control:

- ▶ In the late fifteenth century, Ivan had consolidated Russian power over neighboring Slavic regions.

- ▶ Through both military force and diplomacy, Ivan achieved Moscow's independence in 1480, despite Muscovy's status as a vassal state.

- ▶ He set out to bring other neighboring Slavic and Baltic lands, including Poland-Lithuania, and later, parts of Ukraine, under Russian rule.

- Ivan achieved a centralized, consolidated Russia that was the foundation for an empire and a sovereign nation that sought diplomatic status with Europe.

Figure 1.17. The Forbidden City

A century later, **Ivan the Terrible** set out to expand Russia further, integrate it into Europe, and strengthen Russian Orthodox Christianity. Named the first **tsar**, or emperor, Ivan is known for:

- reforming government, strengthening centralization and administrative bureaucracy and disempowering the nobility
- leading the affirmation of orthodox Christianity, calling councils to organize the church and canonize Russian saints
- reorganizing the military, including promoting officials based on merit rather than status
- expanding and improving foreign policy and relations
- developing Russian culture and religion

However, overextension of resources and his oppressive entourage, the *oprichnina*, depopulated the state and gave him the reputation as a despotic ruler. Despite this, Ivan's reforms strengthened the apparatus of the Russian state.

Farther south in Central Asia, one of Timur's descendants, Babur, laid claim to Timur's dominions. Despite his Mongol roots, Babur identified as Turkic due to

> **DID YOU KNOW?**
>
> The Mughal Emperor Shah Jahan built the Taj Mahal in 1631.

his tribal origins and enjoyed support from the powerful Ottoman Empire in Turkey (see below). He founded the **Mughal Empire** of India:

Figure 1.18. The Taj Mahal

- In 1525, Babur set out for India.

- By 1529, Babur had secured land from Kandahar in the west to Bengal in the east.

- Babur's grandson, Akbar, consolidated the empire, which at the time consisted of small kingdoms.

- The Mughals would rule India until the eighteenth century and nominally control parts of the country until British takeover in the nineteenth century.

During Mughal rule in India, the Ming Dynasty fell in China in 1644 to a peasant revolt and the Qing took over:

- The **Manchu**, a non-Han group from the north, took the opportunity to seize Beijing and take the country.

- Despite their status as non-Han Chinese, the Manchu were accepted, thus beginning the **Qing Dynasty**.

- The first Qing emperor, the Kangxi Emperor, promoted the arts and education.

- Under the reign of the Qianlong Emperor (1736 – 1796), China grew to its largest size, including Tibet, Mongolia, Xinjiang, and parts of Russia.

- Like the Kangxi Emperor, the Qianlong Emperor was a patron of the arts.

- China became the dominant power in East Asia and a successful multi-ethnic state.

- The Qing would be the last of China's imperial rulers after losing power in 1911.

Meanwhile, in Persia, the **Safavids** emerged in 1501 in the wake of the Timurid Empire:

- This dynasty would rule from Azerbaijan in the west through to modern-day Pakistan and Afghanistan.

- A major rival of the Ottoman Empire, the Safavids were a stabilizing force in Asia.

- Following Sufism, the Safavids supported art, literature, architecture, and other learning.

- Their organized administration brought order and stability to Persia throughout their rule, which lasted until 1736, when the **Qajar Dynasty** took over.

Despite the instability inland, Indian Ocean trade routes had continued to function since at least the seventh century.

These oceanic routes connected the following areas:

- the Horn of Africa
- the East African Coast
- the Arabian Peninsula
- Southern Persia
- India
- Southeast Asia
- China

The ocean acted as a unifying force throughout the region, and the **monsoon winds** permitted Arab, Persian, Indian, and Chinese merchants to travel to East Africa in search of goods such as ivory and gold—and people to enslave.

Despite the civilizational achievements of the Islamic Empires, Tang, and later Ming Dynasty China, and the Central Asian and Indian Empires that would emerge from the Mongols, the **East African slave trade** endured until the nineteenth century:

- Arabs, Asians, and other Africans kidnapped African people and enslaved them throughout the Arab world and South Asia.

- Europeans would later take part in the trade as well, forcing Africans into slavery in colonies throughout South and Southeast Asia, and on plantations in Indian Ocean islands like Madagascar.

- The major East African port was Zanzibar, from which gold, coconut oil, ivory, and other African exports—including enslaved people—traveled to Asia and the Middle East.

- Enslaved persons from Sub-Saharan Africa were also forced north overland to markets in Cairo, where they were sold and dispersed throughout the Arab-Islamic, Fatimid, and Ottoman Empires.

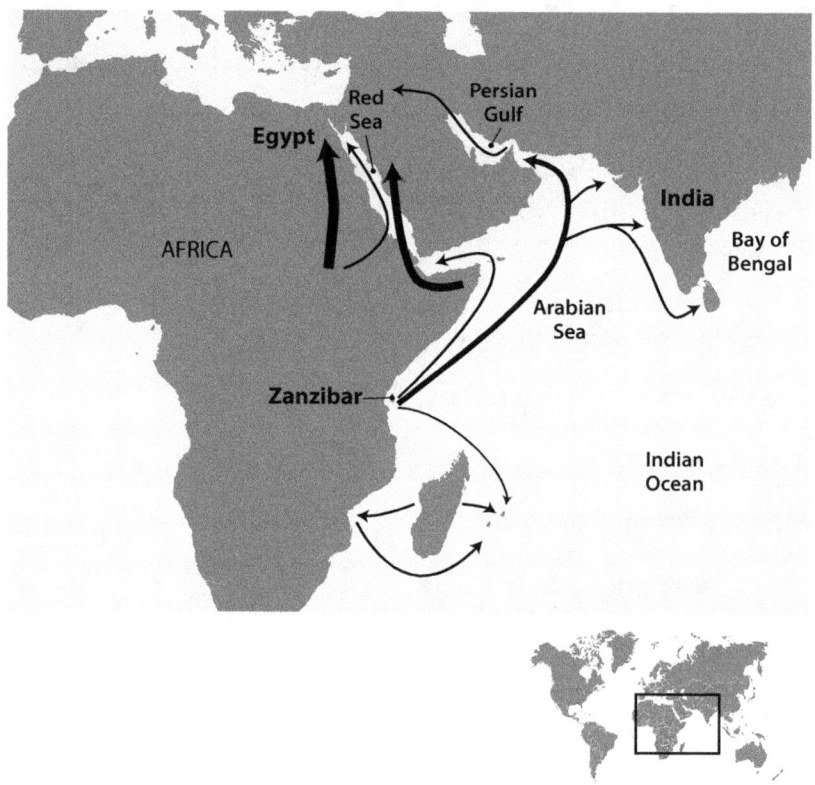

Figure 1.19. Indian Ocean Slave Trade

Islam also spread throughout the African coast and inland. Given the cosmopolitan nature of the coastline, the **Swahili** language adopted aspects of Arabic and other Asian languages.

Farther north, the Ottoman Turks represented a threat to Central Europe:

- After controlling most of Anatolia from the late thirteenth century, the Ottomans spread west into the Balkans.

- They consolidated their rule in 1389 at the Battle of Kosovo.

- In 1453 they captured Istanbul, from which the Ottoman Empire would come to rule much of the Mediterranean world.

- Under the leadership of **Mehmed the Conqueror** and his successors in the fifteenth century, the Ottomans conquered Pannonia (Hungary), North Africa, the Caucasus, the Levant and Mesopotamian regions, western Arabia, and Egypt.

- Under **Suleiman the Magnificent** (1520 – 1566), the **Ottoman Empire** consolidated control over the Balkans, the Middle East, and North Africa and would hold that land until the nineteenth century.

The capture of Istanbul (Constantinople) represented the true end of the Byzantine Empire. The remaining Christian Byzantines—mainly isolated to coastal Anatolia, Constantinople, and parts of Greece—fled to Italy, bringing Greek, Middle Eastern, and Asian learning with them and enriching the emerging European Renaissance.

THE EUROPEAN RENAISSANCE

The **Renaissance**, or *rebirth*, included the revival of ancient Greek and Roman learning, art, and architecture. However, the roots of the Renaissance stretched further back to earlier interactions between Christendom, the Islamic World, and even China, during the Crusades and through Silk Road trade.

Key characteristics of the Renaissance included:

- inspiring new learning and prosperity in Europe
- enabling exploration, colonization, profit, and imperialism
- scientific and religious questioning
- rebellion against the Catholic Church and, later, monarchical governments

Russia would not experience these cultural changes until the eighteenth century, when **Peter the Great** and **Catherine the Great** copied modern European culture, modernized the military, and updated technology, including building the new capital city of St. Petersburg, a cultural center.

Reinvigoration of classical knowledge was triggered in part by Byzantine refugees from the Ottoman conquest of Constantinople, including scholars who brought Greek and Roman texts to Italy and Western Europe.

The fall of Constantinople precipitated the development of **humanism** in Europe:

- Humanism is a mode of thought emphasizing human nature, creativity, and an overarching concept of truth in all philosophical systems (the concept of **syncretism**).
- Emerging in Italy, the seat of the Catholic Church, humanism was supported by some popes, including Leo X.
- In the long term, humanism represented a threat to religious—especially Catholic—orthodoxy, since it allowed religious teaching to be questioned.

- Figures associated with humanism included Dante, Petrarch, and Erasmus.
- Humanism is at the root of the Reformation of the sixteenth century.

Art, considered not just a form of expression but also a science in itself, flourished in fifteenth century Italy, particularly in Florence. Major figures explored design and perspective, innovation in architecture, and anatomy in sculpture:

- Leonardo da Vinci (known for scientific pursuits in addition to artistic achievement)
- Bramante
- Michelangelo
- Rafael
- Donatello

While artists worked throughout Italy and found patrons in the Vatican, among other places, the Florentine **Medici family** supported Renaissance art in that city by funding extensive civic projects, construction, décor, and public sculpture throughout Florence.

Figure 1.20. Michelangelo's *The Creation of Adam*

Meanwhile, scholars like Galileo, Isaac Newton, and Copernicus made discoveries in what became known as the **Scientific Revolution**:

- The Scientific Revolution was rooted in the scientific knowledge of the Islamic Empires, which had been imported through economic and social contact initiated centuries prior during the Crusades.

- Scientific study and discovery threatened the power of the Church, whose theological teachings were often at odds with scientific findings and logical reasoning.

Also in the mid-fifteenth century, in Northern Europe, Johann Gutenberg invented the **printing press**. With the advent of printing, texts could be more widely and rapidly distributed, and people had more access to information beyond what their leaders told them.

Figure 1.21. Gutenberg Bible

Combined with humanism and an increased emphasis on secular thought, the power of the Church and of monarchs who ruled by divine right was under threat. Here lay the roots of the **Enlightenment**, the basis for reinvigorated European culture and political thought that would drive its development for the next several centuries—and inspire revolution.

Transnational cultural exchange had also resulted in the transmission of technology to Europe:

> DID YOU KNOW?
>
> The Bible was the first book to be published using the printing press.

- During the sixteenth century, European seafaring knowledge, navigation, and technology benefitted from Islamic and Asian expertise.

- With this advanced technology, European explorers and traders could now venture beyond the Mediterranean.

- Portuguese and Dutch sailors eventually reached India and China, where they established ties with the Ming Dynasty.

> CHECK YOUR UNDERSTANDING #7
>
> The Scientific Revolution changed European thinking. What was the impact of using reason and scientific methodology rather than religion to understand the world?

- Advances in technology also allowed for trade that was no longer dependent on the Silk Road.

- Improved technology empowered Europeans to explore overseas, eventually landing in the Western Hemisphere, unknown to the peoples of Eurasia and Africa until this time.

MESOAMERICAN AND ANDEAN CIVILIZATIONS

In the Americas, the **Maya**, who preceded the Aztecs in Mesoamerica, came to dominate the Yucatan peninsula around 300 CE:

- The Maya developed a complex spiritual belief system accompanied by relief art and built pyramidal temples that still stand today.

- The Maya developed a detailed calendar and a written language using pictographs similar to Egyptian hieroglyphs.

- Astronomy and mathematics were studied by the Maya.

- Maya political administration was organized under monarchical city-states from around 300 until around 900, when the civilization began to decline.

- There is evidence of interaction throughout Mayan history with the Mesoamerican city-state of **Teotihuacan**, a major city likely comprised of various Mesoamerican peoples such as Toltecs, Mixtecs, Zapotecs, some Mayans, and other peoples.

By around 1400, two major empires dominated Central and South America: the Incas and the Aztecs. These two empires would be the last Indigenous civilizations to dominate the Americas before European colonization of the Western Hemisphere.

As smaller Mesoamerican civilizations had weakened and collapsed, the **Aztecs** had come to dominate Mexico and much of Mesoamerica, throughout which the same calendar was used. Characteristics of the Aztec civilization include the following:

- a military power and militaristic culture that allowed the Aztecs to dominate the region

- a dominance in regional trade in precious objects like quetzal bird feathers

- a main city, **Tenochtitlan**, founded in 1325 that served as a major world city home to several million people at its height

- a society divided on a class basis:
  - slaves
  - indentured servants
  - serfs
  - an independent priestly class
  - military and ruling classes
- upward mobility for classes, especially those who had proven themselves in battle

Figure 1.22. Quetzalcoatl

- sharing many beliefs with the Mayans
- worship of the god **Quetzalcoatl**, a feathered snake, central to its religion

Meanwhile, in the Andes, the **Incas** had emerged. This Indigenous civilization is especially known for the following:

- The Inca civilization was based in **Cuzco**.
- Around 1300, the Incas had consolidated their power and strengthened in the area, likely due to a surplus of their staple crop maize.
- They were able to conquer local lords and, later, peoples farther south.
- Domesticated llamas and alpacas, which allowed the military to transport supplies through the mountains, contributed to their dominance.
- In addition to the citadel of **Machu Picchu**, Inca engineers built imperial infrastructure, including roads throughout the Andes.
- The Incas developed mountain agriculture; they were able to grow crops at high altitudes and maintain way stations on the highways stocked with supplies.
- To subdue local peoples, they moved conquered groups elsewhere in the empire and repopulated conquered areas with Incas.

> **DID YOU KNOW?**
>
> The Incas used a system called *quipus*, knotted cords, to keep track of inventories and other data, such as population.

Figure 1.23. Machu Picchu

COLONIZATION OF THE WESTERN HEMISPHERE

Interest in exploration grew in Europe during the Renaissance period. Numerous factors would eventually lead to the discovery of the Western Hemisphere:

- Technological advancements made complex navigation and long-term sea voyages possible.

- Economic growth resulting from international trade drove interest in market expansion.

- Global interdependence was boosted by Spain when King Ferdinand and Queen Isabella sponsored **Christopher Columbus's** exploratory voyage in 1492 to find a sea route to Asia, in order to speed up commercial trade there.

- Christopher Columbus would instead stumble upon the Western Hemisphere, which was unknown to Europeans, Asians, and Africans to this point.

- Columbus landed in the Caribbean. He and later explorers would claim the Caribbean islands, Central, and South America for Spain and Portugal; however, those areas were already populated by the major American civilizations (discussed above).

Spanish colonization would eventually lead to the fall of the Aztec Empire:

- The Aztec ruler **Montezuma II** led the Aztecs during their first encounter with Spain.

- Explorer **Hernan Cortés** met with Montezuma II in Tenochtitlan after invading other areas of Mexico in 1519.

- Due to Spanish superiority in military technology, Montezuma attempted to compromise with Cortés.

- Cortés was in no position to compromise with the Aztecs: he was seeking wealth and prestige in Mexico and disobeyed Spanish colonial authorities by unlawfully leaving the Spanish stronghold of Cuba.

- A few days later Cortés arrested Montezuma and took over the city.

- Spain was especially interested in controlling Mexican and Mesoamerican gold and subduing the Aztec religion, which included ceremonies with human blood and human sacrifice.

- Spain then began the process of colonizing Mexico and Central America, and the Aztec Empire collapsed.

Though the Inca Empire remained nominally intact for several years after the Spanish gained access to South America, a number of factors would eventually lead to the empire's decline:

- The Spanish accessed the continent in the early sixteenth century and were interested in economic exploitation and spreading Christianity, as was the case in Mexico and Central America.

- In 1533, the Spanish conquistador **Francisco Pizzaro** defeated the Inca king **Atahualpa** and installed a puppet ruler; this marked the decline of the Inca Empire.

- The Spanish desecrated important religious artifacts—such as mummies essential for ancestor worship—installed Christianity, and took economic and political control of the region.

Spreading Christianity was one important reason for European expansion. By taking over the silver- and gold-rich Mesoamerican and Andean territories, as well as the Caribbean islands—where sugar became an important cash crop—Spain also contributed to the development of new economic practices that would eventually lead to the rise of a new era in slavery:

- **Mercantilism** was introduced, whereby the colonizing, or "mother country," took raw materials from the territories they controlled for the colonizers' own benefit.

- Governments amassed wealth through protectionism and increasing exports at the expense of other rising colonial powers, which eventually involved developing goods and then selling them back to those colonized lands at an inflated price.

- The **encomienda** system developed, granting European landowners the "right" to hold lands in the Americas and demand labor and tribute from the local inhabitants. Local civilizations and resources were exploited and destroyed.

- The **Columbian Exchange** began, which enabled mercantilism to flourish.

- Conflict and illness brought by the Europeans—especially **smallpox**—decimated the Native Americans; Europeans were left without labor to mine the silver and gold or to work the land.

- **African slavery** was the Europeans' solution to fill the need for labor.

> **CHECK YOUR UNDERSTANDING #8**
>
> What was destructive about the encomienda system?

Slavery was an ancient institution in many societies worldwide; however, with the Columbian Exchange slavery came to be practiced on a mass scale the likes of which the world had never seen.

Throughout Africa and especially on the West African coast, Europeans traded for slaves with some African kingdoms and also raided the land, kidnapping people. European enslavers took captured Africans in horrific conditions to the Americas; those who survived were enslaved and forced to work in mining or agriculture for the benefit of expanding European imperial powers.

The Columbian Exchange described the **triangular trade** across the Atlantic: European slavers took kidnapped African people from Africa to the Americas, sold them at auction and exchanged them for sugar and raw materials; these materials were traded in Europe for consumer goods, which were then exchanged in Africa for slaves, and so on.

> **DID YOU KNOW?**
>
> The historian Alfred Crosby published *The Columbian Exchange* in the 1970s, coining the term used today to describe the tremendous interchange of people, plants, animals—and diseases—that took place between the hemispheres.

Enslaved Africans suffered greatly and were forced to endure ocean voyages crammed on unsafe, unhygienic ships—sometimes among the dead bodies of other kidnapped people—only to arrive in the Americas to a life of slavery in mines or on plantations.

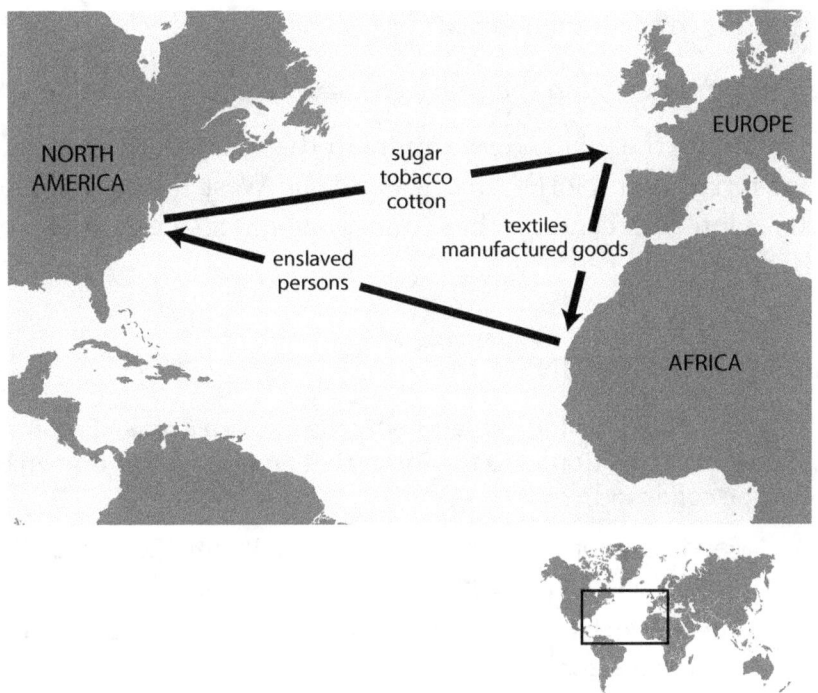

Figure 1.24. Triangular Trade

Throughout this period, Africans did resist both on ships and later, in the Americas:

- **Maroon communities** of escaped slaves formed throughout the Western Hemisphere.

- The **Underground Railroad** in the nineteenth-century United States helped enslaved persons escape the South.

- **Toussaint L'Ouverture** led a successful slave rebellion in Haiti, winning independence from the French for that country in 1791.

Despite this resistance, the slave trade continued for centuries. The colonies and later independent countries of the Western Hemisphere continued to practice slavery until the nineteenth century. Oppressive legal and social restrictions based on race continue to affect the descendants of enslaved African people to this day.

During the eighteenth century, Spain and Portugal were preeminent powers in global trade thanks to colonization and **imperialism**, the possession and exploitation of land overseas. However, Great Britain became an important presence on the seas. It would later dominate the oceans throughout the nineteenth century.

Though Britain would lose its territories in North America after the American Revolution, it maintained control of the resource-rich West Indies and went on to dominate strategic areas:

- South Africa

- New South Wales in Australia

- Mauritius in the Indian Ocean
- Madras and Bengal in the Indian Subcontinent

Britain would further expand its empire in the nineteenth century. Likewise, France gained territory in North America and the West Indies. Despite losses to Britain in the eighteenth century, that country would also expand its own global empire in the nineteenth century.

PRACTICE QUESTIONS

6) Which of the following explains why the Eastern Roman Empire remained stable and transitioned to the Byzantine Empire while Rome in Western Europe collapsed?

   A. Feudalism contributed to instability in Western Europe, so that part of the continent disintegrated into a series of small states.

   B. The schism between the Catholic and Greek Orthodox Churches tore the empire apart.

   C. Muslims entered Constantinople and took it from Christian Roman control.

   D. Imprudent alliances in the West led to Roman collapse, while strong leadership and centralization in the East developed a new empire.

7) Following the death of Muhammad, Muslim leadership became so divided that the religious movement eventually split into Sunnis and Shi'ites. This was due to

   A. disagreement over secession to his place as leader.

   B. disagreement about the importance of conquest.

   C. disagreement over the theological nature of Islam.

   D. disagreement over whether to accept Christians and Jews as *People of the Book*.

8) Which of the following best explains the Atlantic Triangular Trade?

   A. American raw materials were transported to Africa, where they were exchanged for enslaved persons; enslaved persons were taken to the Americas, where they turned raw materials to consumer goods for sale in Europe.

   B. European consumer goods were sold in the Americas at a profit; these goods were also sold in Africa in exchange for raw materials and for enslaved persons, who were taken to the Americas.

   C. European raw materials were sent to the Americas to be transformed into consumer goods by people who had been kidnapped from Africa and enslaved. These consumer goods were then traded in Africa for more slaves.

D. Enslaved African people were traded in the Americas for raw materials; raw materials harvested by slaves went to Europe where they were utilized and turned to consumer goods; European consumer goods were exchanged in Africa for enslaved people.

9) **Despite the violence of the Crusades, they were also beneficial for Europe in that they**

   A. resulted in substantial, long-term land gains for European leaders in the Middle East.

   B. introduced European powers to the concept of nation-states, the dominant form of political organization in the Middle East.

   C. exposed Europe to Islamic and Asian science, technology, and medicine.

   D. enhanced tolerance of Islam throughout Europe.

10) **Which of the following was a result of the rise of the Ottoman Turks?**

    A. Christians left Constantinople for Western Europe, bringing classical learning with them.

    B. European powers were driven to colonize the Americas, fleeing Ottoman approach.

    C. Islam became the dominant religion in Europe, threatening the power of the Catholic Church.

    D. The Vikings ventured deeper into Europe.

Armed Conflicts

Reformation and New Europe

While Spain and Portugal consolidated their hold over territories in the Americas, conflict ensued in Europe. With the cultural changes of the Renaissance, the power of the Catholic Church was threatened. New scientific discoveries and secular Renaissance thought were at odds with many teachings of the Church, eventually leading to the **Reformation**, or movement for reform of the Church:

▶ In 1517, the Catholic monk **Martin Luther** wrote a letter of protest to the pope known as the **Ninety-Five Theses**, which outlined ways he believed the Church should reform.

▶ Luther's ideas gained support, especially among rulers who wanted more power from the Church, triggering the Reformation.

> **DID YOU KNOW?**
>
> Martin Luther translated the New Testament into German. Previously the Bible was in Latin, and priests were usually the only ones able to read it.

- These ideas led to offshoots of new versions of Christianity in Western Europe, separate from the Orthodox Churches in Russia and Greece.

- Protestant thinkers like Luther and **John Calvin** addressed particular grievances, condemning the **infallibility** of the pope (its teaching that the pope was without fault) and the selling of indulgences (guarantees of entry into heaven).

- The English **King Henry VIII** developed the Protestant **Church of England,** further consolidating his own power, famously allowing divorce, and marrying several times himself.

- The reign of Henry VIII, of the **House of Tudor**, initiated a chain of events leading to the consolidation of Protestantism in England, and eventually civil war and the empowerment of Parliament.

In Britain, religious and ethnic diversity between Protestant England and Scotland, and Catholic Ireland, made the kingdom unstable:

- The Catholic **Mary Queen of Scots**, who was the daughter of the Scottish King James V and half French, had been betrothed to Henry VIII's son, Edward; however her guardians canceled the arrangement, causing conflict with England.

- Mary Queen of Scots temporarily married Francis of France, uniting Scotland with that Catholic country, but he quickly died from illness.

- Mary then married her Protestant cousin the Earl of Darnley, with whom she had a son, **James**.

- Darnley forced Mary to abdicate the Scottish throne in 1567 and she fled to England, seeking safety with her Protestant cousin **Elizabeth I**, daughter of Henry VIII and queen of England.

- Mary's son, still a baby, became **King James VI** of Scotland.

- The Tudor Queen Elizabeth imprisoned the Catholic Mary in England as she—and her son—represented a threat to her power.

- Not only was James's male sex a liability for Elizabeth's inheritance to the throne, but their religious identities as Catholics threatened Elizabeth's hold over the Catholics of England and Scotland, as well as her tenuous grip on Catholic Ireland.

- In 1587, Elizabeth had Mary executed following revelations of a Catholic plot to overthrow Elizabeth.

- Despite Mary's execution, James succeeded Elizabeth upon her death in 1603. As **King James I** of England and Ireland, he would usher in the **House of Stuart**.

James I attempted to balance the diverse ethnic and religious groups in England, Scotland, and Ireland, including the Catholic majority in Ireland and the Calvinist Scots, who disagreed on many points with the more liberal Church of England (Anglicans). Despite his efforts at maintaining a delicate political balance, instability grew. In fact, though James's roots were in Catholicism (with his mother having been the Catholic Mary), oppression of Catholics continued. Furthermore, James' daughter married into the Bohemian royal family, forcing English involvement in the Thirty Years' War as that family lost power to Catholics in Central Europe—foreign involvement James was loath to initiate.

> **DID YOU KNOW?**
>
> The Gunpowder Plot to blow up the House of Lords and execute King James in the process was planned by Catholic fighters for November 5, 1605. This plot was conceived by a group including the famous Guy Fawkes, who represents rebellion to this day.

James's son **Charles I** continued the anti-Catholic conflict in 1625 upon his succession to the throne; however, upon his withdrawal in 1630, conservative Protestants in England and Scotland (**Puritans**) began to suspect a royal movement to weaken Protestantism and even restore Catholicism in the kingdom. Many began moving to North America as a result.

Conflict between Protestants and Catholics was fierce on the Continent as well:

- The **Thirty Years' War** (1618 – 1648) began in Central Europe between Protestant nobles in the Holy Roman Empire who disagreed with the strict Catholic Ferdinand II, King of Bohemia and eventually Archduke of Austria and King of Hungary (what was not under Ottoman domination).
    - Elected Holy Roman emperor in 1619, Ferdinand II was a leader of the **Counter-Reformation**, attempts at reinforcing Catholic dominance throughout Europe during and after the Reformation in the wake of the Renaissance and related social change.
    - Ferdinand was closely allied with the Catholic **Habsburg** Dynasty, which ruled Austria and Spain.
- Interference in 1625 by Protestant Denmark and Sweden in Poland and Germany stirred further anti-Catholic discontent among local nobles in Germany, who yearned for independence from the imperial Holy Roman Empire.
    - Despite Danish, Dutch, Swedish, and British support, the imperial military leader Albrecht von Wallenstein took control of most Protestant German states and Denmark.

- Ferdinand II issued the **Edict of Restitution**, restoring rebellious Protestant German territory to imperial, Catholic control.
- The defeat of Denmark in 1629 marked the defeat of Denmark as an important European power at that point in history.

▶ Protestant Sweden engaged in further conflict with Catholic Poland.
- Polish political ambition drove it to take advantage of instability throughout the region, venturing east into Russia until the 1634 Peace of Polyanov.
- After the Peace of Polyanov, Poland battled Sweden for control over Baltic territory.

▶ Sweden quickly reemerged in 1630 to reignite the Protestant cause.
- Allied with the Netherlands, Sweden reestablished a Protestant revival throughout Germany, driving imperial forces south.
- Ferdinand sought aid from the Catholic Spanish Hapsburgs and the Papacy.
- Sweden was defeated at Nordlingen in 1634, and Catholicism was reestablished in the south.

▶ Despite France's status as a Catholic country, it came into conflict with its neighbors—Hapsburg-ruled Spain and Austria.
- Spain's victory in Central Europe in 1634 cemented its power in the region.
- Hapsburg dominance to France's south and east represented a threat to that country, which was now surrounded by a strong military power.
- Despite their religious commonalities, France declared war on Spain in 1635 and, shortly after, the country also declared war on the Hapsburg-supported Holy Roman Empire.
- This political tactic represented a break from the prioritization of religious alliances and a movement toward emphasis on state sovereignty.

▶ The tangled alliances between European powers also resulted in war between Sweden and Austria, with the small states of the weakening Holy Roman Empire caught in the middle.
- The war had been centered on alliances and concerns about the nature of Christianity within different European countries.

- Upon signing the 1648 **Treaty of Westphalia**, the European powers agreed to recognize **state sovereignty** and practice **noninterference** in each other's matters—at the expense of family and religious allegiance.

- The year 1648 marked a transition into modern international relations, when politics and religion would no longer be inexorably intertwined.

The end of the Thirty Years' War represented the end of the domination of the Catholic Church over Europe and the concept of religious regional dominance, rather than ethnic state divisions. Over the next several centuries, the Church—and religious empires like the Ottomans—would eventually lose control over ethnic groups and their lands, later giving way to smaller **nation-states**.

As state sovereignty became entrenched in European notions of politics, so too did conflict between the states, which would eventually reflect the Continent's overseas competition:

- Upon the death of the Hapsburg Holy Roman Emperor Charles VI in 1740, the **War of the Austrian Succession** began, which was a series of Continental wars over who would take over control of the Hapsburg territories; these conflicts would lead to the Seven Years' War.

  - Though there was dispute over whether a woman—Charles's daughter **Maria Theresa**—could inherit the Austrian throne, it is more likely that **Frederick II (or Frederick the Great)** of Prussia took advantage of the instability following Charles's death in 1740 to capture the resource-rich province of Silesia from Hapsburg Austria.

  - Prussia allied with France, Bavaria, and Spain.

  - Maria Theresa sought help from Britain, which would be threatened by French dominance of Europe.

  - Britain and Spain had been in conflict over territory beyond Europe for decades: Britain and France were rivals on the North American continent, in Asia, and in the West Indies.

  - Forced to the negotiating table by dwindling finances, the European powers signed the Treaty of Aix-la-Chappelle in 1748, which granted Maria Theresa most Austrian possessions and gave Silesia to Prussia.

However, it was clear that Austria intended to regain Silesia. In an effort to protect its allies in Hanover during Continental instability, Britain formed a pragmatic alliance with Prussia, despite its traditional friendship with Austria. As a result, Austria allied with its former enemy France, in a development known as the *Diplomatic Revolution*.

In 1756, Austria was set to attack Prussia, but Frederick the Great attacked first, launching the Seven Years' War:

- In Europe, this war further cemented concepts of state sovereignty and delineated rivalries between European powers engaged in colonial adventure and overseas imperialism—especially Britain and France.

- It would kick-start British dominance in Asia and lead to Britain's loss of its North American colonies, nearly bankrupting the Crown (as discussed below).

Frederick the Great invaded Silesia and then Bohemia in 1787; however he was repelled by Austria.

Meanwhile, as the English led a Hanoverian army against the French in the west, they too were defeated and the French marched on Prussia:

- Sweden attacked from the north; Russia attacked from the east.

- Frederick called on Britain for more support.

- William Pitt the Elder, the British political leader (essentially prime minister) authorized enormous financial contributions to Prussia.

- William Pitt the Elder also began focusing the war overseas against France on imperial possessions in the Western Hemisphere and Asia.

Fortunately for the Anglo-Prussian alliance in Europe, changes in Russian leadership led to Catherine the Great's takeover. Catherine ended hostilities with Prussia and focused on development in Russia instead. This time of change in Europe would affect Asia:

- European concepts of social and political organization became constructed around national sovereignty and nation-states.

- European economies had become dependent upon colonies and were starting to industrialize, enriching Europe at the expense of its imperial possessions in the Americas, in Africa, and increasingly in Asia.

- Industrialization and political organization allowed for improved militaries, which put Asian governments at a disadvantage.

- The major Asian powers—Mughal India, Qing China, the Ottoman Empire, and Safavid (and later, Qajar) in Persia—would eventually succumb to European influence or come under direct European control.

While hostilities died down in Europe, the conflict overseas set the stage for the creation of an empire (see below).

THE AGE OF REVOLUTIONS

Monarchies in Europe had been weakened by the conflicts between Catholicism and Protestant faiths. Despite European presence and increasing power overseas, as well as its dominance in the Americas, instability on the continent and in the British Isles made the old order vulnerable.

In England, Puritans and Separatists—strict, conservative Protestants—were suspicious of King Charles I, believing he was weakening Protestantism and even possibly supporting Catholic plots. At the same time, more moderate Protestant leaders, including the weak Parliament and aristocratic class, were upset by Charles' dictatorial reign.

A combination of Enlightenment ideals and political instability would trigger revolution against **absolute monarchy** and mark the early days of the **Age of Revolutions**. Revolutionary actors drew on the philosophies of Enlightenment thinkers:

- John Locke
- Jean-Jacques Rousseau
- Montesquieu
- Voltaire

Core beliefs of Enlightenment thinkers:

- **republicanism** and democracy
- the **social contract** between the people and government
- the **separation of powers**
- the natural **rights of man**

In 1642, the **English Civil War** broke out between the **Royalists**, who supported the monarchy, and the **Parliamentarians**, who wanted a republic:

- Charles I was despotic and sidelined Parliament, causing political and military unrest.
- Conflict between England and Scotland in the late 1630s and an Irish uprising in 1641 weakened Charles further.
- Disgruntled English aristocracy, who felt that Charles had become a tyrannical ruler, withdrew support and began consolidating their own power.
- The Royalists succumbed to the Parliamentarians; Charles was executed in 1649.

Meanwhile, England had lost control over Ireland, and the Parliamentarian military leader Oliver Cromwell was sent to reestablish control over the island:

- Charles II, son of Charles I, had established control as King of Scotland.
- Cromwell defeated him, and England took back control of Scotland in 1651.
- By 1653, England once again controlled Britain and Ireland; Cromwell was installed as Lord Protector.

Following Cromwell's death, Charles II restored the Stuart monarchy; however, stability was short lived once his Catholic brother James II succeeded him in 1685.

By 1688, English Protestants asked the Dutch William of Orange, husband of James II's daughter Mary, to help restore Protestantism in Britain:

- William and Mary defeated James and consolidated Protestant control over England, Scotland, and Ireland under a Protestant constitutional monarchy in the **Glorious Revolution**.
- The 1689 English Bill of Rights established constitutional monarchy, in the spirit of the Magna Carta.

> **DID YOU KNOW?**
>
> Louis XIV built the palace of Versailles, to centralize the monarchy—and also to contain and monitor the nobility.

The **American Revolution**, also heavily influenced by Locke, broke out a century later.

The French Revolution was the precursor to the end of the feudal order in most of Europe. **King Louis XIV**, the *Sun King* (1643 – 1715), had consolidated the monarchy in France, taking true political and military power from the nobility. Meanwhile, French Enlightenment thinkers like Jean-Jacques Rousseau, Montesquieu, and Voltaire criticized absolute monarchy and the repression of freedom of speech and thought. In 1789, the French Revolution broke out.

Numerous factors were in play in the lead-up to the French Revolution:

- The power of the Catholic Church had weakened.
- The Scientific Revolution and the Enlightenment had fostered social and intellectual change.
- Colonialism and mercantilism were fueling the growth of an early middle class: people who were not traditionally nobility or landowners under the feudal system were becoming wealthier and more powerful thanks to early capitalism.
- This new middle class, the **bourgeoisie**, earned their wealth in business and chafed under the rule of the nobility, who had generally inherited land and wealth.

- France had entrenched nobilities and one of the most centralized monarchies in Europe.

- With a growing bourgeoisie and peasant class paying increasingly higher taxes to the nobility, resentment was brewing.

- The problem was most acute in France since it had the largest population in Europe at the time.

- Louis XIV had strengthened the monarchy by weakening the nobility's control over their land and centralizing power under the king.

> **DID YOU KNOW?**
>
> *A Tale of Two Cities*, by Charles Dickens, features a fictional account of the storming of the Bastille. Contrary to popular belief, Victor Hugo's *Les Misérables* takes place several decades after the French Revolution.

- Louis XIV's successors failed to govern effectively or win the loyalty of the people, causing wide resentment of both the nobility and the monarch.

- The bourgeoisie resented their lack of standing in government and society.

- Advances in medicine had permitted unprecedented population growth, further empowering the peasantry and bourgeoisie.

Having supported the American Revolution, the French government was struggling financially. In desperation, the controller-general of finances suggested reforms that would tax the nobility. An unwilling council of nobles instead called for the **Estates-General** to be convened in 1787; this toothless body had not come together since 1614.

The Estates-General was a weak representative assembly that reflected French society:

- the clergy
- the nobility
- the **Third Estate**: the middle class and the poor peasants, or *commoners*

> **DID YOU KNOW?**
>
> The burden of taxation traditionally fell on the Third Estate. In fact, peasants had to **tithe**, paying ten percent of their earnings to the nobles.

After a poor harvest in 1788, unrest spread throughout the country:

- King Louis XVI permitted elections to the Estates-General and some free speech; resentment against the elites gained momentum.

- Disagreement between the nobility and the elite clergy, on the one hand, and the Third Estate and lower-level parish priests, on the other, erupted once the Estates-General convened at Versailles in 1789.
- The two sides came to terms and formed the National Constituent Assembly.
- The king and nobility were suspicious of the other side and Louis XVI planned to dissolve it.

At the same time, panic over dwindling food supplies and suspicion over a conspiracy against the Third Estate triggered the **Great Fear** among the peasants in July 1789:

- Suspicion turned to action when the king sent troops to Paris.
- On July 14 the people stormed the **Bastille** prison in an event symbolic of the overthrow of tyranny and still celebrated in France.
- Peasantry revolt in the countryside resulted in the National Constituent Assembly's official abolishment of the feudal system and tithing.
- The Assembly issued the **Declaration of the Rights of Man and the Citizen**, the precursor to the French constitution assuring liberty and equality, in the model of Enlightenment thought.

Louis XVI refused to accept these developments; as a result, the people marched on Versailles and brought the royals back to Paris, effectively putting the Assembly in charge.

Members of the **Jacobins**, revolutionary political clubs, became members of the Assembly. The more extreme of these political figures would play key roles in the immediate future of the country.

The Assembly continued reforms:

- Lands of the Catholic Church were nationalized to pay off debt, disempowering the Church.
- The administration of the *ancien régime* (the old government) was reorganized and allowed the election of judges.
- When Louis XVI attempted to escape France, he was detained.

The French Revolution inspired revolutionary movements throughout Europe and beyond; indeed, the revolutionary principle of self-determination drove revolutionary France to support its ideals abroad:

- The country declared war on Austria in 1792.
- Following severe defeats by joint Austrian-Prussian forces, the people became suspicious of the unpopular queen **Marie Antoinette**.

- Marie Antoinette was originally from Austria and had encouraged an invasion, hoping to suppress the revolution.
- The people imprisoned the royal family.
- The Jacobins abolished the monarchy, establishing the republic later that year.

War in Europe dragged on into 1793, with considerable French losses against an alliance between Austria, Prussia, and Great Britain.

Within France, the Jacobins—essentially, the government of the Republic—were breaking into two main factions:

- Girondins
  - moderate
  - favored concentrating power in the hands of the bourgeoisie
- Montagnards
  - more extreme
  - led by Robespierre
  - favored radical social policy that empowered the poor

> **DID YOU KNOW?**
>
> An important tenet of the revolutionary ethos in France was the concept of self-determination, or the right of a people to rule themselves, which threatened rulers fearing revolution in their own countries.

Fearful of counterrevolutionaries in France and instability abroad, the republican government created the Committee of Public Safety in 1793:

- Robespierre led the Committee.
- The **Reign of Terror** began in France:
  - Thousands of people were executed by **guillotine**, including Louis XVI and Marie Antoinette.
  - Robespierre himself was executed a year later.

Ongoing war in Europe and tensions in France between republicans and royalists continued to weaken the revolution, but France had military successes in Europe:

- France had continued its effort to spread the revolution throughout the continent.
- These efforts were led by **Napoleon Bonaparte**, who even occupied Egypt in an attempt to threaten British power abroad.
- In 1799, Napoleon took power in France: the revolution was over.

In 1804 **Napoleon Bonaparte** emerged as emperor of France and proceeded to conquer much of Europe throughout the **Napoleonic Wars**, changing the face of the continent:

- French occupation of Spain weakened that country enough that revolutionary movements in its colonies strengthened; eventually Latin American colonies, inspired by the Enlightenment and revolution in Europe, won their freedom.

- Napoleon's movement eastward triggered the collapse of the Holy Roman Empire.
  - The powerful state of **Prussia** emerged in its wake, and a strong sense of militarism and Germanic nationalism took root in the face of opposition to seemingly unstoppable France.
  - Prussia would later go on to unify the small kingdoms of Central Europe that had made up the Holy Roman Empire, forming Germany, as discussed below.

Napoleon was finally defeated in Russia in 1812 and was forced by the European powers to abdicate in 1813. He escaped from prison on the Mediterranean island of Elba and raised an army again, overthrowing the restored monarch of Louis XVIII. Defeated at Waterloo by the British, he was once again exiled, this time to St. Helena in the southern Atlantic Ocean.

By 1815, other European powers had managed to halt his expansion:

- At the **Congress of Vienna** in 1815, a **balance of power** on the continent was agreed upon by European powers that included:
  - unified Prussia
  - the Austro-Hungarian Empire
  - Russia
  - Britain

> **DID YOU KNOW?**
>
> The Congress of Vienna was the first real international peace conference and set the precedent for European political organization, despite Napoleon's brief reemergence.

In the early part of the nineteenth century, Latin American countries joined Haiti and the United States in revolution against colonial European powers. These movements were inspired by the American and French Revolutions.

Independence movements were led or influenced by **Simón Bolivar** in:

- Venezuela
- Colombia (including present-day Panama)

> **CHECK YOUR UNDERSTANDING #9**
>
> How did the emergence of a new middle class—the bourgeoisie—set the stage for revolution in Europe and beyond?

- Ecuador
- Peru
- Bolivia

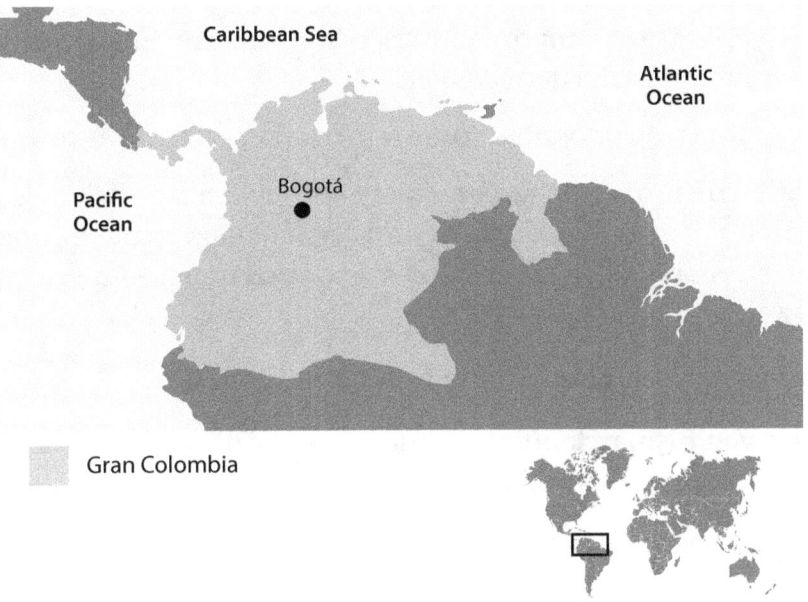

Figure 1.25. Gran Colombia

EUROPEAN DIVISION

The nineteenth century was a period of change and conflict, and the roots of the major twentieth-century conflicts—world war and decolonization—are found in it:

- Nationalism and the nation-state would begin to emerge, becoming a part of modern European social and political norms.
- Economic theories based in the Industrial Revolution like **socialism** and eventually **communism** gained traction.
- **Urbanization** and industry led to stark class divisions (which also helped fuel interest in socialism and communism).

Following the Napoleonic Wars, Prussia had come to dominate the German-speaking states that once comprised the Holy Roman Empire. Prussia, a distinct kingdom within the Holy Roman Empire since the thirteenth century, had become a powerful Central European state by the eighteenth century:

- Prussia became the main rival of Austria for influence in the Germanic lands of Central Europe.
- By the nineteenth century and due in part to emphasis on military prowess, Prussia became an important military power—and a key ally in the efforts against Napoleon.

- Prussia had a particular rivalry with France after losing several key territories during the Napoleonic Wars.
- In 1870, the militarily powerful kingdom went to war against France in the **Franco-Prussian War**.
  - Prussia took control of Alsace-Lorraine, mineral rich and essential for industrial development.

Prussian power would continue to grow in the wake of the Franco-Prussian War:

- **Nationalism** and the **nation-state**—the idea that individuals with shared experience (including ethnicity, language, religion, and cultural practices) should be unified under one government—fueled Prussian power.
- In 1871, the **German Empire** became a united state.
- **Otto von Bismarck** unified those linguistically and culturally German states of Central Europe:
  - Economic cooperation was encouraged.
  - Army reforms were instituted.
  - An image of Prussia as a defender of German culture and nationhood was created.

Nationalism also led to **Italian Unification**:

- Italy, a region of small independent states, was occupied by France and then Austria toward the end of the eighteenth century.
- After being invaded and occupied by Napoleon, the Italian peninsula was divided into three regions.
- Napoleonic concepts of nationalism, freedom, equality, and justice under the law spread throughout the peninsula; what was left of feudalism faded.

Despite re-fragmentation throughout the nineteenth century following the fall of Napoleon, a secret movement for reorganization—the **Risorgimento**—began working toward Italian unification:

- Following the 1859 Franco-Austrian War, Austria's loss of territorial control in northern Italy allowed Italian states to unite via elections.
- Giuseppe Garibaldi led the Northern Italian overthrow of Southern Italian monarchies, uniting the Peninsula with the exception of Rome and Venice.
- The Kingdom of Italy was declared in 1861, under Victor Emmanuel II.

- An Italian alliance with Prussia during the **Austro-Prussian War** in 1866 (in which Austria lost even more territory) allowed Italy to take control of Venice.

- The Kingdom of Italy entered Rome and incorporated that city and the Papal States during the Franco-Prussian War.

CONFLICT IN THE BALKANS

Farther east, as European kingdoms and empires consolidated their power, the Ottoman Empire was in decline:

- The Ottoman Empire had long been a major force in Europe and controlled the bulk of the Balkans.

- The empire had lost land in Europe to the Austrians and in Africa to British and French imperialists.

- In the Balkans, rebellion among small nations supported by European puppet masters would put an end to Ottoman power in Europe for good.

Despite previous conflict between some of these powers, deeper rivalries throughout the continent inspired Russia, Germany, and Austria-Hungary to form the **Three Emperors' League** in 1873:

- If one country went to war, the others would remain neutral, and the powers would consult each other on matters of war.

- The **First Balkan Crisis** in 1874 put an end to this alliance:
  - Bosnia Herzegovina rebelled against Ottoman rule.
  - Christian peasants in Herzegovina were unwilling to submit to Muslim landlords.
  - Regional Christians and Bosnian Muslims were no longer willing to submit to rule by the ethnically different Turks, thus beginning the First Balkan Crisis.

Two years later, the Ottoman autonomous principality of Serbia, joined by Montenegro, rebelled in support of Bosnia:

- Serbian rebellion attracted Russian attention after Serbia came under Russian influence due to Pan-Slavism.
  - **Pan-Slavism** is the concept that Slavic ethnic groups throughout Eastern and Southeastern Europe should embrace their Slavic heritage and turn toward Russia for support.

- When the Ottoman **Sultan Hamid II** refused to institute reforms to protect Balkan Christians, Russia declared war.

- The **Russo-Turkish War** ended in 1878 with the **Treaty of San Stefano**, which favored Russian territorial gains.

- Austro-Hungarian and British objections to the treaty, which threatened their influence in the region, led to the **1878 Congress of Berlin**, hosted by Otto von Bismarck.

- Unfortunately for Russia, which was the militarily and financially weaker power, Britain and Austria-Hungary changed the outcome of the war with the **Treaty of Berlin**, which replaced the Treaty of San Stefano.

  - While the independence of Serbia and Montenegro was decided, Russia lost influence in Bulgaria as well as territorial gains in Asia. These insults would not be forgotten.

Given developments in the Balkans, Germany and Austria-Hungary secretly formed the Dual Alliance to respond to fears of Pan-Slavism. In 1882, Italy asked these countries for assistance against France, which had upset Italian imperial ambition in North Africa; the **Triple Alliance**, a secret political and military alliance was formed.

Stability in the Balkans and among the great powers was further threatened by the 1885 **Second Balkan Crisis**:

- Bulgaria declared unification and independence, violating the Treaty of Berlin and Russian interests.

- Serbia went to war against Bulgaria, requiring Austro-Hungarian support.

Eventually, tension between Russia and Austria-Hungary—which was supported by Germany—led to the breakdown of Russian relationships with those countries. Russian relations improved with Great Britain and France.

> **CHECK YOUR UNDERSTANDING #10**
>
> List some important European alliances in the nineteenth century.

In 1894, Russia and France became allies. Great Britain would join this alliance in the 1907 **Triple Entente**, setting the stage for the system of alliances at the heart of the First World War.

Continued European involvement in the Balkans accelerated the ongoing loss of Ottoman influence there due to phenomena like nationalism, ethnocentrism (Pan-Slavism), military and political power, and religious influence. The small Balkan nations were empowered to continue rebellion against Ottoman rule, and European powers proceeded into the area:

- In 1908, Austria-Hungary annexed Bosnia-Herzegovina, disregarding Russian objections.
- Russia helped form the **Balkan League**, comprised of Serbia, Montenegro, Greece, and Bulgaria, which went to war with the Ottomans in the 1912 **First Balkan War**.
- The Ottomans were defeated and lost nearly all their European possessions.

The following year, disagreement over the division of land led to the **Second Balkan War**:

- The Second Balkan War was between Bulgaria and a Serbian-Greek alliance.
  - Serbia wanted to keep Albanian territory, which Austria-Hungary insisted remain independent.
  - Bulgaria wanted control over more land in Macedonia (which had come mainly under Greek and Serbian rule).
- This instability would eventually lead to the First World War.

IMPERIALISM

Colonialism and imperialism contributed to ongoing tensions between nation-states on the continent of Europe:

Table 1.2. Causes of Colonialism and Imperialism over the Centuries

Century	Colonialism	Imperialism
Fifteenth century	• mercantilism • conquest • Christian conversion	
Sixteenth century		
Seventeenth century		• capitalism • European competition • conceptions of racial superiority
Eighteenth century		
Nineteenth century		

Britain and France, historic rivals on the European continent, were also at odds colonizing North America and in overseas trade, and helped fuel the **Seven Years' War (1756 – 1763)**:

- Britain and France fought in Europe and overseas colonies and interests in North America and Asia.

DID YOU KNOW?

The Seven Years' War is considered by many historians to be the first truly global conflict.

- Alliances:
  - Britain, Prussia, and Hanover
  - France, Austria, Sweden, Russia
- The war's extension into the imperial realm made it a global conflict.

In North America, Britain and France had explored the region and controlled tremendous amounts of territory in what later would become Canada and the United States.

Table 1.3. British and French Control in North America

	Territory	Major Ports	Major Exports
Britain	• Thirteen Colonies (Atlantic coast)	• New York • Philadelphia • Boston	• tobacco • rice • vegetables • various crops
France	• Quebec • Northeastern territories • territory in the Midwest that included interior trade routes through much of **the Great Lakes** region	• Major Ports: • Montreal • Quebec City • St. Lawrence River (leading to Atlantic Ocean) • Detroit River (leading to the St. Lawrence River) • Mississippi River • Port of New Orleans (leading to the Gulf of Mexico)	• beaver pelts (valuable in Europe for their water-repellant properties) • timber • various natural resources

The **French and Indian War**, as the Seven Years' War is called in North America, resulted in net gains for Britain:

- France formed an important alliance with the powerful Algonquin in the Northeast.
- Britain was allied with the Iroquois.
- Strong military leaders like **George Washington** helped Britain take control of French Canada.

The conflict in Europe, however, would put a strain on Britain:

- Financially exhausted from the costly conflict in Europe, Britain ceded control of the Northwest Territories (Michigan, Ohio, Indiana) to various tribes in the **Treaty of Paris in 1763** (agreements later not honored by the United States).

- The financial and military strain suffered by Britain in the Seven Years' War made it particularly vulnerable to later rebellion in the Colonies, helping the Americans win the Revolutionary War there.

According to Pitt the Elder's plan, Britain went to war with France in Asia as well:

- The decline of the **Mughal Empire** in India and the rising power of colonial companies specializing in exporting valuable resources like spices and tea, led to the formation of smaller Indian kingdoms that formed alliances with those increasingly influential corporations.

- By the mid-eighteenth century, violence broke out between the British East India Company and the French East India Company and their allies among the small Indian states in a series of wars known as the **Carnatic Wars** (1746 – 1763).

- With the end of the Seven Years' War, the Treaty of Paris established British dominance in the Subcontinent.

  - France was allowed some trading posts in the region but was forced to recognize British power there.

  - By 1803, British interests effectively took control of the Subcontinent and the Mughals were pushed to the north.

> **DID YOU KNOW?**
>
> The Netherlands was already coming to dominate Indonesia (at the time, the Dutch East Indies) thanks to similar actions by the Dutch East India Company.

Despite losing the Thirteen Colonies, at the dawn of the nineteenth century Britain retained control of Canada, rich in natural resources like beaver pelts and timber. In addition, it controlled the resource-rich and strategically important Indian Subcontinent. Britain would become the strongest naval power in the world and continue to expand its empire, especially in the search for new markets for its manufactured goods to support its industrial economy.

During the reign of **Queen Victoria** (1837 – 1901), the British Empire would expand to lengths not seen up to this time:

- In 1788, Britain had begun sending convicts to the penal colony of Australia.

  - Gold was discovered there in 1851, and British subjects began to voluntarily settle Australia and the Pacific.

- In 1857, the **Indian Mutiny** against private British troops controlled by the East India Company caused the British government to intervene and send in military.
  - Victoria would eventually take the title of **Empress of India**, cementing the imperial nature of government and the Raj (imperial administration).
- In 1877, the British annexed South Africa.
  - Following the Boer Wars, Britain would retain control of diamond- and gold-rich South Africa (see below).
- Victoria chartered the imperialist **Cecil Rhodes** and his company, the British South Africa Company (BSAC) to explore north from South Africa to mine the land.
  - This charter was ordered despite numerous factors:
    - conflicting European claims to the land
    - claims by the Afrikaaners, (see below)
    - the residence of the Matabele, who had lived there for centuries
- Rhodes and the BSAC forcefully took over and brought the following territories under English rule using treaties, diplomacy, and violence:
  - Northern Rhodesia (Zambia)
  - Rhodesia (Zimbabwe)
  - Nyasaland (Malawi)
  - Bechuanaland (Botswana)

In East Africa, the British explorer **David Livingstone** had been working in Kenya; the government had influence over the Sultan of Zanzibar. However, secret German agreements with coastal leaders and the establishment of the German colony of Tanganyika forced the British into more activity in the region. In an agreement with the Germans, the British took control over what would become Kenya and Uganda, while Germany maintained Tanganyika. Borders were drawn without regard for the Kikuyu, Masai, Luo, and other tribes living in the area.

The racist concept of the **white man's burden** drove imperialism. White Europeans were "obligated" to bring what they considered their superior culture to other civilizations around the globe. This idea was popular in Britain and elsewhere in Europe.

Despite its small size, Belgium controlled the Congo, along with its vast resources in Central Africa. Coming into conflict with Rhodes at its southern edges, the Belgian Congo, which reached its heights under **King Leopold II**, was rich in rubber, timber, minerals, and diamonds. Furthermore, this territory was strategically important: controlling the Congo meant controlling the Congo River basin, allowing for the extraction of materials from the interior to the Atlantic Coast.

> **CHECK YOUR UNDERSTANDING #11**
>
> List some of the European powers' justifications for imperialism.

To gain access to closed Chinese markets, Britain forced China to buy Indian opium:

- The Opium Wars ended with the **Treaty of Nanking (1842)**, signed between the British and the increasingly impotent Qing government.

- As a result, China lost great power to Britain and other European countries, which gained:
  - **spheres of influence** (areas of China they effectively controlled)
  - **extraterritoriality** (privileges in which their citizens were not subject to Chinese law)

Even though nominally Chinese leadership still governed, discontent with the Qing Dynasty was growing as Chinese people perceived that their country was coming under control of European imperialists:

- The combination of economic hardship and huge casualties in the Opium Wars and in the **Sino-Japanese War of 1896** (see below) led to a violent uprising.

  - In 1900, the **Boxer Rebellion**, an uprising led by a Chinese society against the emperor, was only put down with Western (including American) help.

  > **DID YOU KNOW?**
  >
  > The Boxers were so called because of their belief that physical exercises, like shadow boxing, would make them impervious to bullets. This rebellion was led by a secret society called the Yihequan, or The Society of Righteous and Harmonious Fists.

  - The Qing were humiliated further by being forced to pay the West enormous reparations for their assistance.

  - Living conditions for Chinese people continued to deteriorate.

The European powers were immersed in what became known as the *Scramble for Africa*. The industrial economies of Europe would profit from the natural resources abundant on that continent, and the white man's burden continued to fuel colonization.

At the **1884 Berlin Conference**, control over Africa was divided among European powers. (Africans were not consulted in this process.)

The **Boer War** (1899–1902) between Afrikaaners of Dutch origin and the English, resulted in Britain officially gaining control of South Africa. Whites would rule the country until the end of **Apartheid** in the early 1990s.

France would eventually control the following:

▶ West Africa

▶ North Africa

　▷ Algeria

　▷ Mali

　▷ Niger

　▷ Chad

　▷ Cameroon

　▷ present-day Republic of the Congo (not to be confused with Belgian Congo, now the Democratic Republic of the Congo)

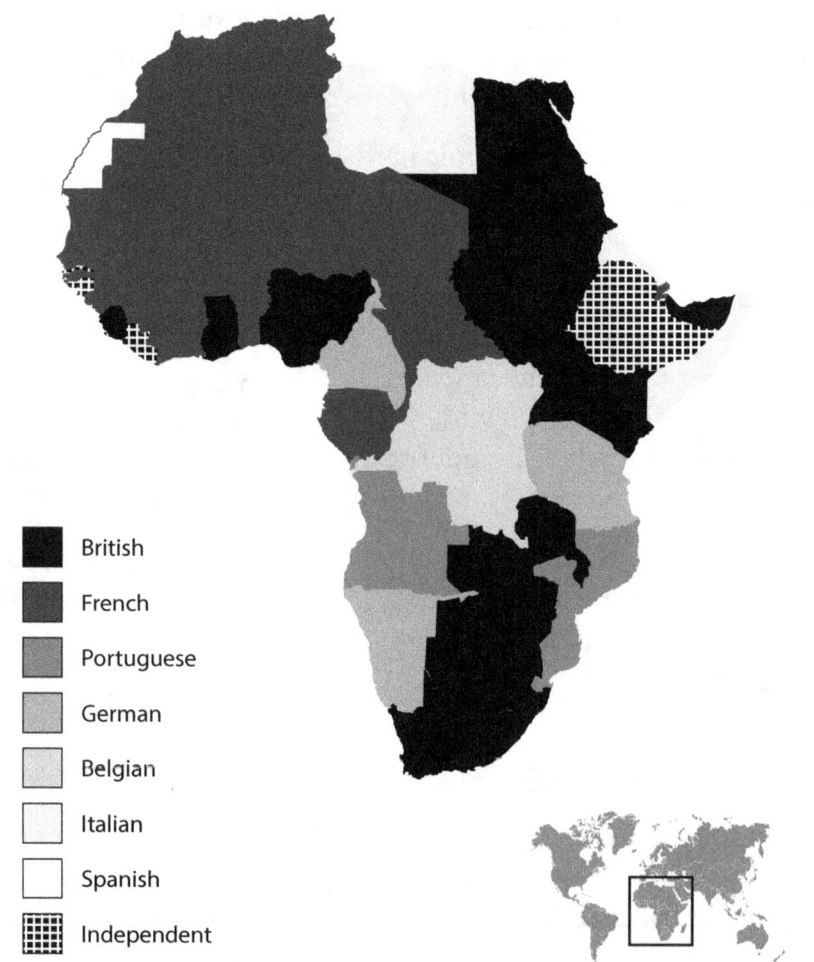

Figure 1.26. Imperial Africa

However, not all non-European countries fell to European imperialism:

- Emperor Meiji promoted the modernization of technology, especially the military, during the **Meiji Restoration** in Japan in 1868.

- Japan proved itself a world power when it defeated Russia in the **Russo-Japanese War** in 1905.

- Japan would go on to play a central role in twentieth century conflict.

INDUSTRIAL REVOLUTION

Throughout this entire period, raw goods from the Americas fueled European economic growth and development, leading to the **Industrial Revolution** in the nineteenth century:

- This economic revolution began with textile production in Britain, fueled by cotton from its overseas territories in North America, and later India and Egypt.

- The first factories were in Manchester, where **urbanization** began as poor people from rural areas flocked to cities in search of higher-paying unskilled jobs in factories.

- Early industrial technology sped up the harvesting and transport of crops and their conversion to textiles.

This accelerated manufacturing was based on **capitalism**, the **laissez-faire** (or **free market**) theory developed by Adam Smith, who believed that an *invisible hand* should guide the marketplace: government should stay out of the economy regardless of abuses since the economy would eventually automatically correct for inequalities, price problems, and any other problematic issues.

Advances in technology also helped accelerate manufacturing:

- The spinning jenny and flying shuttle exponentially increased the amount of cotton that workers could process into yarn and thread.

- The steam engine efficiently powered mills and ironworks; factories no longer had to be built near running water to access power.

Figure 1.27. Spinning Jenny

- Improvement in iron technology allowed for stronger machinery; it would also support the **Second Industrial Revolution** in the late nineteenth and early twentieth centuries, which was based on heavy industry, railroads, and weapons.

To access the raw materials needed to produce manufactured goods, Britain and other industrializing countries in Western Europe needed resources—hence the drive for imperialism as discussed above:

- Cotton was harvested in India and Egypt for textile mills.
- Minerals mined in South Africa and the Congo were used to support metallurgy.

Industrialization and urbanization led to the development of early middle classes in Europe and North America, resulting in increased imports of luxury goods like tea, spices, silk, precious metals, and other items from Asia to meet consumer demand.

Colonial powers also gained by selling manufactured goods back to the colonies from which they had harvested raw materials in the first place, for considerable profit.

Largely unbridled capitalism had led to the conditions of the early Industrial Revolution; workers suffered from abusive treatment, overly long hours, low wages (or none at all), and unsafe conditions, including pollution. The German philosophers Karl Marx and Friedrich Engels, horrified by conditions suffered by industrial workers, developed **socialism**:

- Socialism is the philosophy that workers, or the **proletariat**, should own the means of production and reap the profits.
- The **bourgeoisie**, who had no interest in the rights of the workers at the expense of profit and who did not experience the same conditions, should not own the means of production nor claim its profits.
- Marx wrote *Das Kapital*:
  - He offered arguments for the abolition of the class system, wages, and private property.
  - He favored collective ownership of both the means of production and products, with equal distribution of income to satisfy the needs of all.
- Later, Marx and Engels wrote the *Communist Manifesto*:
  - The *Communist Manifesto* outlined their ideas and called for revolution.
  - It inspired the formation of socialist groups worldwide.

A different version of socialism would later help Russia become a major world power. The Russian intellectuals **Vladimir Lenin** and **Leon Trotsky** would take Marx and Engels' theories further, developing Marxism-Leninism:

▶ They embraced socialist ideals and believed in revolution.

▶ They felt that communism could not be maintained under a democratic governing structure.

▶ Lenin supported dictatorship, more precisely the **dictatorship of the proletariat**, paving the way for the political and economic organization of the Soviet Union.

> **DID YOU KNOW?**
>
> The Communist Manifesto contained the famous words, "Workers of the world, unite!"

PRACTICE QUESTIONS

11) What did the Treaty of Westphalia do?
    A. laid out the final borders of Europe, setting the stage for modern foreign policy
    B. established the notion of state sovereignty, in which states recognized each other as independent and agreed not to interfere in each other's affairs
    C. gave the Catholic Church more power in the affairs of Catholic-majority countries
    D. established the notion of the nation-state, in which culturally and ethnically similar groups would control their own territory as sovereign countries

12) What was an important factor that led to the French Revolution?
    A. the corruption of Louis XIV
    B. the strong organization of the Estates-Genera
    C. support from the United States of America
    D. the anti-monarchical philosophies of Enlightenment thinkers like Rousseau and Voltaire

13) How did Pan-Slavism affect the crises in the Balkans?
    A. Pan-Slavism led Russia to directly intervene militarily throughout the nineteenth century in the Balkans, leading to violent conflict.
    B. Pan-Slavism generally ensured Russian support for Slavic ethnic groups in the Balkans, which contributed to ongoing tensions there already fueled by competing European and Ottoman interests and diverse nationalities.
    C. Russian interests in Slavic groups in the Balkans strengthened its alliance with Turkey.
    D. Pan-Slavism did not have a major effect on the Balkans, as the major Slavic cultures are located farther north in Europe.

14) Which of the following is NOT a way that the white man's burden influenced imperialism?
   A. It inspired Europeans to settle overseas in order to improve what they believed to be "backward" places.
   B. Europeans believed imperialism was in the best interest of Indigenous peoples, who would benefit from adopting European languages and cultural practices.
   C. Europeans believed it burdensome to be forced to tutor non-Europeans in their languages and customs.
   D. Many Europeans supported the construction of schools for colonial subjects and even the development of scholarships for them to study in Europe.

15) Which of the following did Marx and Engels believe?
   A. The proletariat must control the means of production to ensure a wageless, classless society to equitably meet the needs of all.
   B. The workers would control the means of production in the dictatorship of the proletariat.
   C. An organized revolution directed by a small group of leaders was necessary to bring about social change and a socialist society.
   D. The bourgeoisie would willingly give up control of the means of production to the proletariat.

Global Conflicts

Pre-Revolutionary Russia

Russia had gone to war with Japan in 1904 to secure access to the Pacific as well as its interests in Asia. **Tsar Nicholas II**, unpopular at home, also believed that a victory would improve his security as a ruler. Japan, concerned about losing influence in Korea and seeking influence in China, attacked Russia; the **Russo-Japanese War** quickly ended in 1905 due to superior Japanese military technology, including naval technology, training, and leadership.

Russia's loss to Japan in the 1905 Russo-Japanese War was just another example of its difference from other European powers:

▶ While technically a European country, Russia had been slow to industrialize, due in part to its size and terrain.

▶ A largely agrarian country at the turn of the century, **serfdom**, the practice of "tying" peasants to the land and the last vestiges of feudalism, had only been abolished in 1861.

▶ Most Russians were still poor, rural farmers, and industrialization brought wretched conditions to workers in the cities.

- Russia also continued to have an absolute monarchy, unlike many European powers whose governments had shifted during the Age of Revolution.

Numerous factors caused Tsar Nicholas to face dissent at home:

- the humiliating defeat by the Japanese

- discontent fueled by longer-term economic hardship in the face of a strengthening European industrial economy

- limited freedoms in comparison to those enjoyed elsewhere in Europe

As a result, unlawful trade unions appeared, workers began striking, and peasants rose up in protest of oppressive taxation.

Figure 1.28. Bloody Sunday

Still, many Russians blamed the Tsar's advisors and minor officials for conditions, believing that the Tsar himself would act to improve conditions for Russians. These ideas were shattered in 1905 when a peaceful protest of working conditions in St. Petersburg ended in a bloody massacre of civilians by the Tsar's troops. **Bloody Sunday**, as the event came to be called, resulted in the **Revolution of 1905**, during which the Tsar temporarily lost control of Russia and was discredited.

Following the Revolution of 1905, the Tsar made some reforms in Russia, including the establishment of a **Duma**, or Parliament. However, economic hardship and social discontent continued in the country.

While not directly involved with the failed Revolution of 1905, the Marxist Social Democrats—made up of the **Bolsheviks**, led by **Lenin**, and the **Mensheviks**—would gain power. They would eventually take over the country in 1917.

WORLD WAR I

Instability in the Balkans and increasing tensions in Europe culminated with the assassination of the Austro-Hungarian Archduke **Franz Ferdinand** by the Serbian nationalist **Gavrilo Princip** in Sarajevo on June 28, 1914.

In protest of continuing Austro-Hungarian control over Serbia, Princip's action kicked off the **system of alliances** that had been in place among European powers:

- Austria-Hungary declared war on Serbia; Russia came to Serbia's aid.

- As part of the Triple Alliance and an ally of Austria-Hungary, Germany declared war on Russia.

- Russia's ally France prepared for war.

- As Germany traversed Belgium to invade France, Belgium pleaded for aid from other European countries, which led Britain to declare war on Germany.

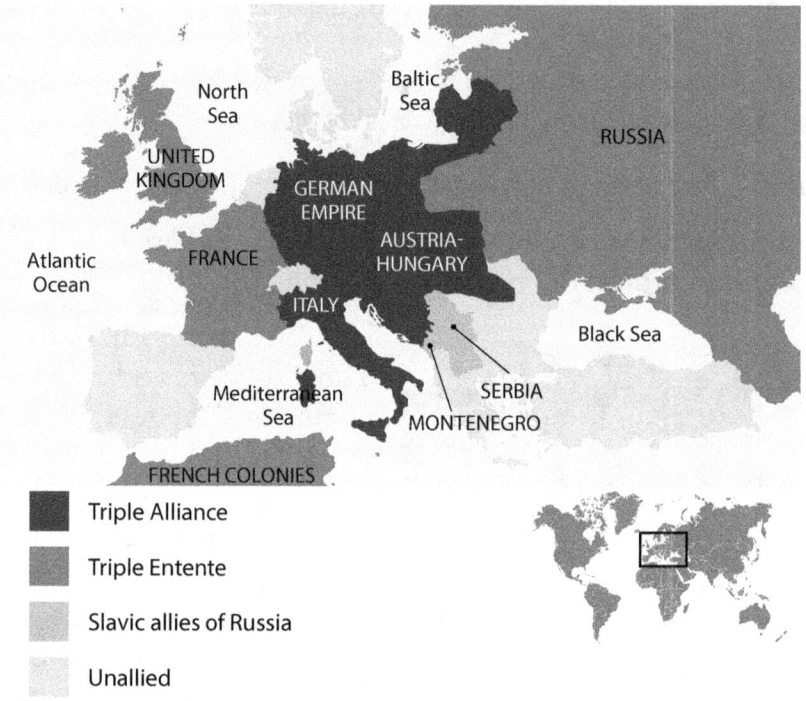

Figure 1.29. WWI Alliances

Germany had been emphasizing military growth since the consolidation and militarization of the empire under Bismarck in the mid-nineteenth century. Germany was a militarized state and an important European power in its own right, and the country was now under **Kaiser Wilhelm II**:

- Wilhelm took over the German Empire in 1888.

- He was the grandson of Frederick II (on his father's side) and Queen Victoria.

- He focused on improving naval power and expanding German territory overseas (including the potential capture of overseas British and French colonies).

Despite Wilhelm's connections to Britain, Germany's threat to British overseas power brought the war beyond Europe to Africa and Asia:

- In Togo, Britain and France took over an important German communications point.

- In China, Japan allied with Britain and France and took control of the German settlement of Tsingtao and German colonies in the Pacific Islands.

- Britain's imperial power allowed it to call on troops from all over the globe—Indians, Canadians, Australians, South Africans, and New Zealanders all fought in Europe.

- France also imported colonial fighters from North Africa.

Table 1.4. Important Military Campaigns of WWI

Battle	Year	Description	Impact
Battle of the Marne	1914	• German, French, and British forces defended France.	• trench warfare that would continue for years, marking the Western Front
Gallipoli	1915	• Australian and New Zealander troops fought the Ottoman Empire, allies of Germany, near Istanbul.	• heavy casualties sustained by the British Commonwealth • The reputation of the Allies' military force was weakened.
Battle of Verdun	1916	• the longest battle of the war	• The Germans failed to defeat the French army.
Battle of Jutland	1916	• The British navy pushed back the German navy. • heavy losses suffered by the British	• Britain was able to ensure that German naval power was diminished for the rest of the war.
Battle of the Somme	1916 (July 1)	• part of an allied effort to repel Germany using artillery to end the stalemate on the Western Front	• After four months, the Front moved only five miles.

Finally, in 1917, the United States learned of the **Zimmerman Telegram**, in which Germany secretly proposed an alliance with Mexico to attack the US. This finally spurred US intervention in the war. Despite Russian withdrawal after the Bolshevik Revolution in October 1917, Germany was forced to surrender in the face of invasion by the US-supported allies.

According to the **Schlieffen Plan**, Germany had planned to fight a war on two fronts against both Russia and France; however, Russia's unexpectedly rapid mobilization stretched the German army too thin on the Eastern Front, while it became bogged down in **trench warfare** on the Western Front against the British, French, and later the Americans.

> **DID YOU KNOW?**
>
> In 1915, a German submarine (U-boat) sank the *Lusitania*, a passenger ship in the Atlantic, killing many American civilians. This event strained relations with a neutral US, which would enter the war in 1917.

Germany lost the war and was punished with the harsh **Treaty of Versailles**, which held it accountable for the entirety of the war:

- The Treaty brought economic hardship on the country by forcing it to pay **reparations**.

- Wilhelm was forced to abdicate and never again regained power in Germany.

- The Treaty resulted in German military failure and consequent economic collapse. These, combined with later worldwide economic depression, set the stage for the rise of fascism and Adolf Hitler.

> **DID YOU KNOW?**
>
> The first international war to use industrialized weaponry, WWI was called "the Great War" because battle on such a scale had never before been seen.

- The Treaty created the **League of Nations**, an international organization designed to prevent future outbreaks of international war. It was largely toothless, especially because the powerful United States did not join.

Change in the Middle East

The end of WWI also marked the end of the Ottoman Empire. A number of factors led to the empire's eventual dissolution:

- An ally of Germany, the Ottoman Empire had been defeated in the war.

- Tremendous losses led to the collapse of many Ottoman institutions.

- Poor organization and refugee movements led to starvation and chaos throughout the region.

- In 1908, the Young Turks, a military government, effectively took over the empire in an effort to modernize it.
  - They were especially concerned with nationalism and promoting *Turkishness*, a focus on Turkish ethnicity and culture, throughout the diverse empire.

- The Ottomans had already lost their North African provinces to France in the mid-nineteenth century.

- From the end of the nineteenth century, the British had been increasing their influence throughout Ottoman territory in Egypt and the Persian Gulf, seeking control over the Suez Canal and petroleum resources in the Gulf.

- In 1916, France and Britain concluded the **Sykes-Picot Agreement**, which secretly planned for the Middle East following the defeat of the Ottoman Empire.
  - The Agreement divided up the region now considered the Middle East into spheres of influence to be controlled by each power; Palestine would be governed internationally.
- In 1917, the secret **Balfour Declaration** promised the Jews an independent state in Palestine, but Western powers did not honor this agreement; in fact it conflicted directly with the Sykes-Picot Agreement. The state of Israel was not established until 1948.
- The Ottoman Empire was officially dissolved in 1923.

At the end of the war the area was indeed divided into **mandates**, areas nominally independent but effectively controlled by Britain and France. The borders drawn are essentially those national borders that divide the Middle East today.

After the First World War, the nationalist **Mustafa Ataturk**, one of the Young Turks who pushed a secular, nationalist agenda, kept European powers out of Anatolia and abolished the Caliphate in 1924, establishing modern Turkey.

After the dissolution of the Ottoman Empire, the future of the Middle East was uncertain.

> **DID YOU KNOW?**
>
> In 1915, the Ottoman Empire launched a genocide against the Christian Armenian people, part of a campaign to control ethnic groups it believed threatened the Turkish nature of the empire. An estimated 1.5 million Armenians were removed from their homes and killed. The Turkish government still denies the Armenian Genocide.

Table 1.5. The Middle East During and After the Ottoman Empire

During the Ottoman Empire	After the Ottoman Empire
- Ottoman caliphate represented the symbolic center of Islam - Ottoman caliphate controlled the holy cities of Mecca and Medina - unifying religious leadership (caliph was entrusted with the leadership of those two holy cities)	- broken up into European-controlled protectorates - Turkey—nationalist, secular, and independent—turned toward Europe - unraveling of the social and political fabric of the region - no longer a caliph/unifying religious leader - refugees and migrants suddenly restricted by international borders from their places of origin - people needed—and lacked—identification papers - ethnic and religious groups divided by what would become the borders of the modern Middle East

France and Britain backed different political factions in their mandates:

- Nominally autonomous Egypt and its ruler, King Fuad, were close allies of the British, having essentially been under their control.
- Husayn ibn Ali (King Hussein), the sharif (ruler) of Mecca, claimed the title of caliph, but was driven out and made king of Jordan by the British. (His family controls the monarchy to this day.)
- The rest of the Arabian Peninsula, where oil had not yet been discovered, was taken by the Saudis, a tribe from the desert which followed an extreme form of Islam, the **Wahhabi Movement**.
  - King Saud would eventually conquer Mecca and Medina but never take the title of Caliph.

The roots of two competing ideologies, Pan-Arabism and Islamism, developed in this context.

- **Pan-Arabism** became an international movement espousing Arab unity in response to European and US influence and presence later in the twentieth century.
  - Arabs and Arabic speakers should be aligned regardless of international borders.
- **Islamism** began as a social and political movement.
  - The Muslim Brotherhood was established in Egypt in the 1920s, filling social roles that the state had abandoned or could not fill.
  - Eventually taking a political role, the Muslim Brotherhood's model later inspired groups like Hamas and Hezbollah.

Russian Revolution

During WWI, a combination of failures at home and on the front only added to widespread dissatisfaction with the rule of the tsar:

- Russia was suffering from widespread food shortages and economic crisis.
- Morale was low due to conscription.
- The military suffered losses and defeats under the command of Nicholas II.

An enormous strike in Petrograd in January 1917 commemorating Bloody Sunday ended in revolt.

- Soldiers refused to fire on protesters.

- The people formed the elected Petrograd Soviet (Petrograd Council) in the **February Revolution**.
- The Tsar was forced to abdicate.
- The revolutionary movement resulted in the fall of his family, the Romanovs.

A weak provisional government was formed until elections could be held.

- It was widely regarded as working in the interests of the elite, making unpopular decisions like continuing to engage in WWI and putting off land reform.
- The Provisional Government was ineffective in solving economic problems.

Meanwhile, other Soviets (councils) formed beyond Petrograd. The elected Soviets seemed to better represent the interests of the workers and peasants who suffered the most, and so they became more powerful. At the same time, the Soviets appealed to discontented soldiers fighting in the unpopular war.

Unlike the Mensheviks, the Bolsheviks, led by Lenin, believed that revolution must be planned and instigated at the right moment—not a phenomenon meant to occur naturally. Consequently, they were not involved in the February Revolution.

Ideologies of Lenin and the Bolsheviks:

- Lenin believed that revolution must be planned, and that the proletariat needed direction in beginning and pursuing a revolution.
- Later in 1917, the Bolsheviks had become a stronger force, and Lenin believed that the time was right to trigger revolution in Russia.

Lenin and the Bolsheviks proposed a number of changes:

- power would be concentrated in the Soviets, not in the Duma
- Russia would make peace and withdraw from European hostilities
- land would be redistributed among the peasants
- economic crises in the cities would be solved

Lenin's plan was to take control of the Petrograd Soviet, of which Leon Trotsky had become chairman.

In the **October Revolution** Lenin, Trotsky, and the Bolsheviks took control of Russia, defeating the Provisional Government in a coup.

In 1918, despite withdrawal from WWI, the **Russian Civil War** was underway:

- The White Armies, former supporters of the Tsar, were in conflict with the Bolshevik Red Army.

- During the war, the communists consolidated their power by nationalizing industry, developing and distributing propaganda portraying themselves as the defenders of Russia against imperialism, and forcefully eliminating dissent.
- For many, it was more appealing to fight for a new Russia with hope for an improved standard of living than to return to the old times under the Tsar.
- Many Russians feared the specter of imperialism or interference by foreign powers.
- By 1921, the Bolsheviks were victorious and formed the **Soviet Union** or **Union of Soviet Socialist Republics (USSR)**.

Following Lenin's death in 1924, Trotsky and the Secretary of the Communist Party, **Josef Stalin**, struggled for power. Stalin ultimately outmaneuvered Trotsky, who was exiled and assassinated.

Under Stalin's totalitarian dictatorship, the USSR became socially and politically repressive:

- The Communist Party and the military underwent **purges** where any persons who were a potential threat to Stalin's power were imprisoned or executed.
- Stalin's paranoia and oppression extended to the general population.
  - Russians suffered under the Great Terror throughout the 1920s.
  - Any hint of dissent was to be reported to the secret police—the NKVD—and usually resulted in imprisonment for life.
- Stalin enforced **Russification** policies, persecuting ethnic groups.
  - People throughout the USSR were forced to speak Russian and limit or hide their own cultural practices.
  - Religious practices were restricted or forbidden.
- In 1931, Stalin enforced the **collectivization** of land and agriculture in an attempt to consolidate control over the countryside and improve food security.
  - He had the *kulaks*, or landowning peasants, sent to the *gulags*, enabling the government to confiscate their land.
  - By 1939, most farming and land was controlled by the government, and most peasants lived on collective land.

- ▷ Collectivizing the farms enabled Stalin to encourage more peasants to leave the country and become industrial workers, produce agricultural surpluses to sell overseas, and eliminate the *kulaks*.
- ▶ Systemic disorganization in the 1920s and early 1930s resulted in famine and food shortages.

As part of modernizing Russia, Stalin focused on accelerating industrial development:

- ▶ He targeted heavy industry with **Five Year Plans**.
  - ▷ Production in industrial materials and staples like electricity, petroleum, coal, and iron increased.
  - ▷ Construction of major infrastructure throughout the country took place from 1929 – 1938.
- ▶ These developments provided opportunities for women, but conditions for the workers were dismal.
- ▶ The USSR quickly became an industrial power, but at the expense of millions of Russians, Ukrainians, and other groups who lost their lives in purges, forced labor camps, and famine.

> **DID YOU KNOW?**
>
> In the 1920s, around twenty million Russians were sent to the gulags, or prison labor camps, usually in Siberia, thousands of miles from their homes. Millions died.

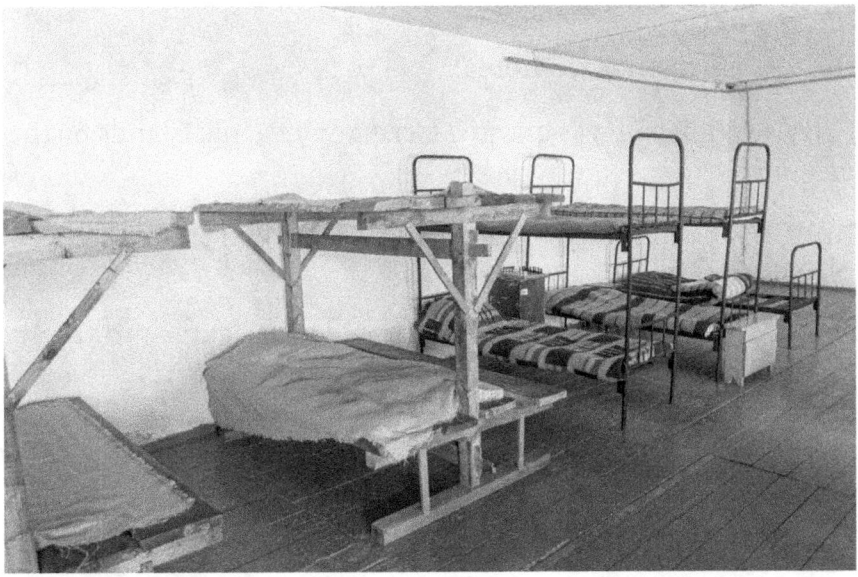

Figure 1.30. Gulag

Change in East Asia

Japan had undergone rapid modernization after being closed off from 1600 until the mid-nineteenth century under the Tokugawa Shogunate.

Following its victory in the Russo-Japanese War, Japan:

- had become more visible internationally in the early part of the twentieth century
- was now recognized as a military power for defeating Russia
- joined a world focused on industry and imperialism

Japan, having already embraced industrialization and modern militarization, turned toward imperialism throughout Asia:

- From 1894 – 1895, Japan fought the **First Sino-Japanese War** with Qing Dynasty China.
- The First Sino-Japanese War revealed Chinese military and organizational limitations and showed Japanese military superiority.
- The 1895 Treaty of Shimonoseki ended the First Sino-Japanese War.
  - It established trading rights for Japan on Chinese territory.
  - Japan gained influence over China's vassal Korea.
  - Japan gained control of Taiwan.

The later **Russo-Japanese War** (1904 – 1905) confirmed Japan's status in the eyes of European empires as a world power. It also solidified Japanese influence in Korea and Manchuria.

- In 1910, Japan annexed Korea.
- After WWI, Japan was granted Germany's Pacific islands by the League of Nations.
- In 1931, Japan invaded Manchuria, creating the puppet state *Manchukuo*.

Following WWI, and despite having provided assistance to the French and British in Asia, Japan began its own imperialist adventure in East and Southeast Asia. Japan intended:

- to gain power
- to access raw materials
- to limit and expel European rule in what Japan considered its sphere of influence

While Japan was building its global reputation, military, and economic strength in Asia, China was undergoing political change.

The Xinhai Revolution broke out in 1911. Led by **Sun Yat-sen**, the revolutionaries had the support of disaffected Chinese people as well as the financial support of millions of Chinese living abroad.

> DID YOU KNOW?
>
> China felt betrayed by European powers, which had awarded German possessions in China to Japan in the Treaty of Versailles. China refused to sign the treaty, and communism became popular among some Chinese leaders.

- The Qing was overthrown.
- Dynastic Chinese rule ended.
- The short-lived **Republic of China** was established.

The Republic of China was recognized by major international powers. But the power vacuum left by the end of imperial China allowed for the rise of warlords throughout the enormous country. Republican government was unable to establish total control. Two major parties would emerge: the **Kuomintang (KMT)** and the **Chinese Communist Party (CCP)**.

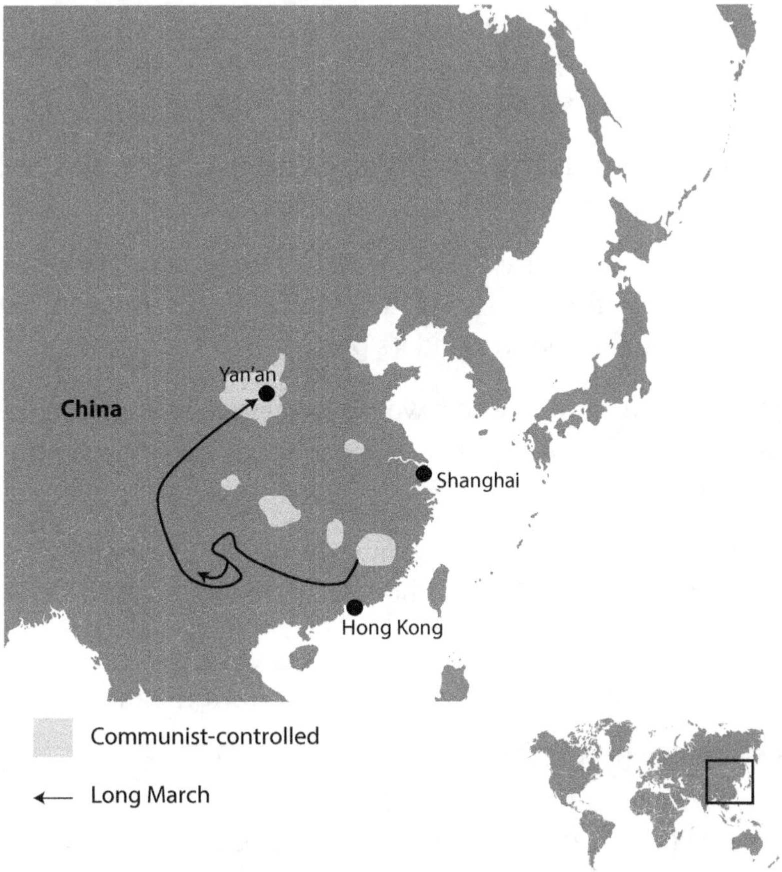

Figure 1.31. The Long March

Table 1.6. The KMT and CCP

Kuomintang (KMT)	Chinese Communist Party (CCP)
• Nationalist Party of the revolutionary government • worked to consolidate government power • KMT leader Chiang Kai-shek (Jiang Jieshi) took back control of much of China from the warlords after Sun Yat-sen's death in 1925. • temporarily worked with the CCP to bring Chinese territory back under the control of the Republic • Chiang turned against the CCP in 1927, driving it south.	• emerged after country felt betrayed by European powers • focused its organizing activities in the countryside on the peasants, becoming powerful in southern China • KMT attacks on the CCP in the south in 1934 forced the CCP to retreat on the **Long March** north. • **Mao Zedong** emerged as the leader of the movement.

World War II

While China was in the midst of political change, Germany was suffering under the provisions of the Treaty of Versailles. In 1919, a democratic government was established at Weimar—the **Weimar Republic**.

Germany was in chaos. The Kaiser had fled, the country was torn apart by the war, and the new government could not bring stability.

▶ Germany was blamed for WWI and owed huge **reparations** according to the treaty to pay for the cost of the war, setting off **hyperinflation** and impoverishing the country and its people.

▶ The rise of communists and a workers' party that came to be known as the National Socialist Party, or **Nazi Party**, led to further political instability.

▶ Following the crash of the stock market in 1929, German unemployment reached six million; furthermore, the United States had called in its foreign loans.

▶ Unemployed workers began supporting communism.

▶ The Nazis, led by **Adolf Hitler**, gained support from business interests, which feared communist power in government, leading the Nazis to become an important force in the Weimar Republic at the beginning of the 1930s.

Hitler maneuvered into the role of chancellor by 1933:

- His charisma and popular platform—to cancel the Treaty of Versailles—allowed him to rise.
- The Nazi Party enjoyed the support of the wealthy and big business, which feared communism (especially with the development of Soviet Russia).
- Nazi ideals appealed strongly to both industry and the workers in the face of global economic depression.
- The Nazi Minister of Propaganda Joseph Goebbels executed an effective propaganda campaign, and would do so throughout Hitler's rule, known as the Third Reich.

In 1934, Hitler became the *Führer*, or leader, of Germany. A series of chaotic events followed:

- a fire in the Reichstag (German Parliament), which allowed Hitler to arrest communist leaders
- the rise of the Gestapo, or secret police (which violently enforced Nazi rule among the people)
- the banning of political parties and trade unions.

As a result of these events, Hitler and the Nazis consolidated total control. They also set into motion their agenda of racism and genocide against "non-Aryan" (non-Germanic) or "racially impure" people.

Jewish people were particularly targeted. Germany had a considerable Jewish population as did the other Central and Eastern European countries that Germany would come to control. Throughout the 1930s, the Nazis passed a series of laws limiting Jewish rights, including:

- jobs that Jewish people could hold
- rights to citizenship
- places they could go
- public facilities they could use
- whom they could marry
- the names they could have

> **DID YOU KNOW?**
>
> **Kristallnacht**, an organized series of attacks on Jewish businesses, homes, and places of worship, took place in 1938. It is so called because the windows of these places were smashed.

Figure 1.32. Aftermath of Kristallnacht

Jewish people would endure continued repression and horrific events in the years to follow:

- In 1939, Jews were forced from their homes into **ghettos**, isolated and overcrowded urban neighborhoods.

- In 1941, they were forced to wear yellow stars identifying them as Jewish.

- Millions of Jewish people were sent to **concentration camps**.

- The Nazis decided on the Final Solution to the "Jewish Question": to murder Jewish people by systematically gassing them at death camps.

- At least six million European Jews were murdered by the Nazis in the **Holocaust**.

Roma, Slavic people, homosexuals, disabled people, people of color, prisoners of war, communists, and others not considered "Aryan" were also forced into slave labor in concentration camps and murdered there. Later, this concept of torturing and killing people based on their ethnicity in order to exterminate them would become defined as genocide.

Hitler was a **fascist**: he believed in a mostly free market accompanied by a dictatorial government with a strong military.

He sought to restore Germany's power and expand its reach by annexing Austria (the *Anschluss*, or *union*) and the Sudetenland, German-majority areas in part of what is today the Czech Republic.

With the collapse of the Weimar Republic and the League of Nations at its weakest state, France and Britain granted the Sudetenland to Hitler in 1938 in a policy called **appeasement** in an effort to maintain stability in Europe and avoid another war. Appeasement failed when Hitler invaded the rest of Czechoslovakia and formed an alliance with Italy the next year.

In 1939 the Soviet Union made a pact with Germany: Germany would not invade the USSR, and the two countries would divide Poland. Germany then invaded Poland. Its 1939 invasion is commonly considered the beginning of the **Second World War**.

War exploded in Europe in 1939 as Hitler gained control of more land than any European power since Napoleon:

- In 1940, Germany took Paris.
- The Battle of Britain began in July 1940.
  - Germany suffered its first defeat and was unable to take Britain.
- Despite staying out of combat, in 1941 the United States enforced the **Lend-Lease Act** which provided support and military aid to Britain.
- The two also released the Atlantic Charter in 1941, which outlined common goals.

When Japan joined the **Axis** powers of Germany and Italy, the **Second Sino-Japanese War of 1937** would also be subsumed under the Second World War, ending in 1945. The **Chinese Civil War** between communists led by Mao Zedong and nationalists led by Chiang Kai-shek was interrupted by the Second Sino-Japanese War, when Japan tried to extend its imperial reach deeper into China, resulting in atrocities like the Rape of Nanking (1937 – 1938).

> **DID YOU KNOW?**
>
> Given the threat posed by the new Soviet Union, Britain and France believed at the time that a stronger Germany would be in their interests.

> **DID YOU KNOW?**
>
> Some historians consider the Japanese invasion of Manchuria in 1931 to be the beginning of WWII.

> **DID YOU KNOW?**
>
> The **Atlantic Charter** described values shared by the US and Britain, including restoring self-governance in occupied Europe and liberalizing international trade.

At this time, Chiang was forced to form an alliance with Mao and the two forces worked together against Japan. By the end of the war, the CCP was stronger than ever, with widespread support from many sectors of Chinese society, while the KMT was demoralized and had little popular support.

In December of 1941, Japan, now part of the **Axis powers** along with Germany and Italy, attacked the United States at Pearl Harbor. Consequently, the US joined the war in Europe and in the Pacific, deploying thousands of troops in both theaters.

Meanwhile, in Asia, Japan continued its imperialist policies. In the early 1940s, it took advantage of chaos in Europe and the weakened European colonial powers to invade and occupy French Indochina, Indonesia, and Burma; it also occupied the Philippines.

Controlling these strategic areas meant the Axis was a direct threat to British India, Australia, and the eastern Soviet Union, not to mention European imperial and economic interests.

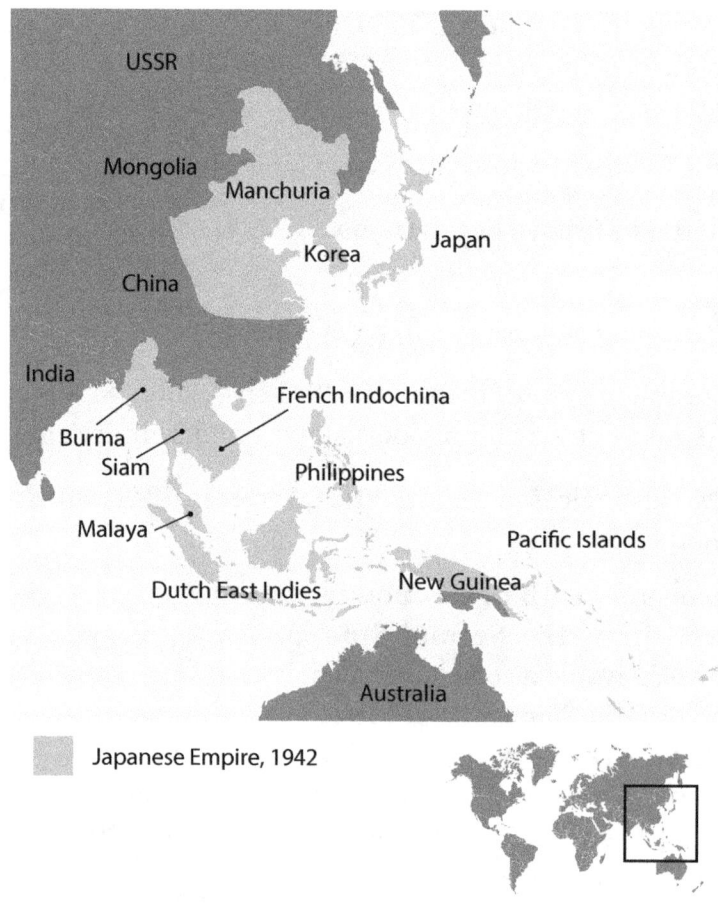

Figure 1.33. Japanese Expansion in Asia

Table 1.7. Major Military Events of WWII

Event	Year	Impact
German invasion of the Soviet Union	1941	Hitler broke his promise to the USSR by invading it, spurring the USSR's alliance with Britain and the US.
Battle of Stalingrad	1942	The USSR defeated Germany, a turning point in the war during which the Nazis were forced to turn from the Eastern Front.
Tehran Conference	1943	• Churchill, Roosevelt, and Stalin met in Tehran to discuss the invasion of Italy. • The Allies took Rome later that year.
D-Day	1944	The Allies invaded France, liberating Paris in August.
Battle of the Bulge	1944 – 1945	• a costly battle that lasted from December 1944 to January 1945 • thousands of US casualties • Hitler's forces were pushed back.
USSR invasion of Berlin; US crosses the Rhine	spring 1945	• Hitler committed suicide. • The Allies accepted German surrender.
Battles of Saipan and Iwo Jima	1944 and 1945, respectively	strategic battles to secure landing strips for American bombers
Battle of Leyte	1944	• The US destroyed most of the Japanese Navy. • Despite casualties of up to 400,000, Japan continued to fight the US for territory in the Philippines.
Battle of Okinawa	1945	• The US planned to use Okinawa as a staging point for an invasion of Japan in order to force Japanese surrender, which would have likely resulted in hundreds of thousands of American troop casualties. • This battle would sway **President Truman** (who succeeded Roosevelt) to drop the atomic bombs to force the Japanese to surrender.
Hiroshima and Nagasaki bombings	1945	The US dropped the atomic bomb on these Japanese cities, causing tremendous civilian casualties, forcing the emperor to surrender, and concluding WWII.

That year in China, the Chinese Civil War recommenced:

- By 1949 the communists had emerged victorious.
- The KMT withdrew to Taiwan.
- Mao and the CCP took over China, which became a communist country.

WWII and the period immediately preceding it saw horrific violations of human rights in Europe and Asia, including the atrocities committed during the Japanese invasions of China, Korea, and Southeast Asia, and the European Holocaust of Jews and other groups like Roma and homosexuals.

The war finally ended with the US atomic bombings of Hiroshima and Nagasaki in 1945, ending years of firebombing civilians in Germany and Japan; devastating ground and naval warfare throughout Europe, Asia, the South Pacific, and Africa; and the deaths of millions of soldiers and civilians all around the world.

The extreme horrors of WWII helped develop the concept of **genocide**—the effort to extinguish an entire group of people because of their ethnicity—and the idea of **human rights**.

The **United Nations** was formed, based on the League of Nations, as a body to champion human rights and uphold international security. Its **Security Council** is made up of permanent member states which can intervene militarily in the interests of international stability.

Allied forces took the lead in rebuilding efforts: the US occupied areas in East Asia and Germany, while the Soviet Union remained in Eastern Europe. The Allies had planned to rebuild Europe according to the Marshall Plan. However, Stalin broke his promise made at the 1945 **Yalta Conference** to allow Eastern European countries to hold free elections. Instead, the USSR occupied these countries and they came under communist control. The **Cold War** had begun.

The Cold War

In February 1945, Stalin, Churchill, and Roosevelt came to numerous agreements at the Yalta Conference:

- the division of Germany
- the free nature of government in Poland
- free elections in Eastern Europe

However, at the Potsdam Conference in July 1945, things had changed:

- Harry Truman had replaced Franklin D. Roosevelt, who had died in office.
- Clement Atlee had replaced Winston Churchill.

- Stalin felt betrayed by the US use of the atomic bomb.

- The US and the British felt that Stalin had violated the agreement at Yalta regarding democracy in Eastern Europe.

Stalin ensured that communists came to power in Eastern Europe, setting up satellite states at the Soviet perimeter in violation of the Yalta agreement. The Soviet rationale was to establish a buffer zone following its extraordinarily heavy casualties in WWII—around twenty million. With Stalin's betrayal of the Allies' agreement, in the words of the British Prime Minister Winston Churchill, an **iron curtain** had come down across Europe, dividing east from west.

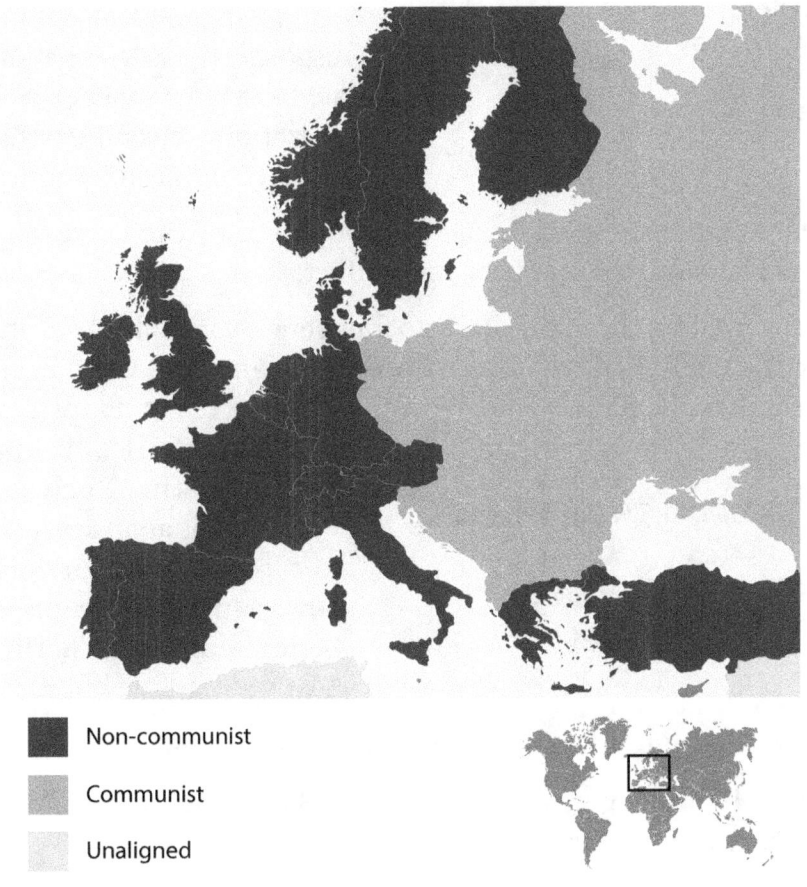

Figure 1.34. Cold War Europe

As a consequence, western states and the Soviet Union created organizations and policies to support their interests:

- Western states formed **NATO**, the North Atlantic Treaty Organization.

  - It served as an agreement wherein an attack on one was an attack on all.

  - It provided for **collective security** in the face of the Soviet expansionist threat.

- The United States adopted a policy of **containment**, the idea that communism should be *contained*, as part of the **Truman Doctrine** of foreign policy.

- The United States also sponsored the **Marshall Plan**, which provided aid to European countries in an effort to restart the European economy and rebuild the continent. Stalin did not permit Soviet-controlled countries to take Marshall aid.

- In response, the Soviet Union created the **Warsaw Pact**, a similar organization consisting of Eastern European communist countries.

> **DID YOU KNOW?**
>
> The concept of **mutually assured destruction**, or the understanding that a nuclear strike by one country would result in a response by the other, ultimately destroying the entire world, may have prevented the outbreak of active violence.

Nuclear weapons, especially the development of the extremely powerful hydrogen bomb, raised the stakes of the conflict.

Germany itself had been divided into four zones, controlled by Britain, France, the US, and the USSR. Berlin had been divided the same way. Once Britain, France, and the US united their zones into West Germany in 1948 and introduced a new currency, the USSR cut off West Berlin in the **Berlin Blockade**. Viewing this as an aggressive attempt to capture the entire city, western powers provided supplies to West Berlin by air in the **Berlin Airlift** for nearly a year.

> **CHECK YOUR UNDERSTANDING #12**
>
> How did the Cold War erupt between the Allies and the Soviet Union?

Berlin continued to be a problem for the USSR:

- Until 1961, refugees from the Eastern Bloc came to West Berlin, seeking better living conditions in the West.

- West Berlin was a center for Western espionage.

- In 1961, the USSR, now led by **Nikita Khrushchev**, closed the border and constructed the **Berlin Wall**.

Following the Second World War, Korea had also been divided:

- In the northern part of the country, the communist **Kim il Sung** controlled territory.

- South of the thirty-eighth parallel, the non-communist Syngman Rhee controlled the rest of the country.

- In 1950, Kim il Sung invaded the south with Russian and Chinese support, intending to create a communist Korea.

According to the Truman Doctrine, communism needed to be contained. Furthermore, according to **domino theory**, if one country became communist, then more would, too, like a row of dominoes falling. Therefore, the United States, by way of the United Nations, became involved in the **Korean War** (1950 – 1953):

- UN troops dominated and led by the US came to the aid of the nearly defeated South Koreans, pushing back Kim il Sung's troops.

- China supported Kim il Sung, and war on the peninsula continued until 1953.

- In 1953, US President Eisenhower threatened to use the nuclear bomb, ending the war in a stalemate.

In 1959, the revolutionary **Fidel Castro** took over in Cuba. Allied with the Soviet Union, he allowed missile bases to be constructed in Cuba, which threatened the United States. During the **Cuban Missile Crisis** in 1962, the world came closer than ever to nuclear war when the USSR sent missiles to Cuba:

- Cuba-bound Soviet ships faced an American blockade and tension grew as the US considered invading Cuba.

- President Kennedy and Premier Khrushchev were able to come to an agreement: the USSR promised to dismantle its Cuban bases as long as the US ended the blockade and secretly dismantled its own missile bases in Turkey.

Figure 1.35. Fidel Castro

- Nuclear war was averted.

Despite this success, the United States engaged in a lengthy violent conflict in Southeast Asia. Supporting anti-communist fighters in Vietnam in keeping with containment and Domino Theory, the United States pursued the **Vietnam War** for almost a decade:

- The **Gulf of Tonkin Resolution** authorized the US president to manage the ongoing conflict without consulting Congress.

  ▷ For a period of years, troops continued to be deployed to the region, fueling the conflict.

- The US became involved in the war after coming to the aid of Vietnam's old colonial master, France.

- Ho Chi Minh, the revolutionary Vietnamese leader, led North Vietnamese forces, including the guerrilla fighters called **Viet Cong**, in a war for independence throughout the 1960s.

  ▷ Despite being outnumbered, Viet Cong familiarity with the difficult terrain, support from Russia and China, and determination eventually resulted in their victory.

- Bloody guerrilla warfare demoralized the American military; the 1968 **Tet Offensive** was a turning point.

  ▷ Despite enormous losses, the North Vietnamese won a strategic victory in this coordinated, surprise offensive.

> **DID YOU KNOW?**
>
> Ho Chi Minh had actually originally approached the Americans for assistance in asserting Vietnamese independence.

- Extreme objection to the war within the United States, high casualties, and demoralization eventually resulted in US withdrawal in 1973.

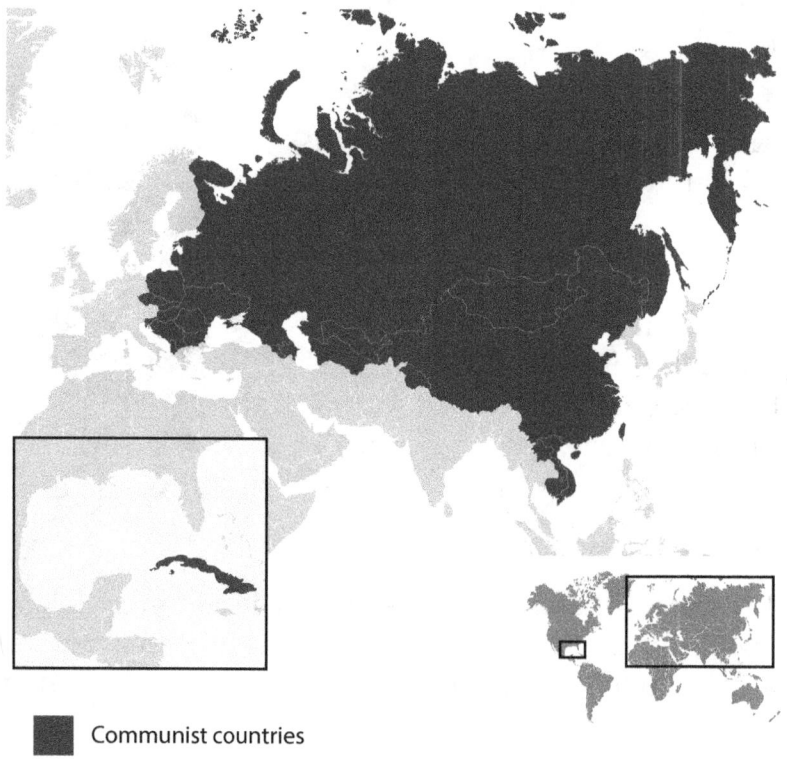

Figure 1.36. The Communist World

Toward the end of the 1960s and into the 1970s, the Cold War reached a period of **détente**, or a warming of relations:

- The US and USSR signed the **Nuclear Non-Proliferation Treaty**, in which they and other nuclear power signatories agreed not to further spread nuclear weapons technology.

- Later, the USSR and the US signed the **SALT 1 Treaty** (Strategic Arms Limitation Treaty), limiting strategic weaponry.

- Some cultural exchanges and partnerships in outer space also took place.

At the same time, the United States began making diplomatic overtures toward communist China. This was, however, part of a different Cold War strategy:

- Despite its status as a communist country, China and the USSR had difficult relations due to their differing views on the nature of communism.

  - While Khrushchev took a more moderate approach to world communism, Mao believed in more aggressive policies.

- Following the **Sino-Soviet Split** of the 1960s, China had lost much Soviet support for its modernization programs, and despite advances in agriculture and some industrialization, Mao's programs like the **Great Leap Forward** had taken a toll on the people.

- In 1972, President Nixon visited China, establishing relations between the communist government and the United States.

  - Communist China was permitted to join the UN. (Previously, China had been represented by the KMT, which was isolated to Taiwan.)

The climate would change again, however, in the 1970s and 1980s:

- The US and USSR found themselves on opposite sides in proxy wars throughout the world (see below).

- The **arms race** was underway.

  - **President Ronald Reagan** pursued a militaristic policy, prioritizing weapons development with the goal of outspending the USSR on weapons technology.

> **DID YOU KNOW?**
>
> Perhaps the most famous proposal in weapons technology during this time was the Strategic Defense Initiative. Popularly known as Star Wars, this outer space-based system would have intercepted Soviet intercontinental ballistic missiles.

DECOLONIZATION

Meanwhile, the former colonies of the fallen European colonial powers had won or were in the process of gaining their independence. One role of the United Nations was to help manage the **decolonization** process.

- In 1949, **Mohandas Gandhi** led a peaceful independence movement in India against the British, winning Indian independence.

- His assassination by Hindu radicals led to conflict between Hindus and Muslims in the Subcontinent, resulting in **Partition**, the bloody division of India.
    - Hindus fled into what is today India.
    - Muslims fled to East Pakistan (now Bangladesh) and West Pakistan.
    - Instability is ongoing on the Subcontinent.

Bloody conflict resulted in many African countries gaining independence in the 1950s, 1960s, and 1970s:

- the Algerian War against France (1954 – 1962)
- the Mau Mau Rebellion against the British in Kenya in the 1950s
- violent movements against Belgium in the Congo

Likewise, strong leadership by African nationalist leaders and thinkers like Jomo Kenyatta, Julius Nyerere, and Kwame Nkrumah contributed to this independence.

The apartheid regime in South Africa, where segregation between races was legal and people of color lived in oppressive conditions, was not lifted until the 1990s; **Nelson Mandela** led the country in a peaceful transition process.

In the Middle East, following the fall of the Ottoman Empire after WWI, European powers had taken over much of the area:

- These **protectorates** became independent states with arbitrary borders drawn and rulers installed by the Europeans.

- The creation of the state of Israel was especially contentious.
    - In the 1917 **Balfour Declaration**, the British had promised the Zionist movement of European Jews that they would be given a homeland in the British-controlled protectorate of Palestine.
    - The US meanwhile assured the Arabs in 1945 that a Jewish state would not be founded there.

- Israel emerged from diplomatic confusion, chaos, and tragedy after the murder of millions of Jews in Europe, and violence on the ground in Palestine carried out by both Jews and Arabs.

- This legacy of conflict lasts to this day in the Middle East.

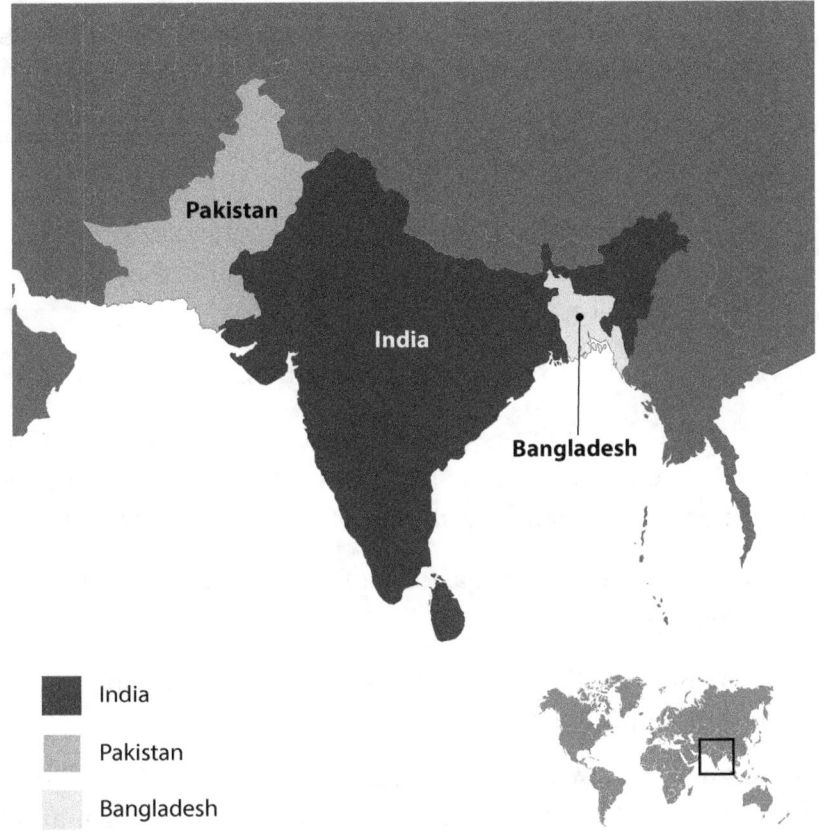

Figure 1.37. Partition

While the Middle East had been divided into protectorates or into nominally independent states like Egypt that were still under strong European influence, these areas had become independent after the Second World War.

Liberal activists against monarchical and dictatorial regimes and popular movements like Pan-Arabism and Islamism put pressure on Middle Eastern monarchies. Countries created by artificial borders based on the Sykes-Picot Agreement and comprised of divided and diverse ethnic and religious groups were already vulnerable to political instability; with added unrest, Middle Eastern governments fell. Furthermore, the Middle East became a Cold War battleground, with regimes courting the support of the Cold War powers:

- In Egypt, Gamal Abdul Nasser led the Pan-Arabist movement in the region, which included creating an Arab alliance against Israel.

- In 1967, Arab allies launched a war against Israel.
  - They were badly beaten in the **Six Day War**, an embarrassing defeat for the Arab states and one from which Nasser never truly recovered.
  - Israel took control of the Sinai Peninsula, the Golan Heights, and the West Bank of the Jordan River.
- During the 1973 **Yom Kippur War**, the US supported Israel while the USSR supported Syria and Egypt.
  - Syria and Egypt had launched a surprise attack on Israel on the holiest day of the Jewish year in an attempt to gain back territory lost years prior.
  - Israel was able to maintain its defenses.
- In 1978, the American president Jimmy Carter was able to broker a peace agreement between the Egyptian leader Anwar Sadat and the Israeli leader Menachem Begin known as the **Camp David Accords**.
  - Other Arab countries, aside from Jordan, did not make peace with Israel.
  - By the 1970s, Pan-Arabism was no longer the popular, unifying movement it had once been.

The **Non-Aligned Movement** arose in response to the Cold War. Instead of the bipolar world of the Cold War, the Non-Aligned Movement sought an alternative: the **Third World**.

> **DID YOU KNOW?**
>
> The bipolar world of the Cold War describes one as democratic, led by the US, and the other communist, led by the USSR.

- Non-Aligned, or Third World countries, wanted to avoid succumbing to the influence of either of the superpowers.
- Many found a forum in the United Nations in which to strengthen their international profiles.

Throughout the Cold War, proxy wars between the US and the USSR were fought around the world:

- In the 1980s, the US began supporting the anti-communist Contras in Nicaragua, who were fighting the communist Sandinista government.

- In 1979, the USSR invaded Afghanistan, an event which would contribute to the Soviet collapse.
    - In response, the US began supporting anti-Soviet *mujahideen* forces, some of whose patrons would later attack the US as part of international terrorist groups.
- the Angolan Civil War
- the Mozambican Civil War

In the Horn of Africa, Somalia was formed when the Italian-administered UN trust territory of Somalia united with the British protectorate of Somaliland in 1960:

- Initially supported by the USSR for its socialist leanings, Somalia and its leader, Mohamed Siad Barre, initiated a war against Ethiopia in 1977.
- The USSR supported Ethiopia.
- The United States supported Somalia.

> **CHECK YOUR UNDERSTANDING #13**
>
> What is a proxy war? Why were proxy wars important in the context of the Cold War?

While never officially colonized, Iran had been under the oppressive regime of the western-supported **Shah Reza Pahlavi** for decades:

- During its imperial era, Britain began exploring petroleum interests in what was then Persia; Western oil companies had remained powerful in that country.
- The Pahlavi Dynasty took over Persia in 1920 from the Qajars, who had ruled since 1785, and who themselves had been important in administration under the Safavids since the sixteenth century.
- By the 1970s, the Shah's corrupt, oppressive regime was extremely unpopular in Iran, but it was propped up by the West.
- Several underground movements worked against the Shah, including communists and Islamic revolutionaries inspired by the Islamism of the early twentieth century.
- In the 1979 **Iranian Revolution**, these forces overthrew the Shah; shortly afterward, Islamist revolutionaries took over the country.
    - The new theocracy was led by a group of clerics led by the Supreme Leader **Ayatollah Khomeini**.

▷ The Ayatollah instituted political and social reforms, including stricter interpretations of Islamic laws and traditions and enforcing those throughout the country as national and local law.

▷ Later that year, radical students who supported the revolution stormed the US Embassy and held a number of staff hostage for over a year. Known as the **Iran Hostage Crisis**, it would humiliate the United States.

Following the Iranian Revolution, the Iraqi leader **Saddam Hussein**, an ally of the United States, declared war against Iran:

> **DID YOU KNOW?**
>
> The revolutionary Iranian government would go on to support Shi'a militants (the Hezbollah, or the Party of God) in the Lebanese Civil War throughout the 1980s; this group is also inspired by Islamism.

- While governed by Sunnis, Iraq was actually a Shi'ite-majority country.
- Saddam feared Iran would trigger a similar revolution there.
- Iraq also sought control over the strategic Shatt al-Arab waterway and some oil-rich territories inland.
- The war raged from 1980 – 1990.

PRACTICE QUESTIONS

16) Which of the following was a weakness of the Schlieffen Plan?
    A. It overstretched the German army.
    B. It failed to anticipate a stronger resistance in France.
    C. It underestimated Russia's ability to mobilize its troops.
    D. all of the above

17) According to the Sykes-Picot Agreement,
    A. Israel would become an independent state.
    B. Husayn ibn Ali would become Caliph.
    C. Ataturk would lead an independent Turkey.
    D. Palestine would be under international supervision.

18) Which of the following led to the rise of the Nazis in early 1930s Germany?
    A. the impact of reparations and the support of German industrialists
    B. the impact of the Great Depression and the support of the workers
    C. support from the international communist movement and the impact of reparations on the German economy
    D. support from German industrialists and strong backing from other political factions in the Reichstag

19) Which of the following describes the roots of the Cold War?

   A. Stalin's unwillingness to cede control of East Berlin to the allies following the fall of the Nazis

   B. the erection of the Berlin Wall

   C. Stalin's failure to honor the Yalta agreement, installing communist regimes in Eastern Europe

   D. the Cuban Missile Crisis

20) Which of the following precipitated the end of the Cold War?

   A. the Iran Hostage Crisis

   B. the Soviet War in Afghanistan

   C. the Iran-Iraq War

   D. the Yom Kippur War

Post-Cold War World

In 1991, the Soviet Union fell when Soviet Premier **Mikhail Gorbachev**, who had implemented reforms like **glasnost** and **perestroika** (or *openness* and *transparency*), was nearly overthrown in a coup. A movement led by **Boris Yeltsin**, who had been elected president of Russia, stopped the coup. The USSR was dissolved later that year and Yeltsin became president of the Russian Federation. The war in Afghanistan and military overspending in an effort to keep up with American military spending had weakened the USSR to the point of collapse, and the Cold War ended.

Figure 1.38. Gorbachev and Reagan

Cold War Consequences

In 1990, Saddam Hussein, the leader of Iraq, invaded Kuwait and took over its oil reserves and production facilities. In response, the United States and other countries went to war—with a UN mandate—to expel Iraq from Kuwait and to defend Saudi Arabia in order to regain control of the world's petroleum reserves in the **Gulf War**. This event cemented the US status as the sole world superpower; the global balance of power had changed.

Despite stability throughout most of Europe, the changes following the fall of the Iron Curtain led to instability in the Balkans:

- In 1992, Bosnia declared its independence from the collapsing state of Yugoslavia, following Croatia and Slovenia.

- Violence broke out in Bosnia between Bosnian Serbs on one side, and Bosnian Muslims (Bosniaks) and Croatians on the other.

- The **Bosnian War** raged from 1992 to 1995, resulting in the deaths of thousands of civilians and another European genocide—this time, of Bosnian Muslims.

Also following the Cold War, proxy wars throughout the world and instability in former colonies continued. In 1994, conflict in Central Africa resulted in the **Rwandan Genocide**. Hutus massacred Tutsis. Violence continued on both sides.

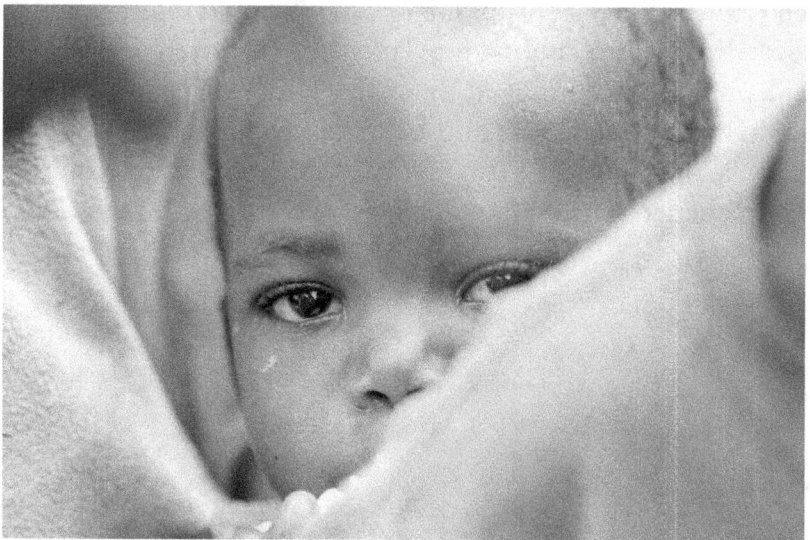

Figure 1.39. Rwandan Genocide

In Zaire, the country descended into instability following the fall of Mobutu Sese Seko, the US-supported dictator, in 1997. Renamed the **Democratic Republic of the Congo**, parts of this country and others in Central Africa would remain wracked by poverty and torn by violence for decades.

In the 1980s, drought in the **Horn of Africa** led to widespread famine. Humanitarian affairs and issues came into the eye of the general public, especially wealthier countries, who became more concerned about providing foreign aid to the suffering.

- The Somali leader Mohamed Siad Barre was overthrown in 1991.

- Somalia was broken up under the control of various warlords and clans.
- The people suffered from starvation with the breakdown of social order.

The United States intervened as part of a UN peacekeeping mission in an attempt to provide humanitarian aid. Strong military resistance from the warlord Muhammad Aideed impacted US public opinion, and the effort failed.

- There is no central government in Somalia, and much of the country is still dependent on aid.
- Some autonomous areas function independently.

COOPERATION AND CONFLICT

Following the end of the Cold War and post-decolonization, the balance of economic and political power began to change:

- The **G-20**, the world's twenty most important economic and political powers, includes many former colonies and non-European countries.
- The **BRICS**—Brazil, Russia, India, China, and South Africa—are recognized as world economic and political leaders.
  - With the exception of Russia, all of these countries were only recently classified as developing countries.
  - While still wrestling with considerable social, economic, and political challenges, the BRICS are world powers in their own right as independent nations—unthinkable developments a century ago.

Steps toward European unification had begun as early as the 1950s:

The **European Union**, as it is known today, was formed after the Maastricht Treaty was signed in 1992. As the former Soviet satellite states moved from communism to more democratic societies and capitalistic economies, more countries partnered with the EU and eventually joined it.

- As of 2015, twenty-seven countries are members, with more on the path to membership.
- European Union countries remain independent but cooperate in international affairs, justice, security and foreign policy, environmental matters, and economic policy.
- Many EU member states share a common currency, the **euro**.
- According to the Schengen Agreement, some EU countries have open borders.

Figure 1.40. European Union Headquarters

Continental integration exists beyond Europe:

- In Africa, the **African Union**, originally the Organization of African Unity, has become a stronger political force in its own right.

    ▷ It organizes peacekeeping missions throughout the continent.

    ▷ Similar to the EU, the AU is a forum for African countries to organize and align political, military, economic, and other policies.

Figure 1.41. African Union Headquarters

In this era of **globalization**, international markets became increasingly open through free-trade agreements. Technological advances such as improvements in transportation infrastructure and the **internet** made international communication faster, easier, and less expensive.

Table 1.8. Free Trade Agreements

Agreement	Description
NAFTA	the North American Free Trade Agreement
Mercosur	the South American free-trade zone
Trans-Pacific Partnership	a proposed free-trade zone between nine countries on the Pacific Ocean
World Trade Organization	international trade oversight

However, more open borders, reliable international transportation, and faster, easier worldwide communication brought risks, too.

In the early twenty-first century, the United States was attacked by terrorists on **September 11, 2001**, resulting in thousands of civilian casualties. Consequently, the US launched a major land war in Afghanistan and another later in Iraq.

Following the attacks on 9/11, the US attacked Afghanistan as part of the **War on Terror**. Afghanistan's radical Islamist Taliban government was providing shelter to the group that took responsibility for the attacks, al Qaeda. Led by **Osama bin Laden**, al Qaeda was inspired by Islamism and the radical Wahhabism of the remote Arabian desert followed by the Saudis.

> **DID YOU KNOW?**
>
> While benefits of international trade include lower prices and more consumer choice, unemployment often rises in more developed countries while labor and environmental violations are more likely in developing countries.

- Bin Laden had fought the Soviets with the US-supported Afghan *mujahideen* during the 1980s.

- Bin Laden and his followers were angered by US presence in Saudi Arabia throughout the 1990s and its support of Israel.

- Osama bin Laden was killed by the United States in 2011.

- Afghan security was turned over from the US to the US-backed government in 2014.

The US began withdrawing troops from Afghanistan in 2020, continuing into 2021. During the withdrawal, the Taliban had a resurgence and officially took control of the country in August 2021.

The Iraq War began in 2003. The US invaded Iraq, arguing that it supported international terrorism, and under faulty premises:

- that Saddam Hussein's regime was involved with al Qaeda
- that Iraq possessed weapons of mass destruction that it intended to use

Iraq descended into chaos, with thousands of civilian and military casualties, Iraqi and American alike. While Iraq technically and legally remains intact under a US-supported government, the ethnically and religiously diverse country is de facto divided as a result of the disintegration of central power.

Elsewhere in the Middle East, reform movements began via the 2011 **Arab Spring** in Tunisia, Egypt, Bahrain, and Syria:

HELPFUL HINT

One consequence of the Syrian Civil War has been enormous movements of refugees into other Middle Eastern countries and Europe.

- Some dictatorial regimes have been replaced with democratic governments; other countries still enjoy limited freedoms or even civil unrest.
- In Syria, unrest erupted into civil war between Bashar al Assad, who inherited leadership from his father, and opposition fighters.

Figure 1.42. Arab Spring

Today, a new group known as the Islamic State of Iraq and al Sham (**ISIS**), referring to Iraq and Syria (or Islamic State of Iraq and the Levant—ISIL), has filled the vacuum in parts of northern and western Iraq and eastern Syria: it has established a de facto state in Iraq and Syria with extremist Islamist policies and presents a global terror threat.

Uprisings in Israeli-occupied West Bank and Gaza have continued sporadically:

- Israel passed control of Gaza to the Palestinian Authority in 2005.
    - Following political divisions within Palestinian factions, Gaza is controlled by Hamas while the Palestinian Authority represents Palestinian interests abroad and in the West Bank.
- In 1999, US President Clinton attempted to broker a final peace deal between the Israelis and Palestinians, delineating borders as part of a two-state solution.
    - These efforts failed and conflict continues.

PRACTICE QUESTIONS

21) Though the US emerged as the sole superpower immediately after the fall of the Soviet Union, which phenomenon in the twenty-first century has characterized global governance so far?

    A. international terrorism
    B. international economic and political organizations
    C. international conflict
    D. the European Union

22) What was one reason for the Bosnian War?

    A. attacks by Bosnian Islamic extremists
    B. the dissolution of Yugoslavia
    C. the separation of Yugoslavia from the USSR
    D. attacks by Middle Eastern Islamic extremists

23) What is one major role that the African Union plays?

    A. The AU is a free trade area.
    B. The AU manages a single currency.
    C. The AU manages several peacekeeping forces.
    D. The AU represents individual African countries in international diplomacy.

24) Which of the following is NOT a reason that the Soviet Union collapsed?

    A. glasnost
    B. perestroika
    C. the war in Afghanistan
    D. the rise of the Taliban

25) **Why did Osama bin Laden sponsor attacks against the United States?**
    A. He opposed US military presence in Saudi Arabia.
    B. He wanted to fight the United States in a proxy war on behalf of Russia.
    C. He wanted to build an empire from Afghanistan overseas.
    D. He wanted oil resources in the Middle East that the United States controlled.

Practice Questions Answer Key

1) **B.** Fresh water permits a reliable food source, which allows for settlement; people need not travel in search of food.

2) **B.** The Sumerians developed cuneiform.

3) **C.** Written Chinese developed under the Shang Dynasty, and the Mandate of Heaven emerged under the Zhou Dynasty; furthermore, traditions like the use of chopsticks also came about during these periods.

4) **A.** The Athenian notion of *demokratia*, or people power, was participatory rather than representative.

5) **C.** The Senate's corruption and weakness, and Caesar's popularity with the plebeians, support of the military, and strong leadership, enabled him to take and retain control.

6) **D.** Security alliances with Germanic and Gothic tribes left Western Rome vulnerable to their attack; meanwhile in the east, centralized power in Constantinople and strong leadership, particularly under Justinian, led to the rise of the powerful Byzantine Empire.

7) **A.** The Meccan elites believed that they should take over leadership of Islam and continue the movement beyond the Arabian Peninsula; however Ali and Fatima, Muhammad's cousin and daughter, believed Ali was Muhammad's rightful successor as his closest living male relative.

8) **D.** American raw materials (like sugar and tobacco) were used in Europe and also turned into consumer goods there. European goods (as well as gold extracted from the Americas) were exchanged in Africa for enslaved persons, who were forced to harvest the raw materials in the Americas.

9) **C.** Europeans who traveled to the Levant to fight returned home with beneficial knowledge and technology.

10) **A.** Byzantine Christians left Constantinople with the rise of the Ottomans. They traveled to Western Europe, bringing classical learning with them.

11) **B.** The Treaty of Westphalia was based on state sovereignty and non-interference, the core principles of modern international relations.

12) **D.** Enlightenment thinking fueled the Age of Revolutions, and revolutionary French thinkers and writers like Rousseau, Voltaire, and others influenced revolutionary French leaders.

13) **B.** Russian support for Slavic ethnic groups in the Balkans—especially Serbia—helped fuel nineteenth century tensions in the region (and continued to do so throughout the twentieth century).

14) **C.** The idea of the white man's burden was not meant to suggest a literal burden; it was a paternalistic concept of responsibility used to justify imperial dominance.

15) **A.** Marx and Engels believed in abolishing wages and the class structure in exchange for a socialist society where the means of production were commonly held and in which income was equally distributed.

16) **D.** All of the answer choices are true.

17) **D.** Sykes-Picot put Palestine under the supervision of various international powers.

18) **A.** The Nazis planned to cease paying reparations, so their nationalist approach appealed to many Germans suffering from the hyperinflation that reparations had triggered. Furthermore, the Nazis had the support of German industrialists, who feared the rise of communism among the working classes.

19) **C.** The Cold War was rooted in Stalin's creation of communist satellite states in Eastern and Central Europe.

20) **B.** The Soviet invasion of Afghanistan and the subsequent ten-year war sapped Soviet financial and military resources—and morale. This draining war, plus the high price of the arms race with the United States, contributed significantly to the fall of the Soviet Union.

21) **B.** While the United States remains a leading world power, the emergence of international organizations like the BRICS, the EU, the G-20, and the AU has empowered other countries; furthermore, international trade agreements are helping mold the international balance of power.

22) **B.** One reason for the Bosnian War was the Yugoslav government's attempt to force the country to stay together; following the end of the Cold War and the collapse of communism, the formerly communist Yugoslavia had started to break up.

23) **C.** The AU organizes and manages peacekeeping forces in Africa; it also cooperates with the United Nations in peacekeeping.

24) **D.** The Taliban did not emerge in Afghanistan until well after Soviet withdrawal from the country.

25) **A.** Bin Laden was against the presence of the United States in Saudi Arabia, especially because that country is home to Mecca and Medina. He also wanted to expand his extremist ideology and opposed US support of Israel.

Check Your Understanding Answer Key

Check Your Understanding #1

social stratification, city-states, administration, irrigation, writing (cuneiform, hieroglyphs), literature (the *Epic of Gilgamesh*), codified rule of law (the Code of Hammurabi), art and architecture (ziggurats, pyramids), the potter's wheel, early astronomy, mathematics, religious thought, metallurgy (weaponry), horsemanship, chariots

Check Your Understanding #2

Greek ideas like reason and democracy informed modern Western thought and governance (rule of law, not rule of man). European literature was inspired by Greek plays and mythology.

Check Your Understanding #3

The republic was divided between the Optimates and the Populare. In addition, the Senate was extremely corrupt. Supported by the Populare, Julius Caesar forced the corrupt Senate to give him control, beginning the transition to an empire.

Check Your Understanding #4

Monotheism is the belief in one god. Major monotheistic religions include Judaism (Yahweh), Christianity (Jesus Christ), and Islam (Prophet Muhammad).

Check Your Understanding #5

The Silk Road spread art, pottery, and goods around Europe and Asia. It also helped Islam and Buddhism spread into China. The Islamic tradition of the hajj spurred cultural interaction as Muslims from around the world came together in Mecca. Islam spread along trans-Saharan trade routes in West Africa, spreading language, literature, goods, and art.

Check Your Understanding #6

There was no real dominant power in Asia. Central Asia lacked one dominant culture. The Abbasids, Seljuks, and Byzantines were in decline, making the Middle East vulnerable.

Check Your Understanding #7

Scientific study and discovery threatened the power of the Catholic Church and monarchs who ruled by divine right.

Check Your Understanding #8

The encomienda system allowed the exploitation and destruction of Indigenous American people and societies.

Check Your Understanding #9

The bourgeoisie earned their wealth but paid taxes and did not have government representation. Resentment grew against the nobility, who inherited wealth and power, driving revolutions.

Check Your Understanding #10

Russia, Germany, and Austria-Hungary (the Three Emperors' League); Germany and Austria-Hungary (the Dual Alliance); Germany, Austria-Hungary, and Italy (the Triple Alliance); Russia, France, Great Britain (the Triple Entente)

Check Your Understanding #11

spreading Christianity, natural resources (gold, opium, tea, beaver pelts, timber, rubber, diamonds); controlling strategic areas, white man's burden

Check Your Understanding #12

Stalin failed to allow Eastern European countries to hold free elections; USSR required a buffer zone in Eastern Europe after WWII; US use of nuclear weapons threatened USSR.

Check Your Understanding #13

In a proxy war, opposing countries fight each other indirectly by supporting sides in a third-party conflict. The US and USSR were never in direct combat during the Cold War, but they fought many proxy wars worldwide.

United States History

NORTH AMERICA BEFORE EUROPEAN CONTACT

Before European colonization, diverse Native American societies controlled the continent. They would later come into economic and diplomatic contact—and military conflict—with European and US colonizers, forces, and settlers.

Civilizations of the Northeast, Midwest, Southeast, Great Plains, Southwest, and Pacific Northwest have played an important and ongoing role in North American history.

THE NORTHEAST

The **Iroquois** and **Algonquin** comprised the major Native American societies in the Northeast. Both would become important allies of the English and French, respectively, in future conflicts.

The Iroquois consisted of five tribes, or the Five Nations:

- Mohawk
- Seneca
- Cayuga
- Oneida
- Onondaga

According to tradition, the Five Nations made peace under the leadership of **Hiawatha**. They organized into the regionally powerful Iroquois Confederacy, bringing stability to the eastern Great Lakes region. The Tuscarora tribe eventually joined, and the union became known as the **Six Nations**.

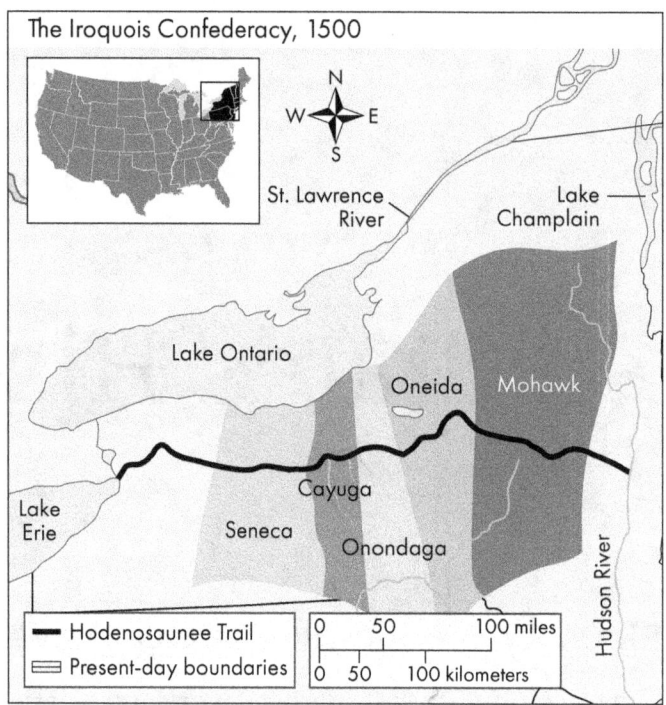

Figure 2.1. Iroquois Confederacy

The Iroquois were known for innovative agricultural and architectural techniques:

▶ farming maize

▶ constructing longhouses

▶ the three sisters tradition of farming, which became used throughout North America

In the three sisters system, maize, beans, and squash, are planted together. These crops complement each other, providing natural protection from pests and the elements, and increasing the availability of nitrogen necessary for growth.

While many Native American, or First Nations, people speak variants of the Algonquian language family, the **Algonquin** people themselves are distinct Indigenous peoples. They have historically been a majority in what is today Quebec and the Great Lakes region.

Active in the fur trade, the Algonquin developed important relationships with French colonizers and a rivalry with the Iroquois. Many Algonquin in French-controlled North America converted to Christianity.

The Midwest

During early western expansion, the young United States would come into conflict with the Shawnee, Lenape, Kickapoo, Miami, and other tribes in present-day Ohio, Illinois, Indiana, and Michigan.

These Algonquin-speaking peoples eventually formed the Northwest Confederacy to fight the United States (see "Revolution and the Early United States," page 17).

- The **Shawnee** were based in the Ohio Valley. However, their presence extended as far as the present-day Carolinas and Georgia.
  - While socially organized under a matrilineal system, the Shawnee had male kings and only men could inherit property.

- The **Lenape**, also a matrilineal society, originally lived in what is today New York, New Jersey, and the Delaware Valley.

- The **Kickapoo** were originally from the Great Lakes region but would move throughout present-day Indiana and Wisconsin.

> **HELPFUL HINT**
>
> The Lenape were eventually forced farther west by European colonization. The Lenape were respected by the Shawnee as their "grandfathers."

- The **Miami** tribe moved from Wisconsin to the Ohio Valley region, forming settled societies and farming maize. They also took part in the fur trade as it developed during European colonial times.

The Southeast

Many major Indigenous peoples of southeastern North America descended from the **Mississippi Mound Builders,** or Mississippian cultures. These societies constructed mounds from around 2,100 to 1,800 years ago. It is thought that these mounds are the remains of burial tombs or the bases for temples.

Figure 2.2. Mississippi Mounds

The Chickasaw were a settled tribe originally based in what is today northern Mississippi and Alabama and western Kentucky and Tennessee. Like the Iroquois, the Chickasaw farmed in the sustainable three sisters tradition.

> **HELPFUL HINT**
>
> The Chickasaw and Choctaw would later form alliances with the British and French, fighting proxy wars on their behalf.

The Choctaw, whose origins trace to Mississippi, Louisiana, Alabama, and Florida, spoke a similar language to the Chickasaw. The Choctaw operated as a matriarchal society. Women were responsible for farming, gathering, and caring for the family. Men were primarily responsible for hunting and defense.

The **Creek**, or **Muscogee**, also descended from the Mississippian peoples, originated in modern Alabama, Georgia, South Carolina, and Florida. Speaking a language similar to those of the Chickasaw and Choctaw, the Creek would later participate in an alliance with these and other tribes—the Muscogee Confederacy—to engage the United States, which threatened tribal sovereignty.

Unlike the Chickasaw, Choctaw, and Creek, the **Cherokee** spoke (and speak) a language of the Iroquoian family. It is thought that they migrated south to their homeland in present-day Georgia sometime long before European contact, where they remained until they were forcibly removed in 1832.

Organized into seven clans, the Cherokee were also hunters and farmers, like other tribes in the region. They too would come into contact—and conflict—with European colonizers and the United States of America.

GREAT PLAINS

Farther west, tribes of the Great Plains would later come into conflict with American settlers as westward expansion continued.

Major Great Plains peoples included:

- Sioux
- Cheyenne
- Apache
- Comanche
- Arapaho

These tribes depended on **buffalo** for food and materials to create clothing, tools, and domestic items. They were nomadic or seminomadic, following the herds. Before horses were introduced to North America, hunters surrounded buffalo or frightened them off cliffs.

SOUTHWEST

In the Southwest, the **Navajo** lived in present-day Arizona, New Mexico, and Utah. The Navajo were descendants of the **Ancestral Pueblo,** or **Anasazi,** who had settled in the Four Corners area and are still known today for stone construction, including cliff dwellings.

> **DID YOU KNOW?**
>
> Horses were introduced to North America by Europeans. Indigenous tribes living on the Great Plains did not access horses until after European contact.

Figure 2.3. Ancestral Pueblo Cliff Palace at Mesa Verde

The Navajo also practiced pastoralism. They lived in semi-permanent wooden homes called *hogans*, the doors of which face eastward to the rising sun. The Navajo had a less hierarchical structure than other Native American societies and engaged in fewer raids than the Apache to the north.

> **DID YOU KNOW?**
>
> Like many other Indigenous peoples, the Ancestral Pueblo practiced three sisters agriculture.

PACIFIC NORTHWEST

In the Pacific Northwest, fishing was a major source of sustenance, and Native American peoples created and used canoes to engage in the practice. First Nations of the Pacific Northwest also created totem poles, which are hand-carved monuments that depict histories.

The **Coast Salish**, whose language was widely spoken throughout the region, dominated the Puget

> **CHECK YOUR UNDERSTANDING #1**
>
> Which North American tribes were traditionally nomadic?

Sound and Olympic Peninsula area. Farther south, the **Chinook** controlled the coast at the Columbia River.

Ultimately, through both violent conflict and political means, Indigenous civilizations lost control of most of their territories and were forced onto reservations by the United States. Negotiations continue today over rights to land, opportunities, and reparations for past injustices.

PRACTICE QUESTIONS

1) Which of the following best describes the political landscape of the Northeast before European contact?

   A. Many small, autonomous tribes scattered throughout the region fought over land and resources.
   B. Several organized tribes controlled the region, including a major confederation.
   C. A disorganized political landscape would facilitate European colonial domination.
   D. The land was largely uninhabited, allowing easy exploitation of resources.

2) Which of the following BEST illustrates tribal interactions before European contact?

   A. Having been pushed westward by the Iroquois, the Lenape are just one example of forced migration in early North American history.
   B. The migration of the Miami from Ontario to the Ohio Valley shows how the Algonquian language family diffused throughout the continent.
   C. Indigenous peoples of the Great Plains forced the Pueblo to move south by consuming resources like buffalo.
   D. Ongoing conflict between the Northwest Algonquin Confederacy and the Iroquois Confederacy resulted in instability that forced tribes to move throughout the region.

3) When Europeans arrived in North America, who was living in what is today the southeastern United States?

   A. the Mississippi Mound Builders
   B. settled tribes who spoke Muskogean and Iroquoian languages
   C. the Chinook and Coast Salish
   D. the Ancestral Pueblo cliff dwellers

4) Tribes living in the Great Plains region were dependent on which of the following for survival?

   A. buffalo for nutrition and materials for daily necessities
   B. domesticated horses for hunting and warfare
   C. access to rivers to engage in the fur trade
   D. three sisters agriculture

5) How were the Navajo influenced by the Ancestral Pueblo, or Anasazi?

   A. The Navajo continued the practice of pastoralism, herding horses throughout the Southwest.
   B. The Navajo expanded control over land originally settled by the Ancestral Pueblo.
   C. The Navajo began building cliff dwellings, improving on the Anasazi practice of living in rounded homes built from wood.
   D. The Navajo developed a strictly hierarchical society, abandoning the looser organization of the Ancestral Pueblo.

COLONIAL NORTH AMERICA

The Americas were quickly colonized by Europeans after Christopher Columbus arrived in 1492. Throughout the sixteenth, seventeenth, eighteenth, and nineteenth centuries, the British, French, and Spanish all controlled major territories in North America.

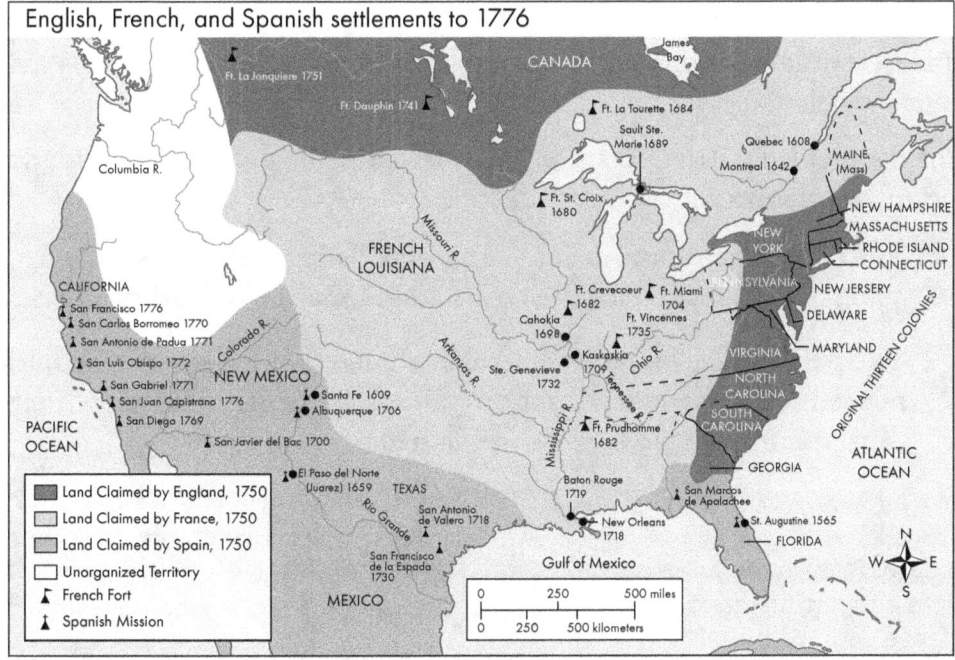

Figure 2.4. European Colonization of North America

Spain in the West and Southwest

Spanish *conquistadors* explored what is today the southwestern United States. They claimed this land for Spain despite the presence of the Navajo and other civilizations. Prominent *conquistadors* included **Hernando de Soto** and **Francisco Vasquez de Coronado**.

Spanish colonization extended beyond controlling and settling land. Spain also intended to spread Christianity. **Missions** were established for this purpose in the West and Southwest, throughout Mexico, and parts of what are today Texas, New Mexico, Arizona, and California.

The Spanish government granted individual European settlers *encomiendas* to establish settlements regardless of the existing local population. Under the European legal system, encomiendas allowed the holder to ranch or mine the land. Colonists used encomiendas to demand tribute and forced labor from Indigenous peoples, essentially enslaving them.

Throughout the Southwest, Spanish colonizers encountered resistance. In 1680, the **Pueblo Revolt**, led by the leader **Popé**, resulted in a two-year loss of land for Spain. Sometimes referred to as part of the ongoing **Navajo Wars**, this revolt included several Native American tribes.

(In the literature and in some primary sources, *pueblo* is often used interchangeably with "Indian" to refer to Native Americans; here, the term refers to Navajo, Apache, and other tribes that came together to resist Spanish hegemony in the region.)

Spain eventually reconquered the territory, subjugating the peoples living in the region to colonial rule.

The conflict led to friction among Spanish thinkers over the means, and even the notion, of colonization.

- The priest **Bartolomé de las Casas**, appalled at the oppression of colonization, argued for the rights and humanity of Native Americans.

- The philosopher **Juan de Sepulveda** argued that Indigenous peoples needed the rule and "civilization" brought by Spain, justifying their cruel treatment at the hands of colonizers.

> **DID YOU KNOW?**
>
> De las Casas lived in the Americas and had firsthand experience with the brutal consequences of colonization. **Juan de Sepulveda** never left Spain.

Despite ongoing conflict between Native Americans and Spanish colonizers, there was social mixing among the people. Intermarriage and fraternization resulted in a stratified society based on race. These racial identities extended in North America and throughout Spanish and Portuguese holdings in the Americas.

According to the *casta* system, an individual's place in societal hierarchy was determined by their race. White people were considered the most privileged. The term *mestizo* referred to people with mixed white European and Indigenous American backgrounds. They, in turn, were more privileged than the Indigenous American peoples.

Indigenous people in Mexico and the Southwest suffered under colonization. Countless people were killed through forced labor and European diseases like **smallpox**, to which they had limited immunity. To exploit these resource-rich lands, Spain (and eventually, other European countries) turned to enslaving African people.

In the trans-Atlantic slave trade, people were kidnapped from Africa to be enslaved in the Western Hemisphere. Torn from their homes and families, they were forced to travel across the Atlantic Ocean in brutal conditions. Upon arriving in the Americas, African people were enslaved in mines and plantations. They were subject to horrific conditions and not compensated. They were considered property, not people.

French Hegemony in the Midwest and Northeast

French explorers such as **Samuel de Champlain** reached what is today Quebec, Vermont, upstate New York, and the eastern Great Lakes region as early as the seventeenth century. While the explorer **Jacques Cartier** had claimed New France (present-day Quebec) for France in the sixteenth century, Champlain founded Quebec City and consolidated control of France's colonies in North America in 1608.

Unlike Spain, which sought not only profit, but also to settle the land and convert Native Americans to Christianity, France prioritized trade.

Beaver pelts and fur from game plentiful in the Northeast were in great demand in Europe. Eventually, France would control much of the Great Lakes and the Mississippi region through Louisiana and New Orleans—valuable trade routes.

French colonists were more likely to establish agreements and intermarry with local Native Americans than other European powers. The term *métis* described mixed-race persons.

Civilizational Contributions of Enslaved Africans

The civilizational contributions of enslaved African people and their descendants to North American society were many and long-lasting. They included the introduction and production of important crops like rice and okra in the Gulf Coast area and American foods enjoyed today like peanut butter and gumbo.

Enslaved Africans and Black Americans also brought traditional music to North America that would evolve into blues music (and later, jazz, rock, and hip hop).

Some West African art and dances evolved into the festive practices seen today in New Orleans and Louisiana during Mardi Gras.

ENGLAND AND THE THIRTEEN COLONIES

In the sixteenth century, Sir Walter Raleigh established the Roanoke colony in present-day Virginia. Roanoke disappeared by 1590, but interest in colonization reemerged as **joint-stock companies** sought royal charters to privately develop colonies on the North American Atlantic coast. The first established colony, **Jamestown**, was also located in Virginia, which became so profitable that the Crown took it over as a colony in 1624.

The colonial leader **John Rolfe** introduced **tobacco** to Virginia farmers, which became the primary cash crop. Tobacco required plantation farming. At first, Virginia used **indentured servants**, who were freed from servitude after a period of work. Some of these indentured servants were from Africa, and in 1660 the **House of Burgesses**, which governed Virginia, declared that all Black people would be enslaved for life.

> **DID YOU KNOW?**
>
> Spanish and French settlers were usually single men looking to trade and were more likely to intermarry with local people. On the other hand, English colonists brought their families and settled in North America, with the goal of establishing agricultural settlements.

The South became increasingly socially stratified, with enslaved persons, indentured servants, landowners, and other classes. The Carolinas and Georgia would also become important sources of tobacco and rice.

South Carolina institutionalized slavery in North America for the next two centuries by adopting the slave codes from Barbados.

While Jamestown and Virginia were comprised of diverse populations of settlers, businessmen, indentured servants, and enslaved people, the demographics were different farther north. In New England, **Separatists**—members of the Church of England who believed it had strayed too far from its theological roots—arrived in North America seeking more religious freedom.

> **CHECK YOUR UNDERSTANDING #2**
>
> List some major exports from colonial North America.

The first group of Separatists, the Pilgrims, arrived on the *Mayflower* in 1620. They drew up the **Mayflower Compact**, guaranteeing government by the consent of the governed.

The Pilgrims were later joined by the **Puritans**, who had been persecuted in England. The colonial Puritan leader **John Winthrop** envisioned the Massachusetts Bay Colony in the model of the biblical *City upon a Hill*, rooted in unity, peace, and what would be a free, democratic spirit; its capital was Boston. These philosophies would later inform the American Revolution.

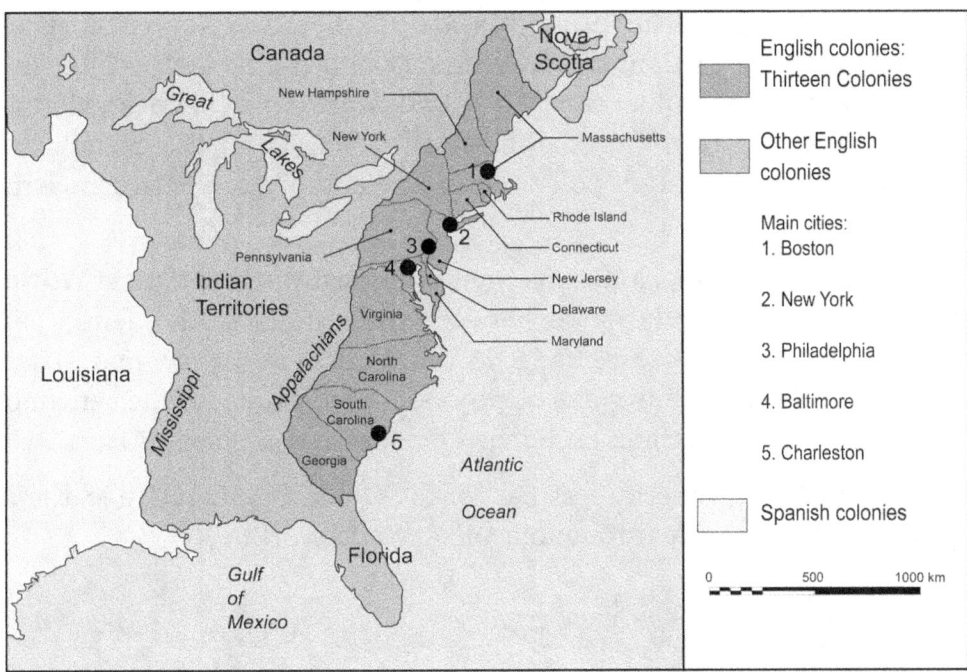

Figure 2.5. The Thirteen Colonies

Despite differences from the South, social stratification existed in New England as well. According to Puritan belief, wealth and success showed that one was a member of the **elect** (privileged by God). Poorer farmers were generally tenant farmers. They did not own land and rarely made a profit.

The mid-Atlantic region, with fertile lands and natural harbors, was well suited for agricultural crops and trade. It was also home to concepts of religious tolerance.

> **HELPFUL HINT**
>
> Slavery was practiced in the northern colonies but not as widely as in the southern colonies. The northern land and climate did not support plantation agriculture. This led to far less demand for slaves than in the south, where labor was needed to harvest tobacco and later, cotton.

The Dutch settlement of New Amsterdam became an important port and trading post. In 1664, England took control of this settlement under terms of surrender from the Dutch that included religious toleration. The settlement was renamed New York.

In 1682, the Quaker **William Penn** founded the city of Philadelphia based on tolerance. Penn had been given the land—later called Pennsylvania—by the British Crown to settle a debt.

Pennsylvania, New Jersey, and Delaware were all founded in the Quaker spirit as part of Penn's **Holy Experiment** to develop settlements based on tolerance.

> **DID YOU KNOW?**
>
> Quakerism promotes equality, community, nonviolence, conflict resolution, and tolerance. These tenets are at the root of the name of Philadelphia, the "City of Brotherly Love."

Earlier in the region, in 1649, the **Maryland Toleration Act** had ensured the political rights of all Christians there, the first law of its kind in the colonies. This was due, in part, to the influence of **Lord Baltimore**, who had been charged by Charles I to found a part of Virginia (to be called Maryland) as a Catholic haven. This helped the king maintain power in an England divided between Catholics and Protestants.

The North American colonial economy was part of the **Atlantic World** and participated in the **triangular trade** between the Americas, Africa, and Europe. Enslaved African people were exchanged in the Americas for raw materials. Raw materials were shipped to Europe to be processed into goods for the benefit of the colonial powers, and sometimes exchanged for enslaved people in Africa.

In this way, North America was part of the **Columbian Exchange**, the intersection of goods and people throughout the Atlantic World.

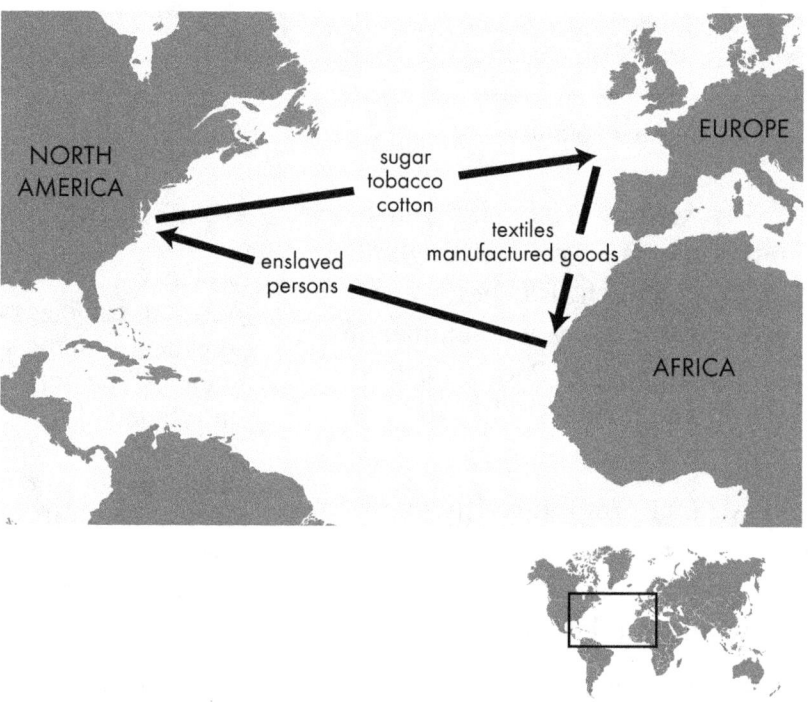

Figure 2.6. Triangular Trade

Exploitation of colonial resources and the dynamics of the Columbian Exchange supported **mercantilism**, the prevailing economic system: European powers controlled their economies to increase global power. Ensuring a beneficial **balance of trade** is essential; the country must export more than it imports.

An unlimited supply of desirable goods obtainable at a low cost made this possible, and the colonies offered just that. In this way,

> **HELPFUL HINT**
>
> Long-term consequences of mercantilism included the decline of feudalism and the rise of capitalism.

European powers would be able to maintain their reserves of gold and silver rather than spending them on imports.

Furthermore, countries with access to more gold and silver—notably, Spain, which gained control of mines in Central America and Mexico—exponentially increased their wealth. This dramatically changed the balance of economic power in Europe.

THE RISE OF COLONIAL DISCONTENT

Throughout the chaos in England during the **English Civil War**, policy toward the colonies had been one of **salutary neglect**, allowing them great autonomy. However, stability in England and an emerging culture of independence in the Thirteen Colonies caught the attention of the British Crown. To ensure that the British mercantilist system was not threatened, England passed the **Navigation Acts** in 1651 and 1660. These restricted colonial trade with any other countries.

An early sign of colonial discontent, **Bacon's Rebellion** in 1676 against Governor Berkeley of Virginia embodied the growing resentment of landowners, who wanted to increase their own profits rather than redirect revenue to Britain.

Following the 1688 Glorious Revolution in England, many colonists thought they might gain more autonomy. However, self-rule remained limited.

American colonists were also increasingly influenced by Enlightenment thought. John Locke's *Second Treatise* was published in 1689. Critical of absolute monarchy, it became popular in the colonies.

Locke argued for **republicanism**, the idea that the people must come together to create a government for the protection of themselves and their property, thereby giving up some of their natural rights. However, should the government overstep its bounds, the people have the right to overthrow it and replace it.

> **HELPFUL HINT**
>
> Locke's concepts of government by consent of the governed and the natural rights of persons eventually became the bedrock of US government.

FRENCH AND ENGLISH CONFLICTS IN NORTH AMERICA

Meanwhile, North America also served as a battleground for France and England. These countries were already in conflict in Europe and elsewhere.

In the mid-seventeenth century, the Algonquin (allied with the French and Dutch) and Iroquois (allied with the English), fought the **Beaver Wars** for control over the fur trade in the northeastern part of the continent.

Given the British alliance with the Iroquois, England would also refer to the

> **HELPFUL HINT**
>
> The Iroquois would ultimately push the Shawnee and other tribes associated with the Algonquin from the Northeast and Great Lakes area farther west to present-day Wisconsin.

Beaver Wars and Iroquois control over the Northeast (today, the Ohio Valley and Great Lakes region) to assert their own claim over this area, which was called the **Northwest Territories**.

Not only did France clash with Britain in the northern part of the continent, but the two colonial powers came into conflict in the South as well. France had come to control the vast **Louisiana Territory**, including the important port city of New Orleans. In 1736, French forces, allied with the Choctaw, attacked the English-allied Chickasaw as part of France's attempts to strengthen its hold on the southeastern part of North America in the **Chickasaw Wars**.

The Seven Years' War broke out in Europe in 1756; this conflict between the British and French in North America was known as the **French and Indian War**. War efforts in North America accelerated under the British leader **William Pitt the Elder**, who invested heavily in defeating the French beyond Europe (see "World History" for details).

Ultimately, Britain emerged as the dominant power in North America. France had allied with the Algonquin, traditional rivals of the British-allied Iroquois. However, following defeats by strong colonial military leaders like George Washington and despite its strong alliances and long-term presence on the continent, France eventually surrendered.

Britain gained control of French territories in North America—as well as Spanish Florida—in the 1763 **Treaty of Paris** which ended the Seven Years' War.

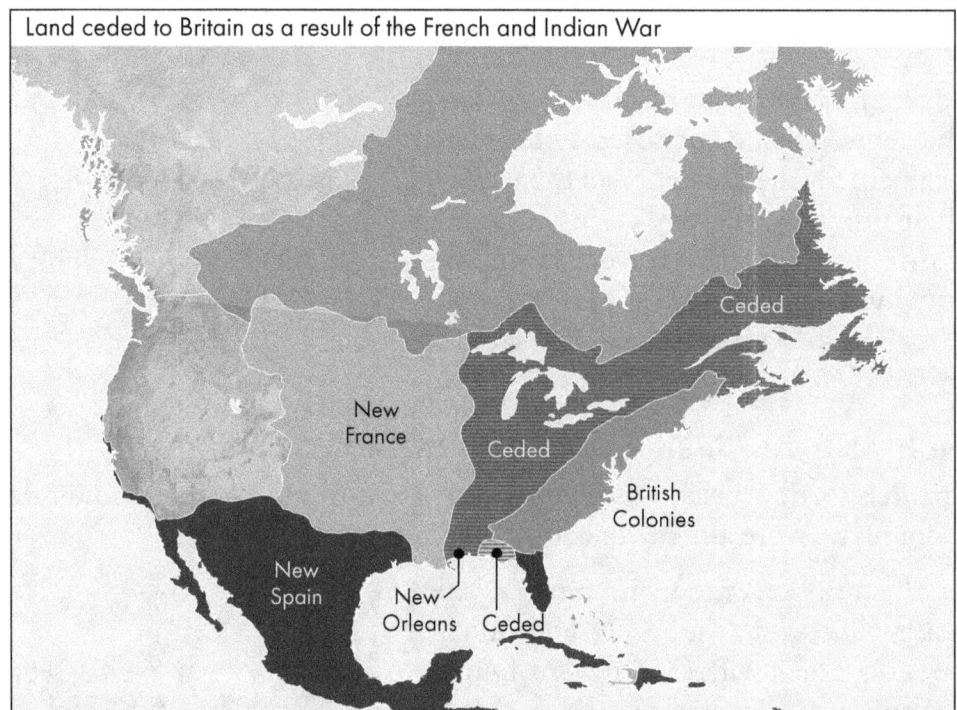

Figure 2.7. British Gains in the French and Indian War

Following another period of salutary neglect in the colonies, in 1754, French and English conflict exploded once again in North America as fighting broke out in the Ohio Valley. The British government organized with North American colonial leaders to meet at Albany. **Benjamin Franklin** helped organize the defensive Albany Plan of Union and argued for this plan in his newspaper, the *Pennsylvania Gazette*, using the famous illustration *Join, or Die*. However, the Crown worried that this plan allowed for too much colonial independence, adding to tensions between the Thirteen Colonies and England.

Figure 2.8. Join, or Die.

In the mid-eighteenth century, a sense of religious fervor called the **Great Awakening** spread throughout the colonies. People broke beyond the confines of traditional Christianity, attracted to traveling preachers and public pronouncements of religious fervor.

- The Great Awakening helped develop a more singularly North American religious culture.

- It also created a divide between traditional European Christianity and emerging North American faiths.

> **DID YOU KNOW?**
>
> Many universities, including some Ivy League schools, were founded during this time to train ministers.

PRACTICE QUESTIONS

6) **What were the differences between Spanish and French colonization in North America?**

   A. Both intermarried with Native Americans; however, the Spanish took a more aggressive approach in spreading Christianity.

   B. Spain sought accord and agreement with Native Americans, while France forced marriages as part of settling the land, resulting in the mixed-race métis class.

   C. France colonized the Southwest; Spain colonized the Northeast and Midwest.

   D. France imported enslaved Africans as part of the Triangular Trade in order to support New France, while Spain mainly exploited local Native American tribes, forcing them to perform labor and essentially enslaving them.

7) How did geography contribute to differences between northern and southern colonies on the Atlantic coast of North America?

   A. Climate and terrain in the south supported plantation agriculture.

   B. Numerous natural ports in the southern colonies led to the development of major cities there.

   C. Mountainous terrain prevented major settlement in northern colonies.

   D. Small farmers in the north grew cotton and tobacco, thanks to the mild climate.

8) Which of the following was a factor in stirring up colonial discontent?

   A. balance of trade

   B. mercantilism

   C. John Locke's *Second Treatise*

   D. the Columbian Exchange

9) Upon what premise were Mid-Atlantic colonies like Pennsylvania, Delaware, and New Jersey founded?

   A. a beacon of unity and humanity, reminiscent of John Winthrop's *City Upon a Hill*

   B. tolerance, as part of William Penn's *Great Experiment*

   C. profit, in accordance with their roots in joint-stock companies seeking profit from the land through royal charters

   D. conquest and conversion, in order to take land from Native American tribes and convert those original inhabitants to Christianity

10) How did the British and French rivalry spill over into North America?

    A. While Britain and France were often on opposite sides in European conflict, they found common ground against Native Americans in North America.

    B. European conflicts between Catholics and Protestants affected Catholic French and Protestant English settlers; related violence from the Hundred Years' War broke out between them as a result.

    C. These European powers engaged in proxy wars, supporting the Iroquois and Algonquin, respectively, as well as the Chickasaw and Choctaw, in jockeying for control of land in the Great Lakes and southeastern regions of North America.

    D. France and Britain formed an alliance to prevent Spain from moving eastward on the continent.

Revolution and the Early United States

The American Revolution

Though victorious in the French and Indian War, Britain had gone into debt. Furthermore, there were concerns that the colonies required a stronger military presence following **Pontiac's Rebellion** in 1763. The leader of the **Ottawa** people, Pontiac, led a revolt that extended from the Great Lakes region through the Ohio Valley to Virginia. This land had been ceded to England from France, with no input from Indigenous residents.

> **CHECK YOUR UNDERSTANDING #3**
>
> Why did Pontiac lead resistance? What was the consequence of Pontiac's Rebellion?

The Ottawa people and other Native Americans resisted further British settlement and fought back against colonial oppression. To make peace, **King George III** signed the **Proclamation of 1763**, an agreement not to settle land west of the Appalachians. Still, much settlement continued in practice.

As a result of the war and subsequent unrest, Britain once again discarded its colonial policy of salutary neglect. In desperate need of cash, the Crown sought ways to increase its revenue from the colonies.

King George III enforced heavy taxes and restrictive acts in the colonies to generate income for the Crown and punish disobedience.

Table 2.1. Controversial Acts and Taxes

Act	Purpose	Consequences
Sugar Act of 1764 (expansion of the Molasses Act of 1733)	taxed sugar and molasses	• sugar, produced in the British West Indies, was widely consumed in the Thirteen Colonies • colonists were heavily impacted
Quartering Act of 1765	required colonists to provide shelter to British troops stationed in the region	• increased resentment among colonials forced to provide shelter to British troops • protests against this act led to the 1770 Boston Massacre
Stamp Act of 1765	taxed all documents by requiring a costly stamp	• first direct tax on the colonists • seen as a violation of rights because they were not represented in British parliament
Townshend Acts	empowered customs officers to search colonists' homes for forbidden goods with **writs of assistance**	• enacted in response to actions of the Sons and Daughters of Liberty • increased resentment • repealed in 1770

continued on next page

Table 2.1. Controversial Acts and Taxes (continued)

Act	Purpose	Consequences
Tea Act of 1773	taxed tea, a popular beverage	• led to Boston Tea Party, a protest when colonists tossed tea from ships into the harbor
Intolerable Acts of 1773	• closed Boston Harbor • put Massachusetts firmly under British control	• colonial leaders held First Continental Congress

Patrick Henry protested the Stamp Act in the Virginia House of Burgesses. In Britain, however, it was argued that the colonists had **virtual representation** and so the Act—and others to follow—were justified.

As a result, colonists began boycotting British goods and engaging in violent protest. **Samuel Adams** led the **Sons and Daughters of Liberty** in violent acts against tax collectors. He led the **Committees of Correspondence**, which distributed anti-British propaganda.

> **DID YOU KNOW?**
>
> The famous phrase "no taxation without representation" originated in John Dickinson's Letters from a Farmer in Pennsylvania and Samuel Adams's **Massachusetts Circular Letter**, which argued for the repeal of the Townshend Acts.

Protests against the Quartering Act in Boston led to the **Boston Massacre** in 1770, when British troops fired on a crowd of protesters. By 1773, in a climate of continued unrest driven by the Committees of Correspondence, colonists protested the latest taxes on tea levied by the **Tea Act** in the famous **Boston Tea Party** by dressing as Native Americans and tossing tea off a ship in Boston Harbor. In response, the government passed the **Intolerable Acts**, closing Boston Harbor and bringing Massachusetts back under direct royal control.

Subsequently, colonial leaders met in Philadelphia at the **First Continental Congress** in 1774. They issued the *Declaration of Rights and Grievances*, presenting colonial concerns to King George III, who ignored it.

> **DID YOU KNOW?**
>
> King George III hired Hessian mercenaries from Germany to supplement British troops. The addition of foreign fighters only increased resentment in the colonies, creating a stronger sense of independence from Britain.

Violent conflict began on April 19, 1775, at **Lexington and Concord**. American militiamen (**minutemen**) gathered to resist British efforts to seize weapons and arrest rebels in Concord. On June 17, 1775, Americans fought the British at the **Battle of Bunker Hill**. Despite American losses, the number of casualties the minutemen inflicted on the British

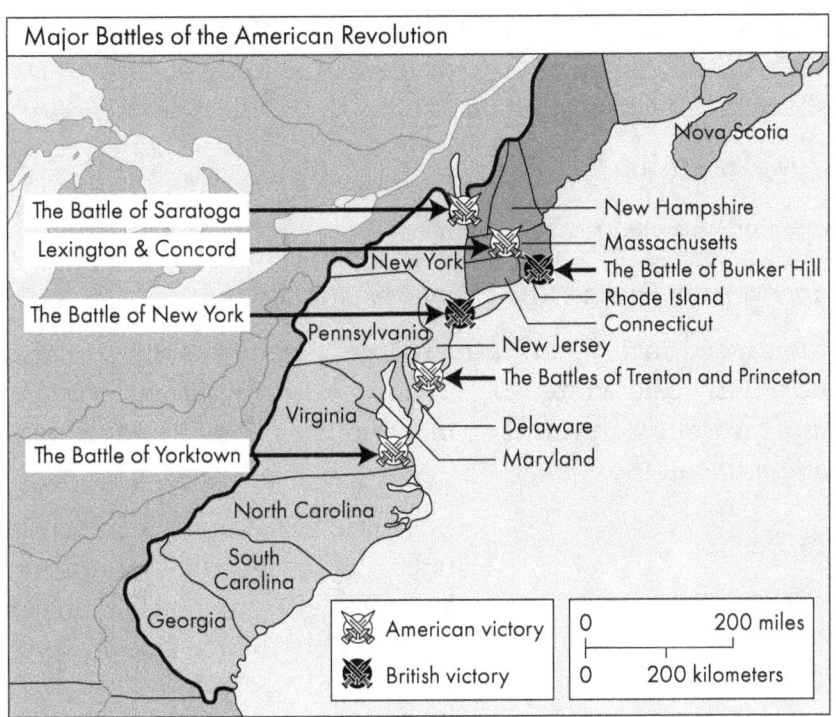

Figure 2.9. Major Battles of the American Revolution

caused the king to declare that the colonies were in rebellion. He deployed troops, and the Siege of Boston began.

In May 1775, the **Second Continental Congress** met at Philadelphia to debate the way forward. Debate between the wisdom of continued efforts at compromise and negotiations versus declaring independence continued.

The king ignored two pleas from the Second Continental Congress:

- *the Declaration of the Causes and Necessities of Taking Up Arms*, which asked him to again consider the colonies' objections

- the **Olive Branch Petition**, which sought compromise and an end to hostilities

> **HELPFUL HINT**
>
> In early 1776, **Thomas Paine** published his pamphlet *Common Sense*. Informed by Locke's concepts of natural rights and republicanism, it popularized the notion of rebellion against Britain.

By summer of 1776, the Continental Congress agreed on the need to break from Britain. On July 4 of that year, it declared the independence of the United States of America and issued the **Declaration of Independence**, drafted mainly by **Thomas Jefferson** and heavily influenced by Locke.

Still, Americans were divided over independence:

- **Patriots** were in favor of independence.

- Tories remained loyal to England.

General George Washington had been appointed head of the Continental Army. He led a largely unpaid and unprofessional body of troops. Despite early losses, Washington gained ground due to:

- strong leadership
- superior knowledge of the land
- support from France, Spain, and the Netherlands

The tide turned in 1777 at **Valley Forge**, when Washington and his army survived the bitterly cold winter to overcome British military forces. The British people did not favor the war, voting so in parliament. The incoming parliamentary majority sought to end the war.

> **HELPFUL HINT**
>
> The American Revolution would go on to inspire revolution around the world.

In the 1783 **Treaty of Paris**, the United States was recognized as a country. It agreed to repay debts to British merchants and provide safety to British loyalists who wished to remain in North America.

THE CREATION OF US GOVERNMENT

Joy in the victory over Great Britain was short-lived. Fearful of tyranny, the Second Continental Congress had provided for only a weak central government by adopting the **Articles of Confederation** to organize the Thirteen Colonies—now states—as a loosely united country.

- A unicameral central government had limited powers:
    - wage war
    - negotiate treaties
    - borrow money
- States could be taxed, but not citizens.
- Westward expansion and the establishment of new states was planned.

> **HELPFUL HINT**
>
> The Northwest Ordinances effectively nullified King George III's Proclamation of 1763, which promised Native Americans that colonization would cease in the Ohio Valley region. Tensions would lead to the Northwest Indian Wars.

The **Northwest Ordinances** of 1787 prohibited slavery north of the Ohio River. Areas with at least 60,000 people could apply for statehood.

However, it soon became clear that the Articles of Confederation were not strong enough to keep the nation united.

The US was heavily in debt. Currency was weak and taxes were high. In Massachusetts,

Daniel Shays led a rebellion. During **Shays' Rebellion**, indebted farmers protested debtor's prisons and aimed to prevent courts from seizing their property.

Such debt and disorganization made the new country appear weak and vulnerable. Furthermore, if the United States were to remain one country, it needed a stronger federal government.

Alexander Hamilton and **James Madison** called for a **Constitutional Convention** to write a constitution as the foundation of a stronger federal government.

Federalists believed in the **separation of powers**, republicanism, and a strong federal government. Madison, Hamilton, and John Adams were important Federalists.

To determine the exact structure of the government, delegates at the convention settled on the **Great Compromise**, a **bicameral legislature**. Two plans had been presented:

- The **New Jersey Plan benefitted smaller states.** It proposed a legislature composed of an equal number of representatives from each state.

- The **Virginia Plan** benefitted larger states. It proposed a legislature composed of representatives proportional to the population of each state.

Enslaved Black Americans had no place in the political process. Still, they were represented in a state's population to determine that state's number of representatives in Congress. States with large enslaved populations accounted for those persons with the **Three-Fifths Compromise**, which counted an enslaved Black American as three-fifths of a person.

Both plans were adopted, and a bicameral legislature was created:

- The **House of Representatives** followed the Virginia Plan model.

- The **Senate** followed the New Jersey Plan model.

Anti-Federalists, like **Thomas Jefferson,** called for even more limitations on the power of the federal government. They were unsatisfied with the separation of powers provided for in the Constitution.

In response, Madison introduced a list of guarantees of American freedoms in the first ten amendments to the Constitution: The **Bill of Rights**. The Federalists considered this a concession to the Anti-Federalists.

To convince the states to ratify the Constitution, Hamilton, Madison, and John Jay wrote the *Federalist Papers*, articulating the benefits of federalism. Likewise, the Bill of Rights helped convince the hesitant.

> **HELPFUL HINT**
>
> The Anti-Federalists would later become the **Democratic-Republican Party** and eventually, the Democratic Party that exists today.

> **DID YOU KNOW?**
>
> Federalists were generally from the North and were usually merchants or businessmen. Anti-Federalists were usually from the South or the rural west and farmed the land.

In 1791, the Constitution was ratified. **George Washington** was elected president, with John Adams serving as vice president. Washington appointed Alexander Hamilton as Secretary of the Treasury and Thomas Jefferson as Secretary of State.

Early American Diplomacy and Legislation

Hamilton prioritized currency stabilization and the repayment of debts. He also believed in establishing a national bank—the **Bank of the United States (BUS)**. President Washington signed the BUS into law in 1791.

Hamilton also favored tariffs and excise (sales) taxes. However, **Democratic-Republicans (Anti-Federalists)** vehemently opposed these. In 1795, rebellion against the excise tax on whiskey broke out. The **Whiskey Rebellion** indicated unrest in the young country and was put down by militia.

Meanwhile, the French Revolution had begun in Europe. However, President Washington issued the **Neutrality Proclamation** in 1793. Despite this action, British and French ships accosted American ships in the Atlantic and forced American sailors into naval service (**impressment**). Several treaties and events marked this era.

Table 2.2. Early American Incidents in Foreign Relations

Major Diplomatic Event	Causes and Consequences
Neutrality Proclamation (1793)	• issued by President Washington • intended to avoid entanglement in the French Revolution and related conflict
Jay's Treaty (1794)	• failed attempt by John Jay to stop impressment of US soldiers in the Atlantic by France and Britain • unsuccessful and unpopular • removed British forts in the western frontier
Pinckney's Treaty (1795)	• treaty with Spain negotiated by Thomas Pinckney • secured US rights on the Mississippi River and Port of New Orleans • defined US border with Spanish Florida • diplomatic success • ratified by all thirteen states • also known as Treaty of San Lorenzo

Major Diplomatic Event	Causes and Consequences
XYZ Affair (1797)	- US diplomats traveled to Paris to negotiate an end to French seizures of US ships - France asked US diplomats for bribes to meet and treated them poorly - resulted in undeclared conflict in the Caribbean until the Convention of 1800
Embargo Act (1807)	- an effort to avoid conflict with European powers at war - only damaged the US economy
Non-Intercourse Act (1809)	- repealed Embargo Act - allowed trade with foreign countries besides Britain and France

The ongoing **Northwest Indian Wars** continued conflict with the Shawnee, Lenape, Kickapoo, Miami, and other tribes in the Ohio region. Following the defeat of allied tribes at the **Battle of Fallen Timbers** in 1794, the Americans gained more territory in Ohio and Indiana.

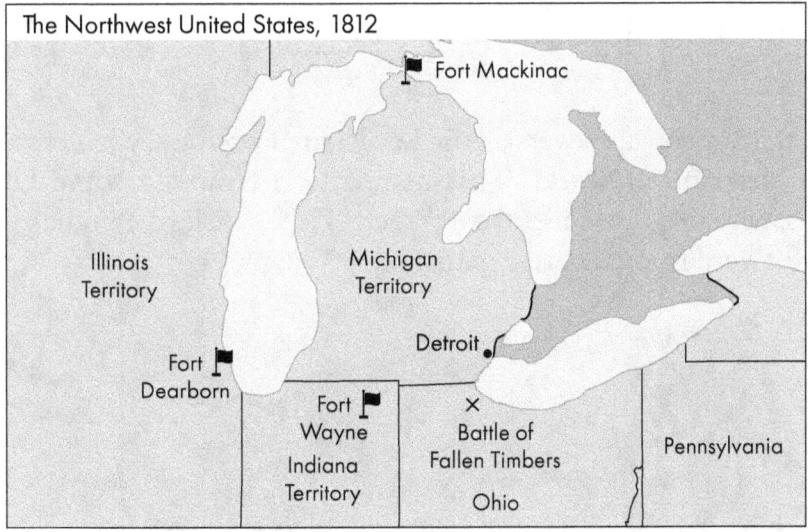

Figure 2.10. Battle of Fallen Timbers

In President Washington's **Farewell Address**, he recommended the United States follow a policy of neutrality in international affairs, setting a precedent for early American history. Vice President John Adams, a Federalist, became the second president.

During the Adams administration, the Federalists passed the harsh **Alien and Sedition Acts**.

Table 2.3. Alien and Sedition Acts

Alien Act	Sedition Act
• allowed the president to deport "enemy aliens" • increased the residency requirements for citizenship	• prohibited criticism of the president • prohibited criticism of Congress

Divisions between the Federalists and the Democratic-Republicans were deeper than ever. Nevertheless, Thomas Jefferson was elected to the presidency in 1801 in a nonviolent transfer of power.

FOUNDATIONS OF WESTWARD EXPANSION

President Jefferson took several actions pleasing Anti-Federalists:

▶ shrank the federal government

▶ repealed the Alien and Sedition Acts

▶ enacted economic policies that favored small farmers and landowners

This contrasted with his predecessors' Federalist policies, which supported big business and cities.

However, Jefferson also oversaw the **Louisiana Purchase**, which nearly doubled the size of the United States. This acquisition troubled some Democratic-Republicans, who saw it as federal overreach. The Louisiana Purchase would be a major step forward in westward expansion.

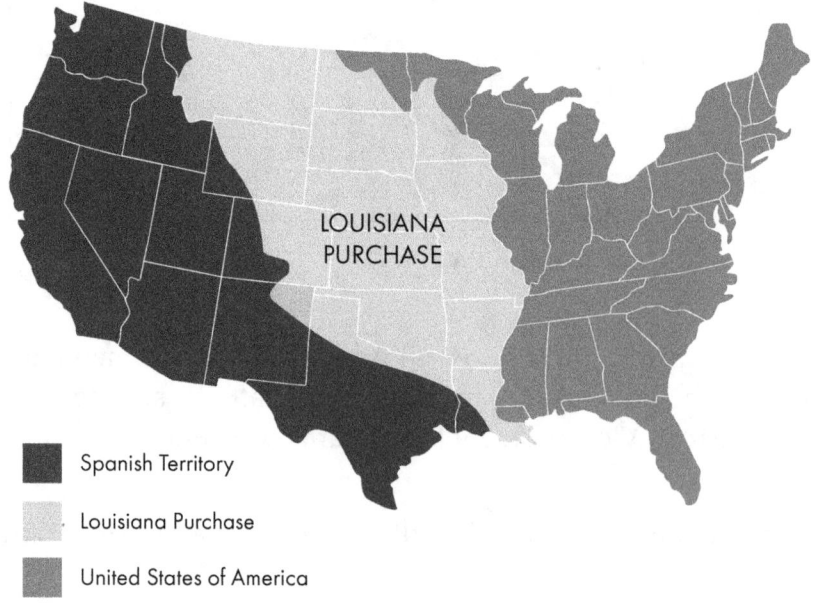

Figure 2.11. Louisiana Purchase

Jefferson hoped to find an all-water route to the Pacific Ocean via the Missouri River. He dispatched **Meriwether Lewis** and **William Clark** to explore the western frontier of the territory. This route did not exist, but Lewis and Clark returned with a deeper knowledge of the territory the US had come to control.

WAR OF 1812

British provocation at sea and in the northwest led to the **War of 1812**. Congress declared war to:

- protect the US from chaotic trade practices
- end the impressment of American sailors
- expand US territory

Growing nationalism in the United States also pressured Madison into pushing for war after the **Battle of Tippecanoe**. In this Indiana battle, **General William Henry Harrison** fought the **Northwest Confederacy**, a group of tribes led by the Shawnee leader **Tecumseh**.

The Shawnee, Lenape, Miami, Kickapoo, and others had come together to form the Northwest Confederacy.

- They wanted to maintain independent territory at the northwest of the United States (present-day Indiana and region).
- They also followed Tecumseh's brother **Tenskwatawa**, who was considered a prophet.

Despite the Northwest Confederacy's alliance with Britain, the United States prevailed.

The War of 1812 resulted in no real gains or losses for either the Americans or the British. Still, the United States had successfully defended itself as a country and reaffirmed its independence. Patriotism ran high.

Figure 2.12. Tecumseh

THE ERA OF GOOD FEELINGS AND THE SECOND GREAT AWAKENING

During the presidency of **James Monroe**, a strong sense of public identity and nationalism grew. This was called the **Era of Good Feelings**. Religious revival became popular. People turned from Puritanism and predestination to Baptist and Methodist faiths, among others, following revolutionary preachers and movements. This period was called the **Second Great Awakening**. In art and culture, romanticism and reform movements elevated the "common man," a trend that would continue into the presidency of Andrew Jackson.

> **HELPFUL HINT**
>
> Federalists strongly opposed the War of 1812 and developed an anti-Republican platform at the Hartford Convention. But by the time they completed their discussions, the War of 1812 had already ended. The Federalists essentially collapsed afterwards.

The country would again struggle economically. The **Tariff of 1816 was meant to boost domestic manufacturing**. But it divided northern industrialists from southern landowners. Industrialists believed in nurturing American industry, whereas southern landowners depended on exporting cotton and tobacco for profit.

Later, following the establishment of the **Second Bank of the United States (BUS)**, the **Panic of 1819** erupted when the government cut credit following overspeculation on western lands. The BUS wanted payment from state banks in hard currency, or **specie**. Western banks foreclosed on western farmers, and farmers lost their land.

Manifest Destiny and the Monroe Doctrine

With the Louisiana Purchase, the country had almost doubled in size. The idea of **manifest destiny** prevailed. According to manifest destiny, it was the fate of the United States to expand westward and settle the continent.

Also in 1819, the United States purchased Florida from Spain in the **Adams-Onis Treaty**. The **Monroe Doctrine**, President James Monroe's policy that the Western Hemisphere was "closed" to further European colonization or exploration, asserted US hegemony in the region.

Westward expansion triggered questions about the expansion of slavery. Southern states depended on enslaving people to maintain the plantation economy. But slavery was increasingly condemned in the North. Furthermore, the Second Great Awakening had fueled the **abolitionist** movement, which sought to abolish slavery.

In debating the nature of westward expansion, Kentucky senator **Henry Clay** worked out a compromise. The **Missouri Compromise**, also known as the **Compromise of 1820**, allowed Missouri to join the union as a slave state, but provided that any other states north of the **thirty-sixth parallel (36°30')** would not permit slavery. Maine would also join the nation as a free state. However, more tension and compromises over the nature of slavery in new states were to come.

Demographics were changing throughout the early nineteenth century. Technological advances such as the **cotton gin** had allowed exponential increases in cotton production. The result: more persons were enslaved than ever before, bringing more urgency to the issue of slavery.

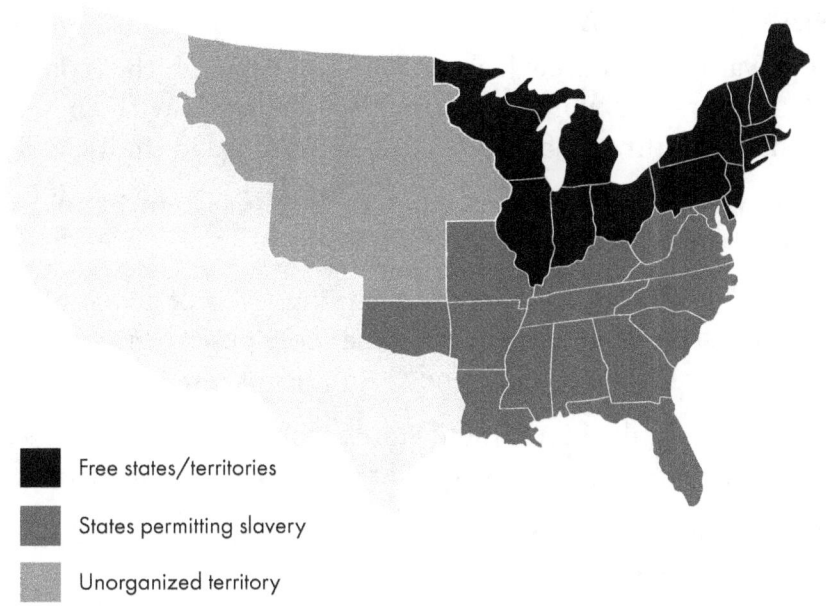

Figure 2.13. Missouri Compromise

Other technological advances like the **railroads** and **steamships** were speeding up westward expansion and improving trade throughout the continent. A large-scale **market economy** was emerging.

With early industrialization and changing concepts following the Second Great Awakening, women were playing a larger role in society, even though they could not vote.

In addition, **immigration** from Europe to the United States was increasing—mainly Irish Catholic and German immigrants. Reactionary **nativist** movements like the **Know-Nothing Party** feared the influx of non-Anglo Europeans, particularly Catholics. Discrimination was widespread, especially against the Irish.

Most states had extended voting rights to white men who did not own land or substantial property: **universal manhood suffrage**. Elected officials would increasingly come to better reflect the electorate.

During the election of 1824, Andrew Jackson ran against **John Quincy Adams**, Henry Clay, and William Crawford. The candidates were all Republicans (from the Democratic-Republican party); John Quincy Adams won.

By 1828, divisions within the party had Jackson and his supporters, then known as Democrats, in favor of states' rights and supporting small farmers and the inhabitants of rural areas. Clay and his supporters became known as **National Republicans** and, later, **Whigs**, a splinter group of the Democratic-Republicans which supported business and urbanization; they also had federalist leanings. The **two-party system** had emerged.

Jacksonian Democracy

Considered a war hero, Andrew Jackson was popular with the "common man"—white, male farmers and workers who felt he identified with them. Thanks to universal manhood suffrage, Jackson had the advantage in the 1828 election.

Jackson rewarded his supporters using the **spoils system**, appointing them to important positions.

Socially and politically, white men of varying levels of economic success and education gained stronger political voices and more opportunities in civil society. Women, Black Americans, and Indigenous Americans remained oppressed.

Opposed to the Bank of the United States, Jackson issued the **Specie Circular**. This devalued paper money and instigated the financial **Panic of 1837**.

Despite his opposition to such deep federal economic control, Jackson was forced to contend with controversial tariffs.

- The **Tariff of 1828** (also known as the **Tariff of Abominations**) benefitted northern industry but heavily affected southern exports.
    - Senator **John C. Calhoun** of South Carolina spoke out in favor of **nullification**, arguing that a state had the right to declare a law null and void if it was harmful to that state.
- The **Tariff of 1832** increased tensions: South Carolina threatened to secede if its economic interests were not protected, causing the **Nullification** Crisis.

Jackson managed the **Nullification Crisis** without resorting to violence. Paradoxically, he protected the federal government at the expense of states' rights by working out a compromise in 1833 that was more favorable to the South.

In the Supreme Court case **Cherokee Nation v. Georgia** (1831), the Cherokee argued for the right to their land —and lost. President Jackson enforced the 1830 **Indian Removal Act**, forcing Cherokee, Creek, Chickasaw, Choctaw, and others from their lands in the southeast.

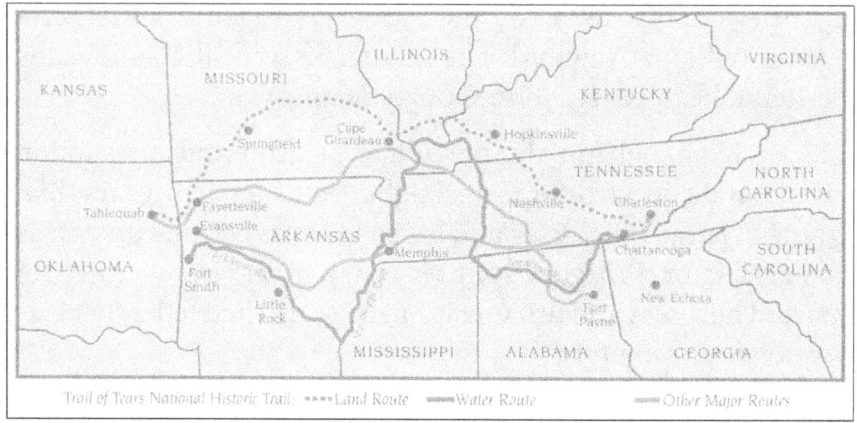

Figure 2.14. The Trail of Tears

To make way for white settlers, thousands of people were forced to travel with all their belongings, mainly on foot, to Indian Territory (today, Oklahoma) on a route that came to be called the **Trail of Tears**. Brutal conditions killed many people.

Throughout the nineteenth century, violent conflicts would continue on the frontier farther west between US forces, white settlers, and the Apache, Comanche, Sioux, Arapaho, Cheyenne, and other tribes.

PRACTICE QUESTIONS

11) **How did the Quartering Act impact the colonists?**
    A. A tax was levied on all documents produced in the Thirteen Colonies, which caused resentment.
    B. Early Americans were forced to build quarters for British soldiers who were stationed locally.
    C. Landowners had to provide one-quarter of their earnings to support British soldiers stationed locally.
    D. Colonists were forced to take British soldiers into their homes, and protests led to the Boston Massacre.

12) **What was the impact of Shays' Rebellion?**
    A. It showed resistance to imposing excise taxes on whiskey and other consumer goods.
    B. It showed the tenuous nature of governmental control in the young United States and illustrated the need for a stronger federal government.
    C. Inspired by *Letters from a Farmer in Pennsylvania*, Daniel Shays and other farmers rose up to protest taxes and the fiscal policies engineered by Alexander Hamilton during the Washington administration.
    D. Shays, who was concerned about strengthened federal powers under the new Constitution, organized radical Democratic-Republicans to protest the fiscal measures espoused by Hamilton, particularly the Bank of the United States.

13) **The United States did not recognize the Proclamation of 1763. What was the impact of that diplomatic reversal?**
    A. Indigenous tribes organized into the Northwest Confederacy, fighting American westward expansion.
    B. The French and British formed the Northwest Confederacy, allying against the United States to control more land in North America.
    C. The British attacked the United States from Canada, starting the War of 1812.
    D. The Northwest Confederacy of British and American soldiers united to drive Indigenous tribes from what is today the Midwest region of the United States.

14) **How did demographics play a part in democratic change during the early and mid-nineteenth century, particularly in the context of Jacksonian Democracy?**

   A. The rising strength of industry in the Northeast, coupled with the beginnings of railroads, strengthened support for pro-business politicians and the business class.

   B. Wealthy European immigrants shifted the balance of power away from the "common man" to business owners and the elites, leading to the rise of the powerful Whig party.

   C. Universal manhood suffrage shifted the balance of political power away from the elites; immigration accelerated westward expansion and began to power early industry and urban development.

   D. Jackson's focus on strengthening the federal government dissatisfied the South, leading to the Nullification Crisis.

15) **Which of the following is true about the Missouri Compromise?**

   A. It illustrated a united approach to westward expansion.

   B. It showed the impact of the abolitionist movement on politics.

   C. It led to increased immigration to the United States.

   D. It eliminated slavery in all new states established in the west.

Civil War, Expansion, and Industry

The Road to Conflict

The Civil War was rooted in ongoing conflict over slavery, states' rights, and the reach of the federal government. Reform movements of the mid-nineteenth century fueled the abolitionist movement. The Missouri Compromise and the Nullification Crisis foreshadowed worsening division to come.

Texas, where there were a great number of white settlers, declared independence from Mexico in 1836. One important reason was that Mexico had abolished slavery. In 1845, Texas joined the Union. This event, in addition to ongoing US hunger for land, triggered the **Mexican-American War.**

As a result of the **Treaty of Guadalupe Hidalgo**, which ended the war, the United States obtained territory in the Southwest: the Utah and New Mexico Territories, and gold-rich California.

The population of California would grow rapidly with the **gold rush** as prospectors in search of gold headed west to try their fortunes. However, Hispanic people who had lived in the region under Mexico lost their land and were denied many rights, despite a promise of US citizenship and equal rights under the treaty. They also endured racial and ethnic discrimination.

Meanwhile, social change in the Northeast and growing Midwest continued. The **middle class** began to develop with the market economy and early industrialization.

Social views on the role of **women** changed:

- extra income allowed them to stay at home
- the **Cult of Domesticity**, a popular cultural movement, encouraged women to become homemakers and focus on domestic skills

Figure 2.15. Seneca Falls Convention

At the same time, middle-class white women were freed up to engage in social activism and became active in reform movements. Activists like **Susan B. Anthony** and **Elizabeth Cady Stanton** worked for women's rights, including women's suffrage. This culminated in the 1848 **Seneca Falls Convention** led by the **American Woman Suffrage Association**.

Women were also active in the temperance movement. Organizations like the Woman's Christian Temperance Union advocated for the prohibition of alcohol. This was finally achieved with the Eighteenth Amendment, although it was later repealed with the Twenty-first.

Reform movements, which ranged from moderate to radical, continued to include abolitionism, which became a key social and political issue in the mid-nineteenth century.

> **HELPFUL HINT**
>
> All American women were denied their right to vote until the ratification of the Nineteenth Amendment in 1920. Black women and American women of color were restricted further until the Voting Rights Act of 1965.

The American Colonization Society wanted to end slavery and send former slaves to Africa.

The writer and publisher **Frederick Douglass**, who had himself been enslaved, also advocated for abolition. However, Douglass was strongly opposed to the American Colonization Society's idea of sending freed slaves—many of whom were born and raised in the US—to Africa.

An activist leader, Douglass publicized the abolitionist movement along with the American Anti-Slavery Society and publications like Harriet Beecher Stowe's *Uncle Tom's Cabin*. The radical abolitionist **John Brown** led violent protests against slavery.

Figure 2.16. Frederick Douglass

The industrial and demographic changes in the North did not extend to the South, which continued to rely on plantations and cotton exports. Differences among the regions grew, and disputes about extending slavery into new southwestern territories obtained from Mexico continued. Another compromise was needed.

Anti-slavery factions in Congress had attempted to halt the extension of slavery to the new territories obtained from Mexico in the 1846 **Wilmot Proviso**, but these efforts were unsuccessful.

The later **Compromise of 1850** admitted the populous California as a free state. Utah and New Mexico joined the Union with slavery to be decided by **popular sovereignty**, or by the residents.

> **DID YOU KNOW?**
>
> Harriet Beecher Stowe planned to illustrate the life endured by enslaved Black Americans through a series of pieces in the abolitionist newspaper *The National Era*. This resulted in over three dozen editorial installments that became published as the two-volume book, *Uncle Tom's Cabin*—outsold only by the Bible in the nineteenth century.

This compromise also reaffirmed the **Fugitive Slave Act**, which allowed enslavers to pursue escaped slaves to free states and recapture them. It would now be a federal crime to assist people escaping slavery. This was unacceptable to many abolitionists.

Shortly thereafter, Congress passed the **Kansas-Nebraska Act of 1854**. This act allowed the Kansas and Nebraska territories to decide slavery by popular sovereignty as well, effectively repealing the Missouri Compromise.

> **CHECK YOUR UNDERSTANDING #4**
>
> List three major consequences of the Compromise of 1850.

As a result, a new party—the **Republican Party**—was formed by angered Democrats, Whigs, and others. Violence broke out in Kansas between pro- and anti-slavery factions in what became known as **Bleeding Kansas**.

In 1856, **Dred Scott**, a Black American who had escaped slavery, sued for freedom at the Supreme Court. Scott had escaped to the free state of Illinois and sought to stay there. Sandford, his enslaver, argued that Scott remained enslaved even though he had escaped to a free state.

The Court heard the case, ***Scott v. Sandford***, and ruled in favor of Sandford. This ruling upheld the Fugitive Slave Act, the Kansas-Nebraska Act, and nullified the Missouri Compromise. The Court essentially decreed that Black Americans were not entitled to rights under US citizenship.

In 1858, a series of debates between Illinois Senate candidates, Republican **Abraham Lincoln** and Democrat **Stephen Douglas**, showed the deep divides in the nation over slavery and states' rights. During the **Lincoln-Douglas Debates**,

Lincoln spoke out against slavery, while Douglas supported the right of states to decide its legality on their own.

In 1860, Abraham Lincoln was elected to the presidency. Given his outspoken stance against slavery, South Carolina seceded immediately. Mississippi, Alabama, Florida, Louisiana, Georgia, and Texas soon followed. On February 1, 1861, they formed the Confederate States of America, or the **Confederacy**, under the leadership of **Jefferson Davis**, a senator from Mississippi.

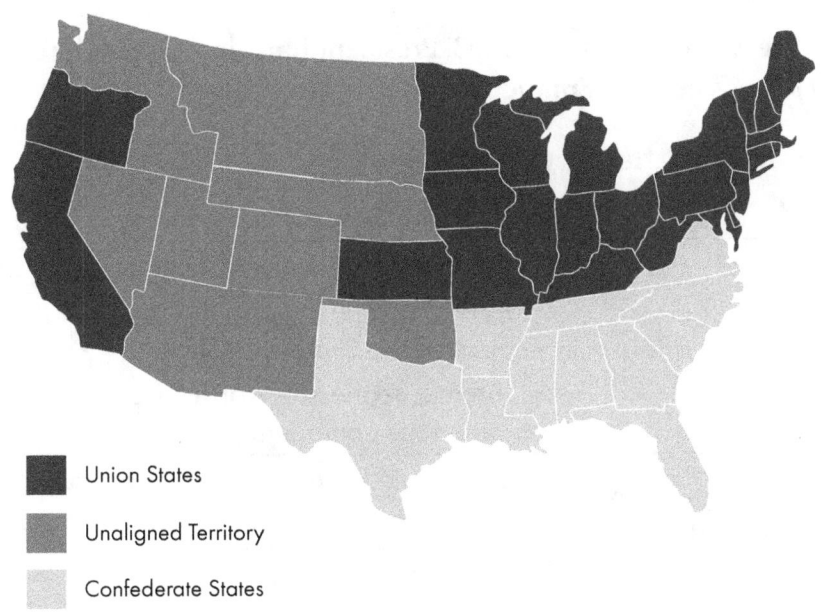

Figure 2.17. Union and Confederacy

THE CIVIL WAR BEGINS

Shortly after the South's secession, Confederate forces attacked Union troops in Charleston Harbor, South Carolina. The **Battle of Fort Sumter** sparked the Civil War. As a result, Virginia, Tennessee, North Carolina, and Arkansas joined the Confederacy.

Both sides believed the conflict would be short-lived. But it became clear that the war would not end quickly.

Realizing how difficult it would be to defeat the Confederacy, the Union developed the **Anaconda Plan**, designed to "squeeze" the Confederacy. The South depended on international trade in cotton for much of its

> **DID YOU KNOW?**
>
> West Virginia was formed when the western part of Virginia refused to join the Confederacy.

income, so a naval blockade would seriously harm the Confederate economy. The Anaconda Plan included:

- a naval blockade of the Confederacy
- Union control of the Mississippi River

Following the **Siege of Vicksburg**, Mississippi, Union forces led by **General Ulysses S. Grant** gained control over the Mississippi River. This completed the Anaconda Plan.

During the war, on January 1, 1863, President Lincoln decreed the end of slavery in the rebel states with the **Emancipation Proclamation**.

Table 2.4. Major Battles of the Civil War

Battle	Impact and Results
Battle of Fort Sumter (1861)	- Confederates attacked Union troops in Charleston, South Carolina - sparked the Civil War - Virginia, Tennessee, North Carolina, and Arkansas joined the Confederacy
First Battle of Bull Run (1861)	- Union failed to rout the Confederacy - showed Civil War would not end quickly
Second Battle of Bull Run (1862)	- Confederate victory - showed strength of Confederate leadership (Robert E. Lee and Stonewall Jackson) - blow to Union morale
Battle of Antietam (1862)	- first battle fought on Union soil - General McClellan prevented Confederate invasion of Maryland - Union did not defeat Confederate forces - Lincoln declared the Emancipation Proclamation
Battle of Gettysburg (1863)	- major Union victory - bloodiest battle in American history up to this point - Confederate army could not recover
Battle of Atlanta (1864)	- final major battle of the Civil War - Union forces penetrated the South - fall of Confederacy
Battle of Appomattox Court House (1865)	- Confederate loss - General Lee surrendered to General Grant, ending the war

The Confederacy had strong military leadership and a vast territory. But the Union prevailed thanks to:

- a larger population (strengthened by immigration)
- stronger industrial capacity (including weapons-making capabilities)
- the naval blockade of Southern trades
- superior leadership

> **DID YOU KNOW?**
>
> President Lincoln delivered the Gettysburg Address onsite at Gettysburg shortly after the battle. He framed the Civil War as a battle for human rights and equality.

AFTERMATH AND RECONSTRUCTION

Bitterness over the Union victory persisted. President Lincoln was assassinated on April 15, 1865. Post-war **Reconstruction** would continue without his leadership.

Before his death, Lincoln had crafted the **Ten Percent Plan**. If ten percent of a Southern state's population swore allegiance to the Union, that state would be readmitted into the Union. However Lincoln's vice president, Andrew Johnson, enforced Reconstruction weakly.

The white supremacist **Ku Klux Klan** emerged to intimidate and kill Black people in the South. Likewise, states developed the oppressive **Black Codes** to limit the rights of freed Black Americans.

As a result, Congress passed the **Civil Rights Act** in 1866, granting citizenship to freed Black Americans and guaranteeing Black American men the same rights as white men.

Eventually former Confederate states also had to ratify the following amendments:

Figure 2.18. Lincoln's Assassination

- the **Thirteenth Amendment**, which abolished slavery
- the **Fourteenth Amendment**, which reaffirmed the Civil Rights Act (equality under the law)
- the **Fifteenth Amendment**, which in 1870 granted Black American men the right to vote

> **DID YOU KNOW?**
>
> Despite ratifying the amendments, Southern states instituted the Black Codes to continue oppression of freedmen, or freed African Americans, who faced ongoing violence.

Conflict over how harshly to treat the South persisted in Congress between Republicans and Democrats. In 1867, a Republican-led Congress passed the **Reconstruction Acts**. These put former Confederate states under the control of the US Army, effectively declaring martial law.

Resentment over the Reconstruction Acts never truly subsided. Military control of the South finally ended with the **Compromise of 1877**, in which:

▸ the disputed presidential election of 1876 was resolved

▸ Rutherford B. Hayes obtained the presidency

▸ troops were removed from the South

Tensions and bitterness existed between Union authorities and Southern leaders. But Reconstruction helped modernize Southern education systems, tax collection, and infrastructure. The **Freedmen's Bureau** was tasked with assisting formerly enslaved Americans and poor whites in the South.

Jim Crow, Segregation, and Civil Rights

> **DID YOU KNOW?**
>
> On June 19, 1865, Union troops arrived in Galveston, Texas. They announced the end of slavery. Many enslaved people in the South had been unaware of the Emancipation Proclamation up to this point. Today the holiday Juneteenth is celebrated in honor of the end of slavery.

Enslaved Black Americans had technically been freed. But many freedmen were unaware of this. Still others remained working on plantations voluntarily—or involuntarily.

Eventually, all enslaved people were freed. But few had education or marketable skills. Furthermore, they could not thrive under oppressive social structures. The **Jim Crow laws** enforced **the separation of races** in the South. Black people's rights were regularly violated.

Black leaders like **Booker T. Washington** and **W.E.B. DuBois** sought solutions.

Table 2.5. Post–Civil War Perspectives on Civil Rights

Booker T. Washington believed in…	W.E.B. DuBois believed in…
• gradual desegregation	• immediate segregation
• vocational education for Black Americans	• higher education and social leadership positions for Black Americans
• the Tuskegee Institute, where he offered vocational education to Black men	• the **National Association for the Advancement of Colored People (NAACP)**, an advocacy group that supported his ideas

These differing views reflected diverse positions within and beyond the African American community over its future.

In 1896, the Supreme Court upheld segregation. Homer Plessy, a Black man, was forced off a whites-only train car. Plessy challenged the law in *Plessy v. Ferguson*, but the Court decided that segregation was constitutional. According to the Court, *separate but equal* still ensured equality under the law. This would remain the law until **Brown v. Board of Education** in 1954.

As part of a broader, ongoing movement known as the **Great Migration**, many Black Americans began leaving the South for better opportunities farther west and in the cities of the north.

Settlement of the West

Throughout the Civil War and the chaotic post-war Reconstruction period, settlement of the West continued. California had already grown in population due to the gold rush. By the mid-nineteenth century, **Chinese immigrants** began arriving in large numbers to California—also in search of gold—but were met instead with racial discrimination.

Meanwhile, the US was opening trade with East Asia, thanks to **clipper ships** that made journeys across the Pacific Ocean faster and easier. In 1853, **Commodore Matthew Perry** had used "gunboat diplomacy" to force trade agreements with Japan. Even earlier, the United States had signed the **Treaty of Wangxia**, a trade agreement, with Qing Dynasty China.

Figure 2.19. Clipper Ship

While Chinese immigrants faced racism, Americans of European descent were encouraged to settle the frontier. The **Homestead Act of 1862** granted 160 acres of land in the West to any pioneer who promised to settle and work it for a certain number of years. However, frontier life proved difficult because the land of the Great Plains was difficult to farm. Ranching and herding cattle became popular and profitable.

White settlers also hunted the buffalo. Mass killings of buffalo threatened Indigenous survival.

The Great Plains and Rocky Mountains were already populated with Sioux, Cheyenne, Apache, Comanche, Arapaho, Pawnee, and others. Conflict between Native American tribes and white settlers was ongoing.

In 1864, US troops ambushed Cheyenne and Arapaho people in Colorado in what became known as the **Sand Creek Massacre**, which triggered even more violence.

The United States came to an agreement with the Sioux in South Dakota, offering them land as part of the **reservation** system. However, by the late nineteenth century, gold was discovered in the Black Hills of South Dakota on the **Great Sioux Reservation**.

The US reneged on its promise, encouraging exploration and seeking control over that gold. The resulting **Sioux Wars** culminated in the 1876 **Battle of Little Big Horn** and General George Custer's "last stand." While the US was defeated in that battle, reinforcements would later defeat the Sioux and the reservation system continued.

Figure 2.20. Ogallala Sioux Ghost Dance at Pine Ridge, 1890

The **Ghost Dance Movement** united Plains tribes in a spiritual movement and in the belief that whites would eventually be driven from the land. In 1890, the military forced the Sioux to cease this ritual. The outcome was a massacre at **Wounded Knee** and the death of the Sioux chief, **Sitting Bull**.

In 1887, the **Dawes Act:**

- ended federal recognition of tribes
- withdrew tribal land rights
- forced the sale of reservations—tribal land
- harmed Indigenous families

Indigenous children were sent to boarding schools, where they were forced to abandon their cultures and languages, and speak English, not their native languages.

PRACTICE QUESTIONS

16) Which of the following BEST describes the roots of the Civil War?
    A. John C. Calhoun developed the doctrine of nullification to uphold slavery.
    B. Early nineteenth century immigration to the North represented a threat to the smaller South.
    C. Lincoln and Douglas provoked pro-war sentiment in their debates around the country.
    D. The country was divided over whether slavery should be permitted as the United States grew.

17) How did the Dawes Act impact Indigenous Americans in the West?
    A. It forced them to move from their ancestral lands to what is today Oklahoma.
    B. It revoked tribal rights to land and federal recognition of tribes, forcing assimilation.
    C. It granted them land on reservations.
    D. It provided 160 acres of land to any settler willing to farm land on the Great Plains.

THE GILDED AGE AND THE PROGRESSIVE ERA

Back in the Northeast, the market economy and industry were flourishing. Following the war, the **Industrial Revolution** accelerated in the United States.

The Industrial Revolution had begun on the global level with textile production in Great Britain, had been fueled in great part by supplies of Southern cotton, and was evolving in the United States with the development of heavy industry—what would come to be called the **Second Industrial Revolution**.

Though products from the US market economy were available in the United States; the country needed more markets abroad to continue to fuel economic growth.

New Imperialism described the US approach to nineteenth and early twentieth century European-style imperialism. Rather than controlling territory, the US sought economic connections with countries around the world.

INCOME INEQUALITY OF THE GILDED AGE

The **Gilded Age** saw an era of rapidly growing income inequality. Inequality was justified by theories like **Social Darwinism**. The **Gospel of Wealth** argued that the wealthy had been made rich by God and were, therefore, socially more deserving of it.

Much of this wealth was generated by heavy industry in what became known as the **Second Industrial Revolution**. Westward expansion required railroads, railroads required steel, and industrial production required oil. These commodities spurred the rise of powerful companies like John D. Rockefeller's Standard Oil and Andrew Carnegie's US Steel.

Figure 2.21. Perspectives on the Senate during the Gilded Age

The creation of **monopolies** and **trusts** helped industrial leaders consolidate their control over the entire economy. A few Americans began holding a huge percentage of income.

Monopolies let the same business leaders control the market for their own products. Business leaders organized into trusts. **Trusts** ensured their control over each other's industries, buying and selling from each other. The results: the economy was dominated by a select few.

These processes were made possible thanks to the vertical and horizontal integration of industries:

- **vertical integration**: One company dominates each step in manufacturing a good, from obtaining raw materials to shipping the finished product.

- **horizontal integration**: This describes the process of companies acquiring their competition, thereby monopolizing their markets.

With limited governmental controls or interference in the economy, American **capitalism**—the free market system—was becoming dominated by a small percentage of wealthy Americans.

> **CHECK YOUR UNDERSTANDING #5**
>
> What was the driving force behind the Second Industrial Revolution?

Government corruption led only to weak restrictive legislation:

- the **Interstate Commerce Act** (1887) was intended to regulate the railroad industry

- the **Sherman Antitrust Act** (1890) was intended to break up monopolies and trusts to create a fairer marketplace

These measures would remain largely toothless until President Theodore Roosevelt's "trust-busting" administration in 1901.

The free markets and trade of the **capitalist** economy spurred national economic and industrial growth. But the **working class**—comprised largely of poor immigrants working in factories and building infrastructure—suffered from dangerous working conditions and other abuses.

Figure 2.22. Triangle Shirtwaist Factory Fire

As the railroads expanded westward, white farmers lost their land to corporate interests. In addition, with limited (or nonexistent) regulations on land use, Mexican Americans and Indigenous Americans in the West were harmed and lost land.

> **DID YOU KNOW?**
>
> In New York City, the Triangle Shirtwaist factory caught fire in 1911, killing 146 employees. It exposed dangerous working conditions and inspired future legislation to protect workers.

Black Americans in the South were also struggling. Under **sharecropping**, many worked the same land for the same landowners who had enslaved them. Black sharecroppers were forced to lease land and equipment at unreasonable rates, essentially trapped in the same conditions they had lived in before.

These harmful consequences led to the development of reform movements, social ideals, and change.

POPULISM AND THE PROGRESSIVE ERA

The 1890 **Sherman Silver Purchase Act** allowed Treasury notes to be backed in both gold and silver. But political conflict, economic troubles, the silver standard, and the failure of a major railroad company led to the financial **Panic of 1893**. President **Grover Cleveland**, who had never been in favor of the silver standard, repealed the Sherman Silver Purchase Act as a result.

In response to corruption and industrialization, farmers, sharecroppers, and industrial workers formed several alliances to improve working conditions and level the economic playing field.

- **The People's (Populist) Party** was formed in response to corruption and industrialization injurious to farmers.
  - Later, it would also support reform in favor of the working class, women, and children.
- **The National Grange** advocated for farmers who were suffering from crushing debt in the face of westward expansion, which destroyed their lands; they were also competing (and losing) against industrialized and mechanized farming.
- **Las Gorras Blancas** was an extremist group that disrupted the construction of railroads to protect farmers and their land from corporate interests.
- **The Greenback-Labor Party** was formed to introduce a silver standard, which farmers believed would inflate crop prices by putting more money into national circulation.
- **The Colored Farmers' Alliance** was formed to support sharecroppers and other Black farmers in the South, who were harmed by Jim Crow laws.

Around the same time, **the labor movement** emerged to support mistreated industrial workers in urban areas.

▶ **The American Federation of Labor (AFL)**, led by **Samuel Gompers**, used **strikes** and **collective bargaining** to gain protections for the workers who had come to cities seeking industrial jobs.

▶ **The Knights of Labor** empowered workers by integrating unskilled workers into actions.

▶ The activist Marry Harris Jones, better known as **Mother Jones**, revolutionized labor by including women, children, and African Americans in labor actions.

Figure 2.23. Mother Jones

With the continual rise of the **middle class**, women took a more active role in advocating for the poor and for themselves. Women activists also aligned with labor and the emerging **Progressive Movement**.

Poor conditions also inspired workers to consider philosophies of reform:

▶ **socialism**: the idea that workers should own the means of production and that wealth should be distributed equally, using economic planning

▶ **utopianism**: the concept of creating utopian settlements with egalitarian societies

▶ **the Social Gospel**: a religious movement believing in the notion that it was society's obligation to ensure better treatment for workers, immigrants, and society's most vulnerable

The Progressive **Theodore Roosevelt** became president in 1901 following the assassination of President William McKinley. The Progressive Era reached its apex.

Roosevelt became known as a *trust-buster*. He enforced the Sherman Antitrust Act and prosecuted the **Northern Securities** railroad monopoly under the Interstate Commerce Act, breaking up trusts and creating a fairer market.

DID YOU KNOW?

The **Sherman Antitrust Act**, despite its intended purpose—to prosecute and dissolve large trusts and create a fairer marketplace—had actually been used against unions and farmers' alliances.

Roosevelt also led government involvement in negotiations between unions and industrial powers, developing the *square deal* for fairer treatment of workers. The Progressive Era also saw a series of acts to protect workers, health, farmers, and children under Presidents Roosevelt and Taft.

The Spanish–American War and US Imperialism

Spanish abuses in Cuba had concerned Americans. But many events were sensationalized and exaggerated in the media. This **yellow journalism** aroused popular concern and interest in intervention in Cuba.

Other causes of the Spanish-American War included the discovery of an insulting letter from the Spanish minister de Lôme, and the mysterious explosion of the United States battleship *USS Maine* in Havana.

> **DID YOU KNOW?**
>
> Sanford Dole led a takeover of the Hawai'i, an independent monarchy. He and other white landowners overthrew Queen Liliuokalani and created the Republic of Hawai'i before US annexation. Today, the Dole Food company still grows and sells fruit worldwide.

The Spanish-American War was the first time the United States had engaged in overseas military occupation and conquest beyond North America, entirely contrary to George Washington's recommendations in his Farewell Address. This **new imperialism** expanded US markets and increased US presence and prestige on the global stage.

The United States did not annex Hawai'i in the Spanish-American war. However, nationalism helped push Pacific imperialism and annexation. White plantation owners had been taking over Hawai'ian land to grow sugar and fruit. They supported annexation of this independent kingdom for economic reasons.

The Treaty of Paris ended the Spanish-American War, granting certain Caribbean and Pacific territories to the United States. At the same time, nationalist sentiment drove US imperialism in strategic areas in the Caribbean, Pacific, and Latin America.

Table. 1.6. United States Expansion in Latin America and the Pacific

Country or Region	Consequences	Legislation or Treaty
Cuba	• Cuba would revert to independence following the war.	**Teller Amendment**
	• The United States effectively took over Cuba (against the wishes of many Americans).	**Platt Amendment**
Panama Canal (Central American Colombia/ Panama)	• England ceded claims in Colombian Central America to the US. • Colombia refused to recognize the treaty. • President Roosevelt engineered a revolution, creating the new country of Panama. • Panama Canal construction began.	**Hay-Pauncefote Treaty**

Country or Region	Consequences	Legislation or Treaty
Philippines	• The United States retained control over the Philippines despite having promised it independence. • Guerilla war resulted as the Philippines resisted US occupation.	**Treaty of Paris (1898)**
Hawai'i	• Hawai'ian Queen Liliuokalani strengthened the monarchy in the face of US sugar and fruit interests. • Supporting US plantation owners, the US annexes Hawai'i in 1898. • Sanford Dole made first Hawai'ian governor under US annexation.	**Newlands Resolution**
Puerto Rico and Guam	• Some Puerto Ricans expected independence. • US had strong foothold in the Caribbean and Pacific.	**Treaty of Paris (1898)**

President Roosevelt continued overseas expansion following the **Spanish-American War**. The **Roosevelt Corollary** to the Monroe Doctrine promised US intervention in Latin America in case of European action there. This essentially gave the US total dominance over Latin America.

PRACTICE QUESTIONS

18) How was a small elite group of wealthy businesspersons able to dominate the economy during the Gilded Age?

    A. The Sherman Antitrust Act put a few expert business leaders in charge of economic policy.

    B. Monopolies and trusts, developed through horizontal and vertical integration, ensured that the same business leaders controlled the same markets.

    C. Industrialization was encouraging the United States to shift to a planned economy in keeping with philosophical changes in Europe.

    D. The silver standard allowed specific businesspeople holding large silver reserves to dominate the market.

19) How did the Progressive Movement change the United States during the Second Industrial Revolution?

   A. Trade unions fought for workers' rights and safety; the Social Gospel, an early philosophy of charity and philanthropy, developed to support the poor and urban disadvantaged.

   B. The Seneca Falls Convention drew attention to the question of women's suffrage.

   C. Progressives argued to extend rights and protections to Native Americans, particularly those displaced by settlement on the Great Plains.

   D. The Supreme Court ruled segregation unconstitutional in *Plessy v. Ferguson*.

20) How did the Spanish-American War change perceptions of the United States?

   A. The United States lost its military, territorial, and economic aspirations as an imperial power.

   B. The United States had begun to prove itself on the global stage as a military power.

   C. United States citizens became dismissive of nationalism.

   D. United States military extended into Europe and the Mediterranean.

THE UNITED STATES BECOMES A GLOBAL POWER

SOCIOECONOMIC CHANGE AND WORLD WAR I

Social change led by the Progressives in the early twentieth century resulted in better conditions for workers, increased attention toward child labor, and petitions for more livable cities.

Continuing economic instability also triggered top-down reform. Banks restricted credit and overspeculated on the value of land and other investments. There was also a conservative gold standard. These led to the **Panic of 1907**.

To stabilize the economy and rein in the banks, Congress passed the **Federal Reserve Act** in 1913 to protect the banking system. Federal Reserve banks were established to cover twelve regions of the country. Commercial banks had to take part in the system, allowing "the Fed" to control interest rates and avoid a similar crisis.

While the United States became increasingly prosperous and stable, Europe was becoming increasingly unstable. Americans were divided over how to respond.

> **DID YOU KNOW?**
>
> Jacob Riis' groundbreaking book and photo essay, *How the Other Half Lives*, revealed the squalor and poverty the poor urban classes—often impoverished immigrants—endured, leading to more public calls for reform.

Following the Spanish-American War, debate had arisen within the US between **interventionism** and **isolationism.** This debate became more pronounced with the outbreak of World War I in Europe.

- interventionism: the belief in spreading US-style democracy
- isolationism: the belief in focusing on development at home

Several inflammatory events triggered US intervention in WWI:

- German submarine warfare in the Atlantic Ocean
- the sinking of the *Lusitania*, which resulted in many American civilian deaths
- the embarrassing Zimmerman Telegram (in which Germany promised to help Mexico in an attack on the US)
- growing American nationalism

With victory in 1918, the US had proven itself a superior military and industrial power. Interventionist **President Woodrow Wilson** played an important role in negotiating the peace. His **Fourteen Points** laid out an idealistic international vision, including an international security organization. The Fourteen Points were not used after WWI, but they informed future international diplomacy.

Divisions between interventionists and isolationists continued.

- Following the Japanese invasion of Manchuria in 1932, the **Stimson Doctrine** determined US neutrality in Asia.
- Congress also passed the **Neutrality Acts** of 1930s in light of conflict in Asia and ongoing tensions in Europe.

> **HELPFUL HINT**
>
> The Neutrality Act of 1939 would allow some financial support to allies, like the United Kingdom. It was used before the United States entered WWII.

ISOLATION, XENOPHOBIA, AND RACISM

On the home front, fear of communists and anarchists, and xenophobia against immigrants led to the **Red Scare** in 1919 and a series of anti-immigration laws. Attorney-General Palmer authorized a series of raids—the **Palmer Raids**—on suspected radicals. This accelerated the hysteria of the Red Scare. Palmer was later discredited.

Xenophobia and isolationism were widespread following the First World War. Congress limited immigration from Asia, Eastern Europe, and Southern Europe with two major racist acts:

- **Emergency Quota Act** of 1921
- **National Origins Act** of 1924

The ongoing Great Migration of Black Americans to northern and western states led to differing views on Black empowerment. Leaders like **Marcus Garvey** believed in self-sufficiency for Black Americans, who were settling in urban areas and facing racial discrimination and isolation.

Garvey's **United Negro Improvement Association** would go on to inspire movements like the Black Panthers and the Nation of Islam. Those radical philosophies of separation were at odds with the NAACP, which believed in integration. Tensions increased with the 1919 race riots. Racist events like the Tulsa race massacre happened throughout the country.

The Ku Klux Klan was growing in power, especially in the South. Black Americans faced intimidation, violence, and death. Black Americans were kidnapped and killed in extrajudicial executions called lynchings. Some lynchings occurred publicly, terrorizing Americans.

> **DID YOU KNOW?**
>
> White residents attacked Black people and businesses on what was known as "Black Wall Street" in the Greenwood area of Tulsa, Oklahoma, on May 31 and June 1, 1931. In what became known as the Tulsa race massacre, a young Black man was accused of assaulting a young white woman. He was arrested, and Black and White residents confronted each other over rumors that he would be lynched. Days of mob violence followed. Black businesses were destroyed, and many people were killed.

THE HARLEM RENAISSANCE AND THE ROARING TWENTIES

Still, African American culture flourished and powered the growth of American popular culture. The **Harlem Renaissance** launched Black music (especially **jazz**), literature, and art into mainstream US culture. So did the evolution of early technology like radio, motion pictures, and automobiles—products that were available to the middle class through credit.

The women's rights movement was empowered by the heightened visibility of women in the public sphere. In 1920, the **Nineteenth Amendment** was ratified, giving all women the right to vote. However, the **Roaring Twenties**, a seemingly trouble-free period of isolation from chaotic world events, would come to an end.

THE GREAT DEPRESSION

Following WWI, the United States experienced an era of consumerism and corruption. The government sponsored **laissez-faire** policies and supported **manufactur-**

ing, flooding markets with cheap consumer goods. Union membership suffered. So did farmers, due to falling crop prices.

While mass production helped the emerging middle class afford more consumer goods and improve their living standards, many families resorted to **credit** to fuel consumer spending. These risky consumer loans, **overspeculation** on crops and the value of farmland, and weak banking protections helped bring about the **Great Depression**, commonly dated from October 29, 1929, or Black Tuesday, when the stock market collapsed.

> **CHECK YOUR UNDERSTANDING #6**
>
> List three reasons for the Great Depression in the United States.

At the same time, a major drought occurred in the Great Plains. American farmers lost their crops in the dust bowl phenomenon and headed to cities. Millions of Americans faced unemployment and poverty.

Figure 2.24. Great Depression

Speculation, or margin-buying, meant that speculators borrowed money to buy stock. Then they sold it as soon as its price rose. Because the price of stocks fluctuated aggressively, buyers would lose confidence in the market and begin selling their shares. This caused the value of stocks to plummet. Borrowers could not repay their loans. As a result, banks failed.

FDR AND THE NEW DEAL

Following weak responses by the Hoover administration, **Franklin Delano Roosevelt** was elected to the presidency in 1932. FDR offered Americans a New Deal: a plan to bring the country out of the Depression.

During the *First Hundred Days* of FDR's administration, a series of emergency acts (known as an *"alphabet soup"* of acts due to their many acronyms) was passed for the immediate repair of the banking system. Notable acts included:

- **Glass-Steagall Act**: established the **Federal Deposit Insurance Corporation (FDIC)** to insure customer deposits in the wake of bank failures.
  - the **Securities and Exchange Commission (SEC)** was later established to monitor stock trading. The SEC also has the power to punish violators of the law

- **Agricultural Adjustment Act (AAA)**: reduced farm prices by subsidizing farmers to limit production of certain commodities

- **Home Owners Loan Corporation (HOLC)**: refinanced mortgages to protect homeowners from losing their homes

- **Federal Housing Administration (FHA)**: insured low-cost mortgages

- **Tennessee Valley Authority (TVA)**: the first large-scale attempt at regional public planning and a long-term project despite being part of the First Hundred Days.

The New Deal addressed more than economic issues. Several acts provided relief to the poor and unemployed. The federal government allotted aid to states to be distributed directly to the poor through the **Federal Emergency Relief Act**. The New Deal especially included legislation designed to generate jobs:

- **Public Works Administration (PWA)**: used by the federal government to distribute funding to states for the purpose of developing infrastructure and to provide construction jobs for the unemployed.

- **Civilian Conservation Corps (CCC)**: created to offer employment in environmental conservation and management projects.

> **DID YOU KNOW?**
>
> The TVA was intended to create jobs and bring electricity to the Tennessee Valley area. But one of its true objectives was to accurately measure the cost of electric power, which had been supplied by private companies. The TVA was the first public power company and still operates today.

- **Works Progress Administration (WPA):** established during the **Second New Deal** and a long-term project that generated construction jobs and built infrastructure throughout the country.

- **Federal Writers' Project** and **Federal Art Project:** part of the WPA; created jobs for writers and artists, who wrote histories, created guidebooks, developed public art for public buildings, and made other contributions.

- **Wagner Act:** designed to address labor issues as well; ensured workers' right to unionize and established the **National Labor Relations Board (NLRB)**. Strengthening unions guaranteed collective bargaining rights and protected workers.

Despite the recovery afforded by acts passed during the First Hundred Days, millions of Americans, still unemployed, were critical of the New Deal. Fearing a third-party challenge in the 1936 election, FDR requested Congress to pass additional New Deal legislation, often referred to as the Second New Deal.

FDR was a Democrat in the Progressive tradition. The Progressive legacy of social improvement was apparent throughout the New Deal and his administration. The New Deal and its positive impact on the poor, the working class, unions, and immigrants led these groups to support the Democratic Party, a trend that continues to this day.

> **DID YOU KNOW?**
>
> The Federal Writers' Project enlisted unemployed writers to interview Black Americans who had been enslaved. The outcome was a compilation, *Born in Slavery: Slave Narratives from the Federal Writers' Project, 1936 – 1938* that is available at the Library of Congress. These narratives are some of the few recorded histories of Black Americans who had been enslaved, in their own words and from their perspective.

PRACTICE QUESTIONS

21) Which of the following precipitated US entry into the First World War?
    A. the sinking of the *Lusitania*
    B. the Great Depression
    C. the attack on the *Maine*
    D. the New Deal

22) How did the New Deal repair the damage of the Great Depression and help the United States rebuild?

- A. Immediate economic reforms stabilized the economy during the First Hundred Days; later, longer-term public works programs provided jobs to relieve unemployment and develop infrastructure.
- B. Social programs put into effect during the First Hundred Days provided jobs for Americans; measures to protect homeowners, landholders, and bank deposits followed to guarantee financial security.
- C. Programs like the Tennessee Valley Authority helped the government determine proper pricing and institute price controls for important public goods.
- D. FDR proposed supporting banks and big business with federal money to reinvigorate the market by limiting government intervention.

23) How did the United States change in the 1920s?

- A. The Great Migration ceased.
- B. African American culture became increasingly influential.
- C. The Great Depression caused high unemployment.
- D. Thanks to the New Deal, millions of Americans found jobs.

THE UNITED STATES AND WORLD WAR II

COOPERATION WITH EUROPE

The entire world suffered from the Great Depression, and Europe became increasingly unstable. With the rise of the radical Nazi Party in Germany, the Nazi leader, Adolf Hitler, became a threat to US allies after bombing Britain and leading German takeovers of several European countries.

However, the United States was weakened by the Great Depression and reluctant to engage in international affairs. Public and political support for isolationism continued and was reinforced by the Neutrality Acts. The US remained militarily uncommitted in the war.

> **CHECK YOUR UNDERSTANDING #7**
>
> List some reasons for US reluctance to enter WWII.

The Neutrality Act of 1939 did, however, allow cash-and-carry arms sales to combat participants. In this way, the United States could militarily support its allies (namely, the United Kingdom).

FDR was increasingly concerned about the rise of fascism in Europe, seeing it as a global threat. To ally with and support the United Kingdom without technically declaring war on Germany, FDR convinced Congress to enact the **Lend-Lease Act**. The Lend-Lease Act directly supplied Britain with military aid, in place of cash-and-carry.

FDR and the British Prime Minister **Winston Churchill** met in response to the nonaggression pact between Hitler and Stalin to sign the **Atlantic Charter**, which laid out the anti-fascist agenda of free trade and self-determination.

To garner support for his position, FDR spoke publicly about the **Four Freedoms**:

- freedom of speech
- freedom of religion
- freedom from want
- freedom from fear

THE US ENTERS WWII

After the Japanese attack on **Pearl Harbor** on December 7, 1941, the US entered the war. Even though the United States had been directly attacked by Japan, it focused first on the European theater. The US and other Allied powers (the United Kingdom and the Soviet Union) agreed that Hitler was the primary global threat.

The United States focused on eliminating the Nazi threat in the air and at sea, destroying Nazi U-boats (submarines) that threatened the Allies throughout the Atlantic. The US also engaged Germany in North Africa, defeating its troops to approach fascist Italy from the Mediterranean.

On June 6, 1944, or **D-Day**, the US led the invasion of Normandy, invading German-controlled Europe. After months of fighting, following the deadly and drawn-out **Battle of the Bulge** when the Allies faced fierce German resistance, the Allies were able to enter Germany and end the war in Europe.

Figure 2.25. Battle of the Bulge

The US was then able to focus more effectively on the war in the Pacific. The US had been able to break the Japanese code. But Japan had been unable to crack US code thanks to the **Navajo Code Talkers**, who used the Navajo language, which Japan was unable to decipher.

The US strategy of **island hopping** allowed it to take control of Japanese-held Pacific islands, proceeding closer to Japan itself despite **kamikaze** attacks, in which Japanese fighter pilots intentionally crashed their planes into US ships.

President **Harry Truman** took power following FDR's death in 1945. Rather than force a US invasion of Japan, which would have resulted in huge numbers of casualties, he authorized the bombings of **Hiroshima** and **Nagasaki**, the only times that **nuclear weapons** have been used in conflict. The war ended with Japanese surrender on September 2, 1945.

> **DID YOU KNOW?**
>
> Executive Order 9066 targeted Americans of Japanese descent, but other Americans suspected of having ties to the enemy due to their ethnicity, like German Americans, Italian Americans, and even some Aleutian Americans, were also forced into internment during WWII.

In the United States, Japanese Americans were forced to live in internment camps. Under FDR's Executive Order 9066, these Americans were forced to give up their belongings and businesses and live in harsh military camps scattered throughout the West until the end of the war. They were surrounded by barbed wire and armed guards.

Fred Korematsu argued that Executive Order 9066 was unconstitutional and fought to the Supreme Court for the rights of Japanese Americans. But the Court upheld FDR's order in *Korematsu v. United States*. Congress issued a formal apology to the survivors in 1988.

THE POSTWAR WORLD

The **United Nations** was formed in the wake of the Second World War, modeled after the failed League of Nations. Unlike the League, however, it included a **Security Council** comprised of major world powers, with the authority to militarily intervene for peacekeeping purposes in unstable global situations. Most of Europe had been destroyed, and the victorious US and the Soviet Union emerged as the two global **superpowers**.

In 1945, Stalin, Churchill, and Roosevelt met at the **Yalta Conference** to determine the future of Europe. The Allies had agreed on free elections for European countries following the fall of the fascist regimes.

After the war, however, the USSR occupied Eastern Europe, preventing free elections. The US saw this as a betrayal of the agreement at Yalta. Furthermore, while the US-led **Marshall Plan** began a program to rebuild Europe, the USSR consolidated its presence and power in eastern European countries, forcing them to reject aid from the Marshall Plan. This division would destroy the alliance between the Soviets and the West, leading to the **Cold War** between the two superpowers and the emergence of a **bipolar world**.

PRACTICE QUESTIONS

24) Why did the United States and the Soviet Union turn against each other after the Second World War?
    A. Stalin felt that the Marshall Plan should have been extended to the Soviet Union.
    B. Because of the fear of communism in the United States, the US had considered invading the USSR following the occupation of Nazi Germany.
    C. Despite assurances to the contrary, the USSR occupied Eastern European countries, preventing free elections in those countries.
    D. The Soviet Union was concerned that the United States would use the nuclear bomb again.

25) What was the purpose of the United Nations Security Council?
    A. to provide a means for international military intervention in case of conflict that could threaten global safety, in order to avoid another world war
    B. to provide a forum for the superpowers to maintain a dialogue
    C. to provide a means for countries to counter the power of the US and USSR to limit the reach of the superpowers
    D. to develop a plan to rebuild Europe and Japan

POSTWAR AND CONTEMPORARY UNITED STATES

COLD WAR AT HOME AND ABROAD

With the collapse of the relationship between the USSR and the US, distrust and fear of **communism** grew. Accusations of communist sympathies against public figures ran rampant during the **McCarthy Era** in the 1950s, reflecting domestic anxieties.

President Harry S Truman's **Truman Doctrine** stated that the US would support any country threatened by authoritarianism (communism). This led to the **Korean War** (1950 – 1953), a conflict between the US and Soviet-backed North Korean forces, which ended in a stalemate.

> **DID YOU KNOW?**
>
> Truman never requested an official declaration of war. Instead, fighting in the Korean War was backed by the United Nations. The US would drop more explosives on Korea during this conflict than throughout the entirety of those used in the Pacific during WWII.

US foreign policy was defined by two ideologies:

- **Containment**: the need to contain Soviet (communist) expansion
- **Domino theory**: once one country fell to communism, others would quickly follow

Other incidents continued under the administration of the popular President **John F. Kennedy**:

- the **Bay of Pigs** invasion in Cuba (1961), a failed effort to topple the communist government of Fidel Castro
- the **Cuban Missile Crisis** (1962), when Soviet missiles were discovered in Cuba and military crisis was narrowly averted

Meanwhile, in Southeast Asia, communist forces in North Vietnam were gaining power. Congress never formally declared war in Vietnam but gave the president authority to intervene militarily there through the **Gulf of Tonkin Resolution** (1964).

This protracted conflict—the **Vietnam War**—led to widespread domestic social unrest. Social unrest increased as US deaths rose, especially after the Vietnamese-led **Tet Offensive** (1968). The US ultimately withdrew from Vietnam. North Vietnamese forces, led by **Ho Chi Minh**, took over the entire country.

Figure 2.26. The Tet Offensive

CIVIL RIGHTS AND SOCIAL CHANGE

During the 1960s, the US experienced social and political change, starting with the election of the young and charismatic John F. Kennedy in 1960. Following JFK's assassination in 1963, President **Lyndon B. Johnson**'s administration saw the passage of liberal legislation in support of the poor and of civil rights.

The **Civil Rights Movement**, led by activists like the **Rev. Dr. Martin Luther King Jr.** and **Malcolm X**, fought for Black American rights, including the abolition of segregation in southern states and better living standards for Black people in northern cities.

In 1954, the Supreme Court heard the case **Brown v. Board of Education**, against segregating schools. Under Chief Justice Earl Warren, the Court found segregation unconstitutional and overturned its decision in *Plessy v. Ferguson*. *Brown* occurred shortly after the desegregation of the armed forces. Public support for civil rights and racial equality was growing.

The **Southern Christian Leadership Conference (SCLC)** and Dr. King, a religious leader from Georgia, believed in civil disobedience, nonviolent protest. In Montgomery, Alabama, **Rosa Parks**, an African American woman, was arrested for refusing to give up her seat to a white man on a bus. Buses were segregated at the time, and leaders including Dr. King organized the **Montgomery Bus Boycott** to challenge segregation. The effort was ultimately successful.

Building on their success, civil rights activists, now including many students and the **Student Nonviolent Coordinating Committee (SNCC)**, led peaceful demonstrations and boycotts to protest segregation at lunch counters, in stores, and other public places.

The movement grew to include voter registration campaigns organized by CORE, the Congress of Racial Equality. White and Black students and activists from around the country supported CORE. These students and activists became known as the **Freedom Riders**, so-called because they rode buses from around the country to join the movement in the Deep South.

> **CHECK YOUR UNDERSTANDING #8**
>
> What was the initial goal of SCLC?

SNCC and activists organized to protest segregation at government and public facilities and on university campuses. The movement gained visibility as nonviolent protesters were met with violence by the police and state authorities, including attacks by water cannons and police dogs in Alabama. Undaunted, activists continued to fight against segregation and unfair voting restrictions on African Americans.

The Civil Rights Movement gained national public attention and had become a major domestic political issue. Civil rights workers organized the **March on Washington** in 1963, when Dr. King delivered his famous *I Have a Dream* speech.

Widespread public support for civil rights legislation was impossible for the government to ignore. In 1964, Congress passed the **Civil Rights Act**, which outlawed segregation.

Figure 2.27. March on Washington

Meanwhile, **Malcolm X** was an outspoken proponent of **Black empowerment**, particularly for African Americans in urban areas. Unlike Martin Luther King Jr., who supported integration, Malcolm X and other activists, including groups like the **Black Panthers**, believed that Black Americans should stay separate from White Americans to develop stronger communities.

The Voting Rights Act

Despite the successes of the Civil Rights Movement, African Americans' voting rights were still not sufficiently protected. According to the Fifteenth and the Nineteenth Amendments, all Black Americans—men and women—had the right to vote. But many southern states had voting restrictions in place, like literacy tests and poll taxes, which disproportionately affected African Americans.

To draw attention to this issue, Dr. King and civil rights workers organized a march from Selma to Montgomery, Alabama. Marchers were attacked by police. In 1965, led by President Lyndon B. Johnson, Congress passed the **Voting Rights Act**, which prohibited restrictions on voting, including literacy tests. Separately, the **Twenty-Fourth Amendment** made poll taxes unconstitutional.

> **DID YOU KNOW?**
>
> Today, some states have instituted voter identification laws that disproportionately affect minorities. Many Americans believe these laws are similar to literacy tests and poll taxes. Debate continues in Congress and in the public sphere over the constitutionality of voter ID laws.

Civil Rights for More Americans

The Civil Rights Movement extended beyond the Deep South. **Cesar Chavez** founded the **United Farm Workers (UFW)**, which organized Hispanic and migrant farm workers in California and the Southwest to advocate for unionizing and collective bargaining. Farm workers were underpaid and faced racial discrimination. The UFW used boycotts and nonviolent tactics similar to those used by civil rights activists in the South. Cesar Chavez also used hunger strikes to raise awareness of the problems faced by farm workers.

The Civil Rights Movement also included **feminist** activists who fought for fairer treatment of women in the workplace and for women's reproductive rights. The **National Organization for Women** and feminist leaders like **Gloria Steinem** led the movement for equal pay for women in the workplace. The landmark case of *Roe v. Wade* struck down federal restrictions on abortion.

The **American Indian Movement (AIM)** brought attention to injustices and discrimination suffered by Native Americans nationwide. Ultimately it was able to achieve more tribal autonomy and address problems facing Native American communities throughout the United States.

In New York City in 1969, the **Stonewall riots** occurred in response to police repression of the gay community. These riots and subsequent organized activism are seen as the beginning of the Lesbian, Gay, Bisexual, Transgender, and Queer (LGBTQ) rights movement.

THE WAR ON POVERTY

President Kennedy had envisioned a liberal United States in the tradition of the Progressives. His youth and charisma were inspiring to many Americans, and his assassination in 1963 was a shock.

Kennedy's vice president, Lyndon B. Johnson, continued the liberal vision with the **Great Society**. LBJ embraced **liberalism**, believing that government should fight poverty at home and play an interventionist role abroad (in this era, by fighting communism).

Johnson launched a **War on Poverty**, passing reform legislation designed to support the poor and vulnerable:

> **DID YOU KNOW?**
>
> In a commencement address delivered to University of Michigan graduates in 1964, LBJ outlined his vision of the Great Society and challenged the new graduates to join him in tackling issues in cities, the environment, and classrooms to advance the quality of life in America.

- **Medicare Act:** provided medical care to American senior citizens
- **Department of Housing and Urban Development:** increased the federal role in housing and urban issues
- **Head Start:** provided early intervention for disadvantaged children before elementary school
- **Elementary and Secondary Education Act:** increased funding for primary and secondary education

During LBJ's administration, the **Immigration Act of 1965** was also passed. It overturned the racist Emergency Quota Act.

While taking steps to combat poverty at home, LBJ's overseas agenda was becoming increasingly unpopular. Adhering to containment and domino theory, Johnson drew the United States deeper into conflict in Southeast Asia.

The **Vietnam War** became extremely unpopular in the US due to:

- high casualties
- the unpopular draft (which forced young American males to fight overseas)
- confusion over the purpose of the war

Student activists, organizing in the mold of the Civil Rights Movement, engaged in protest against the Vietnam War. The rise of a **counterculture** among the youth added to a sense of rebellion among Americans, usurping government authority and challenging traditional values. Aspects included:

- the development and popularity of **rock and roll music**

- the culture of **hippies**
- changing concepts of drug use and sexuality

PRACTICE QUESTIONS

26) **Why did the Civil Rights Movement continue to push for legislative change even after the passage of the 1964 Civil Rights Act?**
   A. While the Civil Rights Act provided legal protections to African Americans and other groups, many believed it did not go far enough since it did not outlaw segregation.
   B. Leaders like Malcolm X believed further legislative reform would ensure better living conditions for blacks in cities.
   C. Civil rights leaders wanted legislation to punish white authorities in the South who had oppressed African Americans.
   D. Legal restrictions like literacy tests, poll taxes, and voter registration issues inhibited African Americans from exercising their right to vote, especially in the South.

27) **Which of the following best describes liberalism under LBJ?**
   A. Liberalism was the philosophy that the government should be deeply involved in improving society at home and committed to fighting communism abroad.
   B. According to liberalism, the US should devote its resources to improving life at home for the disadvantaged but refrain from direct intervention in international conflict.
   C. Liberals believed in moderate social programs with limited spending.
   D. Liberalism frowns upon conflict intervention, as shown by the mass demonstrations against the Vietnam War in the 1960s.

POLITICAL CONSERVATISM, SOCIAL LIBERALISM, AND THE TWENTY-FIRST CENTURY

Radical social change in the 1960s, coupled with the toll of the Vietnam War on the American public—many of whom had lost loved ones in the war or themselves served in combat—led to backlash against liberalism.

Conservatism strengthened in response to several factors:

- the heavy role of government in public life throughout the 1960s
- high rates of government spending
- social challenges to traditional values

Due in great part to the escalation of the Vietnam War, LBJ announced his intention not to run for another term. The conservative **Richard Nixon** became president in 1970.

Economic and International Crises

During President Richard Nixon's administration, the conflict in Vietnam ended, and a diplomatic relationship with China began. Nixon also oversaw economic reforms. He lifted the gold standard in an effort to stop **stagflation**, a phenomenon when both unemployment and inflation are simultaneously high. Ending the gold standard reduced the value of the dollar in relation to other global currencies and foreign investment in the United States increased.

However, the Nixon administration was found to have engaged in corrupt practices. A burglary at the Democratic National Headquarters, based at the Watergate Hotel, was connected to the Oval Office. The **Watergate scandal** eventually forced Nixon to resign, and Vice President **Gerald Ford** took office for one term. Nixon's resignation further destroyed many Americans' faith in their government.

> **CHECK YOUR UNDERSTANDING #9**
>
> Define *stagflation*.

During the 1970s, the economy suffered due to US involvement in the Middle East. US support for Israel in the Six Day War and 1973 Yom Kippur War caused **OPEC** (the Organization of Petroleum Exporting Countries), led by Saudi Arabia and other allies of Arab foes of Israel, to boycott the US. As a result, oil prices skyrocketed. In the 1979 Iranian Revolution and the resulting **hostage crisis**, when the US Embassy in Tehran was taken over by anti-American activists, the economy suffered from another oil shock.

While President Jimmy Carter had been able to negotiate peace between Israel and Egypt in the **Camp David Accords**, he was widely perceived as ineffective. Carter lost the presidency in 1980 to the conservative Republican **Ronald Reagan**.

Reagan championed domestic tax cuts and an aggressive foreign policy against the Soviet Union. The Reagan Revolution revamped the economic system, cutting taxes and government spending. According to supply-side economics (popularly known as *Reaganomics*), cutting taxes on the wealthy and providing investment incentives, would result in a "trickle down" of wealth to the middle and working classes and the poor. But tax cuts forced Congress to cut or eliminate social programs that benefitted millions of those same Americans. Later, the **Tax Reform Act** of 1986 ended progressive income taxation.

Reagan and the Arms Race

Despite promises to lower government spending, the Reagan administration invested huge sums of money in the military. This investment in military technology—the **arms race** with the Soviet Union—helped bring about the end of the Cold War with the 1991 fall of the USSR and, later, a new era of globalization.

In addition to funding a general arms buildup and supporting measures to strengthen the military, the Reagan administration funded and developed advanced military technology to intimidate the Soviets, despite having signed the **Strategic Arms Limitation Treaties (SALT I and II)** limiting nuclear weapons and other strategic armaments in the 1970s. Ultimately, the US would outspend the USSR militarily, a precipitating factor to the fall of the Soviet Union.

The Reagan Revolution also ushered in an era of conservative values in the public sphere. After the Civil Rights Era, whose victories had occurred under the auspices of the Democratic Johnson administration, many southern Democrats switched loyalties to the Republican Party. At the same time, the Democrats gained the support of African Americans and other minority groups who benefitted from civil rights and liberal legislation.

During the Reagan Era, conservative Republicans espoused a return to "traditional" values. **Christian fundamentalism** became popular, particularly among white conservatives. Groups like **Focus on the Family** lobbied against civil rights reform for women and advocated for traditional, two-parent, heterosexual families.

THE END OF THE COLD WAR AND GLOBALIZATION

The administration of **George H.W. Bush** signed the **Strategic Arms Reduction Treaty (START)**, with the Soviet Union in 1991, shortly before the dissolution of the USSR. Later, it would enter into force in 1994 between the US and the Russian Federation as an agreement to limit the large arsenals of strategic weapons possessed by both countries.

With the collapse of the Soviet Union, the balance of international power changed. The bipolar world became a unipolar world, and the United States was the sole superpower.

A major crisis occurred in the Middle East when Iraq, led by **Saddam Hussein**, invaded oil-rich Kuwait. This threatened international access to petroleum.

The US intervened with the blessing of the United Nations and the support of other countries. The resulting **Gulf War**, or **Operation Desert Storm** (1991), cemented US status as the world's sole superpower. Saddam's forces were driven from Kuwait, and Iraq was restrained by sanctions and no-fly zones.

With the election of President **Bill Clinton** in 1992, the US took an active role in international diplomacy, helping broker peace deals in the former Yugoslavia, Northern Ireland, and the Middle East.

Clinton's election also indicated a more socially liberal era in American society. While conservative elements remained a strong force in politics and sectors of society, changing attitudes toward minorities in the public sphere and increased global communication (especially with the advent of the internet) were a hallmark of the 1990s.

As part of **globalization**—the facilitation of global commerce and communication—the Clinton administration prioritized free trade. The United States signed the **North American Free Trade Agreement (NAFTA),** which removed trade restrictions with Mexico and Canada and created a free trade zone throughout North America.

The Clinton administration also eased financial restrictions in the US, rolling back some of the limitations provided for under Glass-Steagall. These changes were controversial: many American jobs went overseas, especially manufacturing jobs, where labor was cheaper.

Furthermore, globalization began facilitating the movement of people, including undocumented immigrants seeking a better life in the United States. **Immigration reform** would be a major issue into the twenty-first century.

Clinton faced dissent in the mid-1990s with a conservative resurgence. A movement of young conservatives elected to Congress in 1994 promised a **Contract with America**, a conservative platform promising a return to lower taxes and traditional values. Clinton also came under fire for personal scandals: allegations of corrupt real estate investments in the Whitewater scandal and inappropriate personal behavior in the White House. These scandals fueled social conservatives and Christian fundamentalists who favored a return to the conservative era of the 1980s.

Despite these controversies and political division, society became increasingly liberal:

- New technology like the **internet** facilitated national and global communication, media, and business.
- Minority groups like the LGBTQ community engaged in more advocacy.
- Environmental issues became more visible.

The Twenty-First Century

By the end of the twentieth century, the United States had proved itself as the dominant global economic, military, and political power. Due to its role in global conflict from the Spanish-American War onwards, the US had established military bases and a military presence worldwide: in Europe, Asia, the Pacific, and the Middle East.

The US also dominated global trade: American corporations established themselves globally, taking advantage of free trade to exploit cheap labor pools and less restrictive manufacturing environments (at the expense of American workers).

American culture remained widely popular as well. Since the early twentieth century, American pop culture—music, movies, television shows, and fashion—was enjoyed by millions of people around the world.

However, globalization also facilitated global conflict. While terrorism had been a feature of the twentieth century, the United States had been relatively untouched by large-scale terrorist attacks. That changed on **September 11, 2001**, when the terrorist group **al Qaeda** hijacked airplanes, attacking New York and Washington, DC, in the largest attack on US soil since the Japanese bombing of Pearl Harbor.

The 9/11 attacks triggered an aggressive military and foreign policy under the administration of **President George W. Bush**, who declared a War on Terror, an open-ended global conflict against terrorist organizations and their supporters.

Figure 2.28. Attacks of September 11, 2001

Following the attacks, the US struck suspected al Qaeda bases in Afghanistan, beginning the **Afghanistan War**, during which time the US occupied the country. Suspected terrorist fighters captured there and elsewhere during the War on Terror were held in a prison in **Guantanamo Bay**, Cuba, which was controversial because it did not initially offer any protections afforded to prisoners of war under the Geneva Conventions.

President Bush believed in the doctrine of **preemption**: if the US is aware of a threat, it should preemptively attack the source of that threat. Preemption would drive the invasion of Iraq in 2003, when the US attacked the country, believing that it held **weapons of mass destruction** that could threaten the safety of the United States. This assumption was later revealed to be false. Still, the United States launched the **Iraq War**, deposing Saddam Hussein and supporting a series of governments until it withdrew its troops in 2011, leaving the country in a state of chaos.

At home, Congress passed the **USA Patriot Act** to respond to fears of more terrorist attacks on US soil. This legislation gave the federal government unprecedented—and, some argued, unconstitutional—powers of surveillance over the American public.

Tax cuts and heavy reliance on credit (especially in the housing market, which fueled the **Subprime Mortgage Crisis**) during the Bush administration helped push the country into the **Great Recession**.

Despite the tense climate, social liberalization continued in the US.

In 2008, the first African American president, **Barack Obama**, a Democrat, was elected. Under his presidency, the US emerged from the recession, ended its major combat operations in Iraq and Afghanistan, passed the Affordable Care Act, which reformed the healthcare system, and legalized same-sex marriage.

The Obama administration also oversaw the passage of consumer protection acts, increased support for students, and safety nets for homeowners. His administration was not without challenge, though. Over the course of his two terms, the Democratic party would go on to lose more than 1,000 seats to Republicans in state legislatures, Congress, and at the gubernatorial level.

PRACTICE QUESTIONS

28) Which of the following BEST describes globalization?
    A. cutting taxes to induce a "trickle down" of wealth to the middle class and the poor
    B. free trade among countries and easier international communication
    C. increased visibility and importance of environmental issues
    D. open-ended global conflict against terrorist organizations and their supporters

29) How did Reagan's economic policies affect working class and poor Americans?
    A. They had little effect on these classes because the United States has a free market economy.
    B. They increased taxes by eliminating the progressive income tax and cut social programs needed by many disadvantaged people.
    C. They benefitted the working and middle classes by cutting taxes and increasing investment opportunities.
    D. Despite Reagan's tax cuts, the government was able to fund all social programs, so lower income Americans who used them were unaffected by changes in revenue.

30) How did the Bush doctrine of preemption affect US foreign policy in the early twenty-first century?

    A.   The US believed that to contain terrorism, it had to occupy countries that might harbor terrorists.

    B.   Fearing that the entire Middle East would succumb to terrorists, the Bush administration established a presence in the centrally located country of Iraq to avoid a "domino effect" of regime collapse.

    C.   The Bush administration justified international intervention and foreign invasion without previous provocation to preempt possible terrorist attacks.

    D.   The US held prisoners captured during the War on Terror at Guantanamo Bay, where they were not given the protections and privileges entitled to prisoners of war under the Geneva Conventions.

Practice Questions Answer Key

1) **B.** Powerful tribes controlled trade and territory; among these were the powerful Iroquois Confederacy.

2) **B.** The Algonquin people were primarily located in what is today Quebec and southern Ontario, but the Algonquian language was spoken widely throughout North America among both settled and semi-settled non-Algonquin peoples.

3) **B.** The Choctaw, Creek, Chickasaw, and others were Muskogean-speaking peoples; the Cherokee spoke an Iroquoian language. Both tribes were settled.

4) **A.** The Great Plains tribes depended on buffalo, which were plentiful before European contact and settlement, for food; they also used buffalo parts for clothing and to make necessary items.

5) **B.** The Ancestral Pueblo had settled in what is today the Four Corners region. The Navajo came to control land extending through present-day Arizona, New Mexico, and Utah.

6) **A.** Spain established missions to spread Christianity, in addition to settling and exploiting the land; France worked to establish networks of trade and did not concentrate on religious conversion (although the Church was present and at work in its colonies). Both intermarried locally.

7) **A.** The southern colonies featured a climate conducive to plantation agriculture. Crops like tobacco, cotton, and rice grew easily there, and led to demand for enslaved people.

8) **C.** John Locke's *Second Treatise* was critical of absolute monarchy and became popular in the colonies.

9) **B.** William Penn founded these colonies in the spirit of his tolerant Quaker faith.

10) **C.** The Beaver Wars, the Chickasaw Wars, and later the French and Indian War (which was part of the Seven Years' War) are all examples of British-French conflict playing out in North America.

11) **D.** Anger at being forced to provide shelter for British soldiers led

to protests; in 1770, British soldiers fired on protests against the Quartering Act in what came to be called the Boston Massacre.

12) **B.** Shays' Rebellion, in which Daniel Shays led a rebellion of indebted farmers shortly after the end of the Revolution, showed the need for a stronger federal government to ensure national stability and was a major factor in planning the Constitutional Convention.

13) **A.** Westward expansion accelerated after US independence. The Shawnee, Lenape, Miami, Kickapoo, and others organized to form the Northwest Confederacy.

14) **C.** Universal manhood suffrage allowed all white males, whether or not they owned property, to vote; the "common man" had a voice in government, and Jackson enjoyed their support. Likewise, an influx of poor European immigrants changed the country's demographics, providing more workers for early industry, more settlers interested in populating the west, and a stronger voice in government against the wealthy.

15) **B.** The Missouri Compromise allowed Missouri to join the union as a slave state but prohibited enslavement in any other new states north of the thirty-sixth parallel. By limiting the permissibility of enslaving people in new states, the Missouri Compromise showed how strongly the abolitionist movement affected politics.

16) **D.** Legislation like the Missouri Compromise, the Compromise of 1850, and the Kansas-Nebraska Act represented ongoing efforts to bridge the gap between differences in views over slavery in determining the future of the country.

17) **B.** The punitive Dawes Act forced assimilation by revoking federal recognition of tribes, taking lands allotted to tribes and dissolving reservations, and forcing children into assimilationist schools (thereby dividing families).

18) **B.** Horizontal and vertical integration of industries allowed the same companies—and people—to control industries, or create monopolies. Those elites who monopolized specific markets organized trusts so that one group controlled entire sectors of the economy.

19) **A.** Unions improved conditions for industrial workers; the Social Gospel imparted a sense of social responsibility that eventually manifested in laws and regulations protecting the rights and safety of workers, farmers, the poor, and others.

20) **B.** US military successes showed European powers and other countries its strength as a military power.

21) **A.** The sinking of the *Lusitania*, which resulted in numerous civilian deaths, was one factor causing the US to enter WWI.

22) **A.** FDR focused on immediate economic stabilization upon taking office, then attacked poverty and unemployment on a sustainable basis.

23) **B.** The Harlem Renaissance is one example of the emergence of African American culture in the public imagination; as US popular culture developed, African American contributions had a strong influence.

24) **C.** Stalin's refusal to permit free elections or democracy in the countries of Eastern Europe was seen as a betrayal of the agreement reached by the Allies at Yalta, and a major reason for the collapse of the US-Soviet relationship.

25) **A.** While the UN was modeled in part after the League of Nations, the Security Council was (and is) able to militarily intervene in cases of armed conflict that could pose a global threat, an ability the League of Nations did not have.

26) **D.** Despite the end to legal segregation, discrimination was deeply entrenched, and laws still existed to prevent African Americans from voting. Civil rights activists worked to ensure the passage of the Voting Rights Act in 1965.

27) **A.** LBJ believed in forming a Great Society and launched a War on Poverty, initiating federal government-sponsored social programs to support the disadvantaged; he also actively waged a war against the spread of communism in Southeast Asia, ultimately unsuccessfully.

28) **B.** Globalization is the facilitation of global commerce and communication.

29) **B.** Supply-side economics theorized that low taxes on the wealthy would encourage investment in the economy; as a result, wealth would "trickle down" to the middle and working classes and the poor. However, in practice, lower taxes meant less government revenue and many social programs that were needed by poor Americans were cut.

30) **C.** Preemption was used to justify the 2003 invasion of Iraq, on the assumption that Iraq had weapons of mass destruction it intended to use or to provide for terrorist attacks against the United States.

Check Your Understanding Answer Key

Check Your Understanding #1

Great Plains peoples (e.g., **Sioux, Cheyenne, Apache, Comanche, Arapaho**)

Check Your Understanding #2

tobacco, rice, beaver pelts, fur

Check Your Understanding #3

Pontiac's Rebellion showed resistance to colonial incursions, accelerated European concerns that a stronger military presence was needed in the North American colonies, and resulted in an agreement not to settle land west of the Appalachians (Proclamation of 1763).

Check Your Understanding #4

1) admitted California as a free state; 2) allowed legality of slavery to be decided by popular sovereignty in Utah and New Mexico; 3) upheld the Fugitive Slave Act; 4) abolished the slave trade (but not slavery) in Washington, DC; 5) fixed the boundaries of Texas along its current lines

Check Your Understanding #5

heavy industry, petroleum/oil, westward expansion (railroads and steel)

Check Your Understanding #6

consumer credit, overspeculation on crops/land, weak banking protections

Check Your Understanding #7

economic weakness from the Great Depression, support for isolationism, the Neutrality Acts

Check Your Understanding #8

The initial goal of the Southern Christian Leadership Conference (SCLC) was desegregation.

Check Your Understanding #9

both unemployment and inflation are high at the same time

(Usually, when unemployment is low, inflation is high, and vice versa.)

Texas History

According to the US Census as of July 2015, Texas is the second-largest state in the United States. With a population of over 27.4 million, it is also the second-fastest growing state in the country.

Major Texas cities like Houston, Austin, San Antonio, and Dallas-Fort Worth are among the top ten fastest growing cities in the nation. Furthermore, with a land area of 268,596 square miles, Texas is second in geographical size only to Alaska.

With a rich and unique history, rule by "six flags"—six different countries, including an independent Republic of Texas—and a singular place in the United States today, the state of Texas has a distinctive story to tell. Indeed, understanding the history of Texas is key to understanding the history of the United States—and even North America—as a whole.

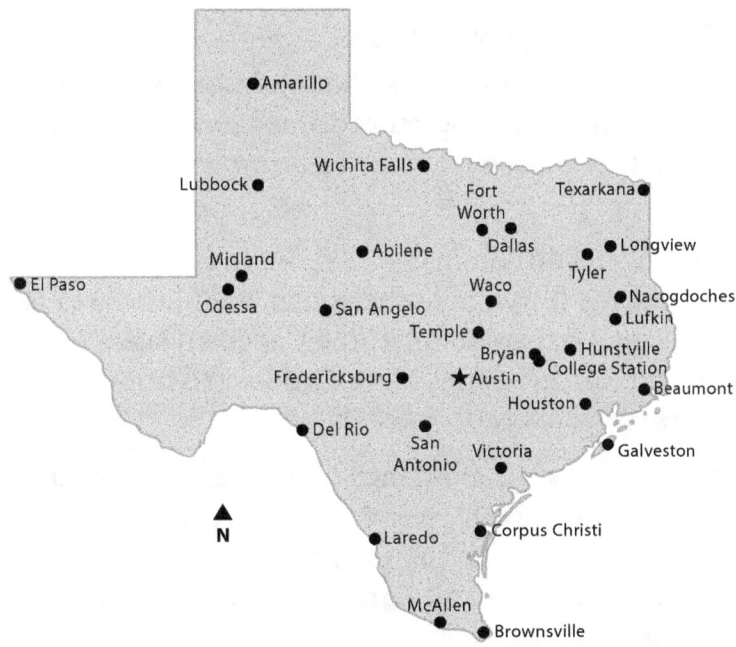

Figure 3.1. Political Map of Texas

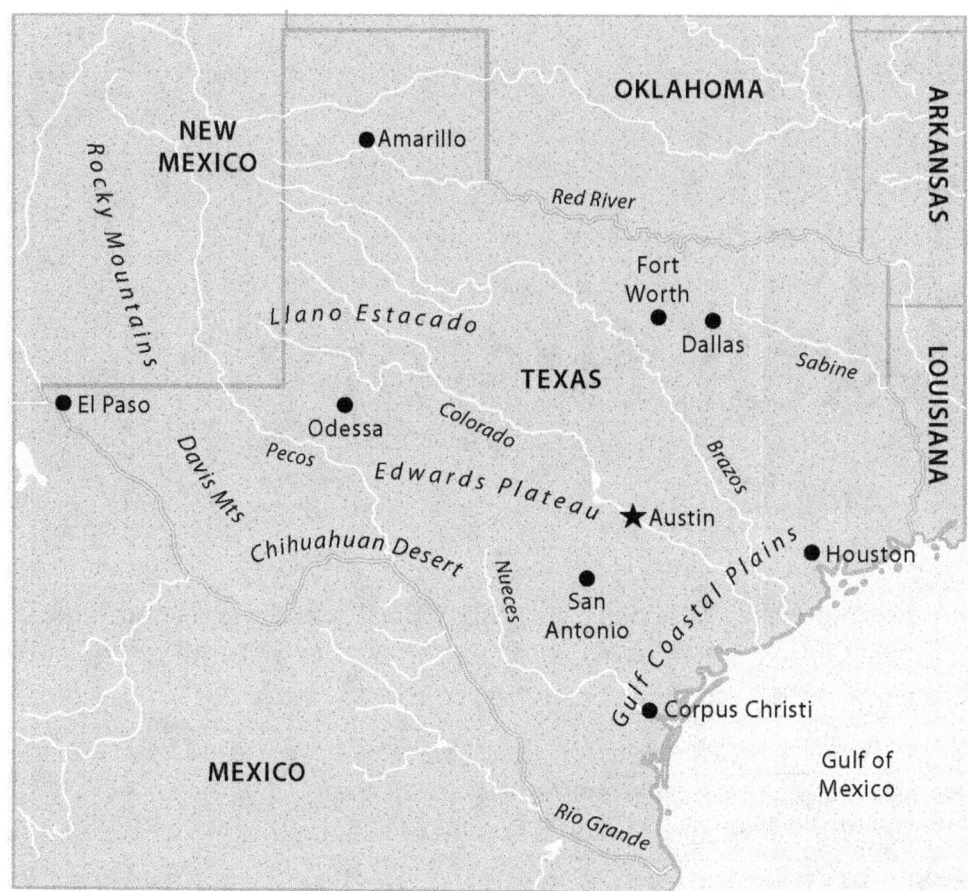

Figure 3.2. Physical Map of Texas

Precolonial to Texas Revolution

Texans before European Contact

Before the arrival of European explorers and colonists, Texas was populated by a number of Indigenous tribes. The migratory **Karankawa** lived along the Gulf Coast; fishers and hunter/gatherers, they moved via canoe and were among the first to encounter Europeans.

Farther inland, the **Caddo** dominated East Texas, living in settled communities and practicing agriculture throughout the region and in the area around the Red River. Organized in the **Hasinai** alliance, the Caddo engaged in brisk trade, and Europeans took part in this economy. Many Caddo died from diseases introduced by European settlers.

Farther west, tribes like the **Comanche**, **Apache**, and **Kiowa** dominated the Great Plains and moved into northern and western Texas. These migratory tribes adopted horses after the introduction of these animals by Europeans. Violent encounters between these tribes and European, Mexican, Texan, and American settlers were common until the late nineteenth century.

Spain in Texas

Spain's search for gold in the Americas spurred its exploration throughout the region north to Texas. In 1519 the Spanish explorer who discovered Texas, **Alonso Àlvarez de Piñeda**, recommended colonization (though he never actually set foot on the land, only viewing it from his ship as he explored the Gulf Coast). An expedition to Florida led by **Pánfilo Naváez** became stranded on the Texas coast after attempting to return to Mexico; seven years later, the survivors, led by **Cabeza de Vaca**, were rescued. Returning to Mexico, they passed on rumors of gold farther inland in Texas, inspiring exploratory expeditions by **Francisco Vasquez de Coronado** and **Hernando de Soto** in 1540, and **Juan de Oñate** in 1598. None were successful in the search for gold, but they did confirm that the land was suitable for raising cattle.

Ultimately, Texas was less valuable than Mexico and other territories because it proved devoid of gold and silver; however Spain was wary of French incursions southwestward. As France became entrenched north in Québec and the Great Lakes region, French explorers headed south through the Mississippi region. In the seventeenth century, René Robert Cavalier, Sieur de La Salle, led an expedition for France down the Mississippi River, claiming land from the Great Lakes to the Gulf of Mexico and as far west as the Rocky Mountains for France in 1682. **La Salle** called the territory **Louisiana** in honor of King Louis XIV.

La Salle continued farther south, establishing **Fort St. Louis** at Matagorda Bay. While the settlement was eventually destroyed by the local Karankawa, and while La Salle himself was killed by his own men shortly afterward, Spain saw the settlement as a threat.

Consequently, the Spanish established missions and presidios to create a buffer zone in Texas to repel French interests in North America. The influential and committed priest **Fray Damian Massanet** founded **Mission San Francisco de las Tejas** near San Antonio in 1690, the first mission in Texas, with **Don Alonzo de León**, governor of the region (at the time called Coahuila and New Philippines).

Spain closed San Francisco de las Tejas two years later. However missions remained important and influential due to the zeal of missionaries, despite their failure to convert Native Americans. **Father Francisco Hidalgo** reached out to the French in spite of the political climate, and Lamothe Cadillac, governor of Louisiana, sent Louis Juchereau de St. Denis to trade in Texas.

France and Spain jointly founded six other missions and reopened Mission San Francisco de las Tejas in 1716. **Father Antonio Jesus de Margil** controlled the missions of East Texas; however, by the end of the decade, missionaries were becoming disheartened with the difficulty of the work and the reluctance of the Native Americans to convert. The 1721 Spanish expedition led by **Marque de Aguayo** reinvigorated Spanish presence in the area, which would remain a buffer zone throughout the eighteenth century.

Following the French and Indian War and the decline of French power in North America, after 1754 the **Marquis de Rubi** issued the **New Regulation of the Presidios** moving them to San Antonio. San Antonio thus became the frontier and the presence of presidios to the north was reduced. This reorganization would improve consolidation of efforts against the Apache and Comanche, who attacked Spanish outposts from the north and west. However, Spanish control over its territories north of Mexico was tenuous.

Consequently, in order to strengthen control over Texas, **Governor Francisco Bouiligny** of Upper Louisiana and **Governor Bernardo de Galvez** of Lower Louisiana secretly agreed to permit White Anglo settlers in Texas as long as they converted to Catholicism and became Spanish subjects. The **Spanish Conspiracy** was in violation of policy that only encouraged Spanish immigration to New Spain, but it began to strengthen Texas economically. Whites from the United States began immigrating west in search of opportunities in the region. **Moses Austin** left Connecticut with other settlers for the colony of **New Madrid**, now in Missouri; he prospered by mining lead for ammunition in Mine à Breton.

The **Adams-Onís Treaty** of 1819, which delineated the border between the United States and Spain, left New Madrid in United States territory.

- Moses Austin asked the governor in San Antonio for permission to immigrate to Texas and introduce settlers.
- He intended to duplicate the New Madrid model.
- Spain eventually granted him land and permitted settlement in Texas.
- Moses Austin died in 1821, and his son Stephen Austin would carry out this project.

Meanwhile, other Anglo (White) settlers had been flowing into Texas without explicit permission from Spain. Also known as **filibuster settlers**, they immigrated for personal gain but at the same time furthered a US national policy: westward expansion, or the ideal of Manifest Destiny, regardless of borders.

Mexican Texas

Following Mexican independence from Spain, Mexico established the **empresario** system, in which *empresarios*, or land brokers were granted cheap land and given six years to bring families to settle it as long as they enforced Mexican law. Anglos were permitted to colonize the land in order to better secure it for Mexico under the **Colonization Law of 1825**.

His family's previous agreements with Spain voided following the revolution, **Stephen F. Austin**, Moses Austin's son and an able diplomat, negotiated the first *empresario* arrangement with the new Mexican government and attracted 300 Anglo families to Texas. Settlers could receive, for a low rate, either 4,000 acres of land for ranching or approximately 177 acres for farming—consequently, many became ranchers. In return, they had to demonstrate evidence of "good reputations" (for example, prove they had no criminal background), convert to Catholicism, and become Mexican citizens. However they would not have to pay taxes for seven years.

Mexico wanted foreign settlers to purchase Texas land at only a thirty-dollar down payment with ten years tax-free to encourage settlement. Yet Anglo settlers did not always consider themselves Mexican and also wanted to bring enslaved persons of African origin, a dilemma because Mexico prohibited slavery. As a result, Mexico began encouraging Mexican settlement in Texas to counter this movement.

Still, by the late 1820s, Anglo settlers outnumbered Mexican settlers and others of Spanish and Spanish-speaking origin (called **Tejanos** and **Tejanas**). Anglo-Tejano relations were active: arguably the strongest example was between Stephen F. Austin and **Martin DeLeon**, the first Mexican *empresario*, from Nuevo Santander. DeLeon and his settlers colonized the land near what is today Victoria, Texas. Austin and DeLeon established active relations, including a postal service, between their colonies.

Tensions were developing between the Mexican government and Anglo-dominated Texas. In 1825, US **President John Quincy Adams** proposed the US purchase of Texas. Mexico rebuffed the offer, increasingly suspicious of Anglo Texan and United States intent in the region. In 1826, following disputes over land rights, the *empresario* Haden Edwards formed an alliance with the Cherokee and led the **Fredonia Rebellion** in northeast Texas, declaring independence from Mexico in protest of revocation of land grants. While unsuccessful, these actions contributed to consolidation of political power over the region.

Following growing tensions and violence in northeast Texas, Mexico passed the **Law of April 6, 1830**, which:

- placed severe restrictions on Texas
- closed immigration from the United States, severing commercial and family ties with the country
- encouraged Mexican and European settlement in Texas to counter Anglo settlement
- provided for customs collections in Texas
- augmented military presence in the region
- further restricted slavery

Some Tejanos were also against the Law of 1830; it threatened their economic interests by interfering with business ties to the United States. They also wanted to separate Texas from the rest of its province (Coahuila) and desired better protection from Native American raids. Furthermore, like many other Mexican citizens, they were resentful of the centralized military dictatorships that had replaced the brief Mexican republic.

The law also settled convicts in Texas. Because *empresarios* and colonists had originally needed to demonstrate evidence of good reputations, this caused resentment; so did the fact that colonists now needed to pay taxes (although the seven-year exemption was to end anyway). Finally, instability in the Mexican government alarmed Mexicans, Tejanos, and Anglo Texans alike; Anglo Texans, many of whom maintained strong ties to the United States, were concerned about violent changes of government in Mexico City in contrast with ongoing democratic elections in the United States.

With the introduction of a strong military presence in Texas, violent clashes began throughout the region reflecting tensions between the centralist, military government and federalists. In 1832, the federalist governor of Texas and Coahuila, **Jose Maria Latona** reopened the region to Anglo settlement in violation of the Law of 1830; in response, **Captain Juan (John) Davis Bradburn** arrested his representatives near the border with Louisiana and closed Texas ports. Bradburn and his 150 soldiers had been sent by the Mexican government to occupy Anahuac, near Galveston. Although he reopened the ports, he later arrested the Anglo attorney **Willian Barret Travis** and his partner Patrick Jack.

Texans demanded Bradburn release Travis and Jack during the first disturbance of 1832 in the **Turtle Bayou Resolution**, in which they also protested the Law of 1830 and reaffirmed their allegiance to the original **Constitution of 1824**. In response, Colonel Jose de las Piedras left Nacogdoches, where he had been stationed with a force of 350, and relieved Bradburn of command, releasing Travis and Jack. However, Austin had already approached Velasco to take a cannon to use at Anahuac, clashing with Colonel Domingo de Ugartechea, stationed there with a force of 150. This clash marked the second disturbance of 1832 and the first real violence of the Texas Revolution.

Upon returning to Nacogdoches, de las Piedras ordered Texans to turn in their firearms; instead, they attacked him and on August 2, 1832, he surrendered and was taken to San Antonio.

Despite the violence of the **Disturbances of 1832**, Austin presented them as efforts in support of the 1824 constitution to protest government centralization and the Law of 1830. On October 1, 1832, Anglo Texans and some Tejanos held the **Convention of 1832**. Electing Austin as head of the governing council of San Felipe, where they met, they drafted a resolution calling for the establishment of Texas as a separate state of Mexico, for self-rule, and for the repeal of the Law of 1830.

Though the resolution was rejected, Texans tried again at the **Convention of 1833**; in April of that year, fifty-six representatives drafted a resolution asking the Mexican government to end restrictions on slavery in Texas, allow increased Anglo immigration from the United States, provide Texans more protection from the Apache and Comanche, improve mail service, and separate Texas from Coahuila.

Meanwhile, the Mexican military leader **Antonio López de Santa Anna**, upon becoming president of Mexico, nullified the 1824 constitution (and its similarities to the US constitution) in favor of a more restrictive one that centralized federal power. Santa Anna dissolved the Mexican Congress and state legislatures; he also violently put down rebellions in several Mexican states. Finally, Santa Anna dismissed self-rule in Texas.

Stephen F. Austin traveled to Mexico City to present Texas' proposals to the government directly, and was imprisoned. Even after Mexico repealed the Law of 1830, Texas was still not granted its own statehood.

At the same time, filibuster settlers continued moving from the United States to Texas and tensions continued to rise. General Martin Perfecto de Cos was appointed military commander of the northern Mexican provinces, including Texas and Coahuila. He sent troops to collect customs at Anahuac, spurring more violence when William Travis led volunteers against Mexican military there. In response, de Cos increased military presence in Texas.

By Austin's release and return to Texas in 1835, tensions were building toward rebellion.

PRACTICE QUESTION

1) **How did the Law of 1830 reflect tensions between Texas and the Mexican government?**
    A. The law was intended to protect Tejanos from Anglos.
    B. Mexico would no longer tolerate the practice of slavery.
    C. External threats to Mexican control of Texas inspired the Law of 1830; this established a new empresario system whereby Mexico could settle Mexicans and Europeans in the region, rather than attracting whites from the United States.
    D. Anglo dominance in Texas, strong ties with the United States, weak identification with Mexico, and the US policy of westward expansion threatened Mexican control over Texas.

REVOLUTION TO STATEHOOD

THE TEXAS REVOLUTION

The refusal of Colonel John H. Moore and his company to return a cannon to the Mexican military at the **Battle of Gonzales** on October 2, 1835 (wheeling it out with the flag "Come and Take It") is generally considered the beginning of the Texas Revolution. More volunteers assembled and continued to San Antonio, intending to take the city and de Cos.

The volunteers besieged the city; **Ben Milam** led the assault that began the **Battle of San Antonio** (December 5 – 10, 1835) after which de Cos surrendered.

During the siege, delegates met to determine the way forward. They chose **Sam Houston,** the former governor of Tennessee, to lead an army; however other armed groups of volunteers had already sprung up under **James Bowie** in San Antonio, **James Fannin** in Goliad, and elsewhere. As a result, Houston had difficulty organizing and imposing authority beyond the northeast.

Figure 3.3. Detail of a Mural Depicting the "Come and Take It" Flag at Gonzales, Texas

By February 1836, Santa Anna himself entered Texas with six thousand troops in an attempt to subdue the uprising. On February 23, San Antonio was besieged again. Meanwhile, during the chaos fifty-nine delegates, among them two Tejanos, signed the **Texas Declaration of Independence** on March 1, 1836, at Washington-on-the-Brazos. Adopting it the next day, they also wrote the first **Texas Constitution**. The delegates confirmed Sam Houston's command of the army and appointed **David Burnet** as interim president of the Republic of Texas.

A few days later, on March 6 Santa Anna attacked the Alamo. **David Crockett**, a former Tennessee congressman and volunteer colonel and William B. Travis led the defense against Santa Anna (James Bowie was either dead or dying at the time within the Alamo), but ultimately Mexico prevailed in the **Battle of the Alamo**; those not killed in the attack were executed, aside from a few whom Santa Anna freed to warn other Texans.

> **DID YOU KNOW?**
>
> Santa Anna entered Texas shortly after subduing another uprising in Zacatecas; resistance to his rule was not isolated to Anglo Texans.

Upon hearing the news in Gonzales and facing the Mexican advance, Sam Houston evacuated the city in the **Runaway Scrape**. Meanwhile, James Fannin remained at Goliad despite orders to join Houston; defeated by Santa Anna, Fannin's army was executed, too.

Santa Anna pursued Houston, who moved north. On April 20, Houston's and Santa Anna's forces briefly met on the battlefield at the San Jacinto River and White Oak Bayou.

The next day, during the **Battle of San Jacinto**, Houston surprised the Mexicans by attacking in the afternoon rather than the morning. Lasting only eighteen minutes, the battle was won by the Texans. Houston's army captured Santa Anna and while nine Texans died, an estimated 630 Mexicans were killed.

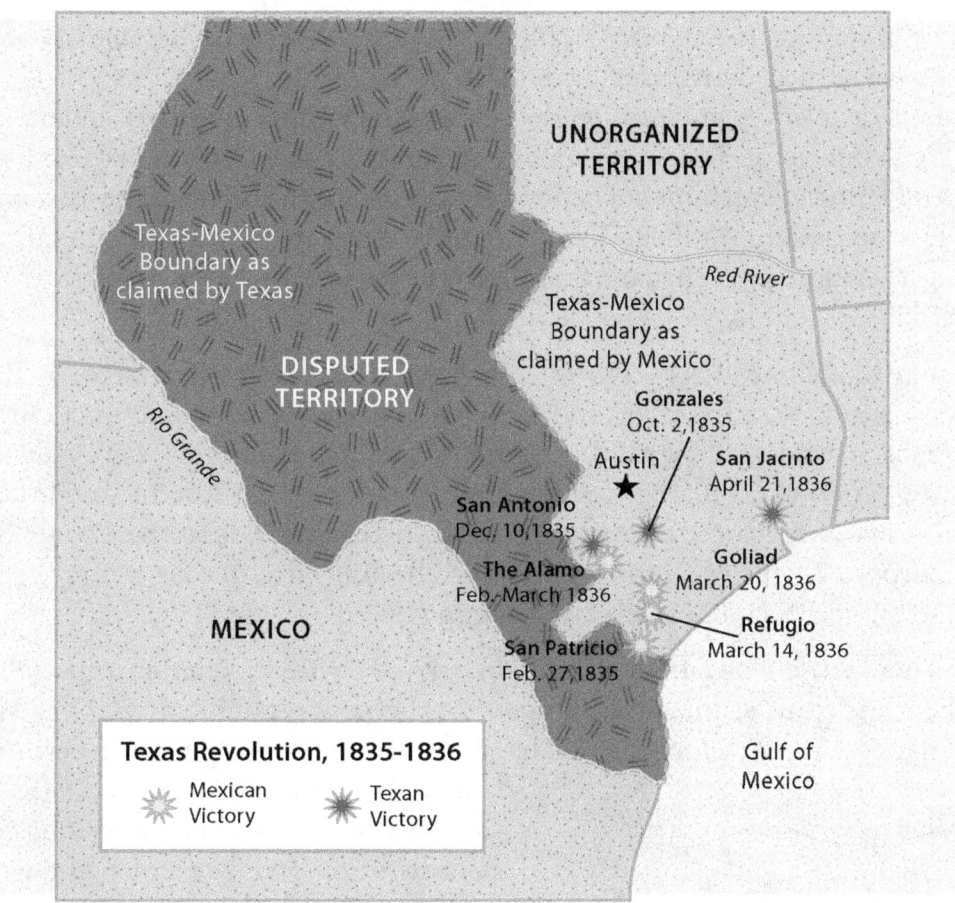

Figure 3.4. Battles of the Texas Revolution

A few weeks later, on May 14, Santa Anna agreed to the **Treaty of Velasco**, which granted Texas independence. Texas thus became an independent republic.

THE REPUBLIC OF TEXAS

Sam Houston was elected President of the Republic of Texas in September, 1836; **Mirabeau Lamar** became vice president; and Stephen Austin became secretary of state. Land near the village of Waterloo (more centrally located than Houston) was chosen as the location for the new capital, which was named Austin in honor of the secretary of state, who had died shortly after taking office.

Houston had been elected in a landslide, despite running against Austin; many voters were recent immigrants from the United States who were familiar with him from his military and political service there, and were not familiar with Austin's deep history in Texas.

Figure 3.5. Flag of the Republic of Texas

The Republic faced major challenges. Texas was bankrupt and in enormous debt—over one million dollars—with only five hundred dollars in the treasury at one point. Houston established rangers and militia in place of a costly army and enforced customs collections at Galveston. He also sold the Texan naval fleet. His successor, Mirabeau Lamar, printed three million dollars in currency, causing its value to plummet and making his planned investments in infrastructure impossible.

To raise income, Texas continued to exploit its greatest resource: land. The Houston administration gave land away and even issued **land scrip,** a currency redeemable in land, in order to attract settlers. The goal was to raise national income by taxing landowners. Lamar reintroduced the *empresario* system, and attracted more immigrants from the north, including recent arrivals to the United States from Europe. Texans of German and Czech heritage live in east-central Texas to this day, around New Braunfels and LaGrange.

As new settlers of European descent arrived in Texas, relationships between people of different ethnicities changed. In the new republic, only male Anglos and Tejanos were considered citizens. Black people (whether enslaved or free), native North Americans, and women of any ethnicity were not. According to the Constitution, free Black men and women could not even live in the country.

Rapidly rising numbers of White immigrants saw Tejanos as a threat or as Mexican agents. At the same time, Texas' relationship with Mexico remained unstable.

DID YOU KNOW?

Samuel McCulloch Jr. had fought in the Texas Revolution and was wounded at Goliad; however, he was deprived of Texas citizenship because he was a free Black man.

- In 1842 Mexico raided Texas and occupied San Antonio twice.
- In response, Texas raided the northern Mexican towns of Laredo and Guerrero.
- Meanwhile, Texas maintained its small naval force of schooners in the Gulf of Mexico to protect trade routes with New Orleans.
- Texas also provided support to Yucatan when it rebelled against the Mexican government.

As Texas' relationship with Mexico deteriorated, new White settlers believed Tejanos—even those who had supported the revolution—to be a threat. Many Tejanos were forced to leave or face a reduced quality of life, living as second-class citizens in an environment of prejudice.

> **DID YOU KNOW?**
>
> Juan Erasmo Seguin was unfairly accused of leading the Mexican attack on the city because of his ethnicity. Seguin had been a captain in the Texas army, a senator in the Texas congress, and mayor of San Antonio.

Tense relations also persisted between Texas and Native American tribes. Although Houston had maintained a stable relationship with the Cherokee in the east, Lamar forcibly removed the Cherokee from their land. He also sent military into Comanche land to protect Anglo settlements.

Texas' foreign relations and borders were also complex. In an attempt to extend its sovereignty to the Rio Grande in New Mexico, Texas troops were halted by the US Army in 1843. However, Texas had a strong relationship with the United States. Sam Houston had fought with the current President Andrew Jackson in the War of 1812; under Jackson, the

> **DID YOU KNOW?**
>
> Sam Houston had lived with the Cherokee in his youth and even been married to a Cherokee woman; he supported diplomacy in relations with Native Americans, not violence or removal.

United States had recognized the Republic of Texas in 1837. Jackson, a proponent of Manifest Destiny, was strongly in favor of Texas joining the Union. But abolitionists were not, given that slavery was an entrenched institution in Texas.

Houston supported joining the United States; Lamar did not, envisioning Texas as a North American power rivaling the US and Mexico alike. Texas did establish relations with Great Britain, the Netherlands, and France. But Houston and others recognized that the United States, its policy of westward expansion, and its ideal of Manifest Destiny would be threatened by any strong relationships between Texas and European powers, particularly Great Britain.

Fearful of a Texan alliance with Great Britain, the Tyler administration was open to annexation, and President Houston encouraged President John Tyler in this venture. Tyler first proposed annexation in the form of a treaty; however, treaties must be ratified by the US Senate, which rejected it.

Before leaving office, Tyler again proposed annexation to Congress as a joint resolution. This time, the resolution passed. On the Texan side, Congress approved annexation on July 4, 1845; the people confirmed their approval in October. On February 19, 1846, Texas joined the United States as the twenty-eighth state.

ANNEXATION AND THE US-MEXICAN WAR

Texas became a state during the administration of President James Polk. For the United States, annexation was part of its policy of westward expansion. Texas' population grew exponentially, with settlers coming mainly from the South—including enslaved people.

Viewing annexation as a provocation, Mexico recalled its ambassador from the United States. Mexico sent troops to the Rio Grande under the command of General Mario Arista; President Polk sent troops under the command of General Zachary Taylor to the Nueces River 200 miles north. Finally, clashes on April 24, 1846, triggered the **Mexican-American War.**

After two years of conflict, the United States and Mexico negotiated the **Treaty of Guadalupe Hidalgo,** in which the United States gained territory in exchange for fifteen million dollars. Mexico would also abandon any claims to Texas. That same year, Zachary Taylor became president.

Territories gained by the US under the treaty included:

- New Mexico
- Arizona
- Colorado
- Utah
- Nevada
- California

Under the Treaty of Velasco, the Rio Grande had formed the boundary between Texas and Mexico. With US gains following the war with Mexico, Texas saw fit to claim land as far west as parts of New Mexico and Colorado, in keeping with that treaty. However New Mexicans, with a more entrenched regional history and cultural identity, resisted. At the same time, westward expansion continued to drive debate over slavery in the United States. The American people and government were fiercely divided over whether to permit or forbid slavery in the enormous new territory obtained following the war.

According to the **Compromise of 1850**:

- Congress agreed to admit California as a free state.
- The legality of slavery would be decided by popular sovereignty in the Utah and New Mexico Territories.
- The Fugitive Slave Act was strengthened.
- Trade in enslaved persons was abolished in Washington, D.C.
- The borders of Texas were established as they stand today.
    - In exchange, Texas received ten million dollars.
    - Given that the US government had not taken on Texas' public debt at annexation, Texas benefitted from the arrangement.

Figure 3.6. Texas' Borders after the Compromise of 1850

THE STATE OF TEXAS

James Pickney Henderson was elected the first governor of Texas following annexation. The state was organized in accordance with a constitution written during the last year of the Republic under the guidance of **Thomas Jefferson Rusk**, with many similarities to the US Constitution. It maintained protections for slavery and also retained the **Homestead Law**, which prohibited the seizure of indebted owners' property and protected women's property rights. Rusk and Sam Houston were elected to represent Texas in the US Senate. Henderson appointed **John Hemphill** as the first chief justice of the Texas Supreme Court. Meanwhile, Texas' population continued to grow, primarily via the migration of White southerners and the Black Americans they enslaved.

> **HELPFUL HINT**
>
> While most new Texans were southerners, many were new immigrants from Europe, including Czechs, Poles, French, Swiss, and numerous Germans. Their cultural heritage persists to this day in central Texas, where some locals spoke German as a first language even into the 1970s.

Galveston became the largest city in Texas (with approximately 6,000 inhabitants) and an important American port—some claimed it would rival New Orleans and New York City. As the largest port in Texas, Galveston was the gateway for Texas goods, which were in demand elsewhere in North America and in Europe.

Table #.1. Products Traded at the Port of Galveston

Texas Exports	Texas Imports
▸ cotton	▸ manufactured goods
▸ sugar	▸ luxury imports (like clothing)
▸ molasses	▸ furniture
▸ cattle	▸ tools
▸ cattle products	▸ early industrial implements

Enslaved Black people were also traded at the Port of Galveston.

Texas used the funding from the Compromise of 1850 to settle debts and invest in infrastructure and education. Under the administration of **Governor Elisha M. Pease** (1853 – 1859), the state invested in roads, improvement in river navigability and management, and education. Texas also sought ways to lower taxes for its residents, a tradition that continues. Pease requested a US military presence in the state to protect settlers on the frontier from attacks by the Kiowa, Comanche, and other Native Americans; migration into Texas, mainly from the South, had tripled during the 1850s, and the institution of slavery became more entrenched as a result.

Meanwhile, the entire nation continued to become more divided over slavery. In Washington, Senator Houston voted against the controversial **Kansas-Nebraska Act** of 1854, which opened that territory up to settlement with the legality of slavery to be decided by popular sovereignty. This essentially nullified the Missouri Compromise of 1820, which had forbidden slavery north of the thirty-sixth parallel.

At the time, US senators were chosen by state legislatures (direct election of senators would not take effect until the ratification of the Seventeenth Amendment in 1913). Disapproving of Houston's vote, the Texas State Legislature indicated it would not return him to office, so he returned to Texas to run for governor.

Despite his anti-slavery position, which clashed with supporters of states' rights who believed in the rights of states to determine the legality of slavery, Houston was elected as governor of Texas in 1859.

PRACTICE QUESTION

2) Following the Texas Revolution, who of the following were considered citizens of the Republic of Texas?

   A. Black, Tejano, and White men
   B. Tejano and White men only
   C. Tejano and White men and women
   D. White men and women only

Civil War and Reconstruction

Division and Secession

Most White Texans, whether or not they themselves enslaved other people, supported the practice of slavery. Many believed in notions of white supremacy, aspired to enslave people themselves, or refused federal oversight of state laws at all costs. Therefore in the elections of 1860, opposition to Abraham Lincoln and the Republicans was widespread among those able to vote—White males. Lincoln was not even listed on the ballot in Texas and an alternative, vehemently pro-slavery candidate, Vice President John Cabell Breckinridge, beat Lincoln's opponent Stephen Douglas in a landslide in the state.

Following Lincoln's victory in the presidential election of 1860, South Carolina quickly seceded, followed by Georgia, Alabama, Mississippi, Louisiana, and Florida. Texas followed shortly thereafter. (After Texas joined, the remainder of the Confederate states—Arkansas, Virginia, North Carolina, and Tennessee—followed once war broke out.)

Governor Houston opposed secession, but secessionist leaders like John M. Ford called for special elections for delegates to a convention to consider it. Elections were held on January 8, 1861. Most delegates enslaved people and many were already state representatives. The convention was scheduled for January 28, 1861.

Despite calling an extraordinary meeting of the legislature on January 21 in order to prevent a convention, Houston was essentially without recourse; the legislature failed to act, and the Secession **Convention,** led by Oran M. Roberts, later voted overwhelmingly for an **Ordinance of Secession** (with a vote of 166 to eight) on February 1. Texans ratified the ordinance in a special vote on February 23; it passed by 44,317 to 13,020, with only a few counties near the Red River and German-dominated Central Texas voting against. The Secession Convention also wrote a new constitution, specifically stipulating the legality of slavery. A few weeks later, Texas troops forced the Union General David E. Twiggs to surrender at the Alamo; military supplies were taken for Texas.

Texas had not yet joined the Confederacy, and at the time was temporarily once again an independent country. On March 2, Texas Independence Day, secessionists met in Austin to officially declare secession from the United States and allegiance to the Confederate States of America. Despite his decades of service, Governor Sam Houston refused to pledge allegiance to the Confederacy and was replaced by **Lieutenant Governor Edward Clark**. Finally, Texas sent observers to attend the meeting of Confederate delegates in Montgomery, Alabama, determining the organization of the Confederacy.

Texas at War

While no major fighting took place in Texas, many Texans participated in the Confederate army: 60,000 to 70,000 served, and most were volunteers. Battle did, however, occur in New Mexico. Jefferson Davis permitted Brigadier General Henry Hopkins Sibley, to invade the Union Southwest in search of gold in Colorado and to extend Confederate territory to the Pacific. Having raised a force composed primarily of Texans, Sibley defeated the Union at Valverde and held Santa Fe. Ultimately the Texans were forced to retreat from New Mexico after the Union destroyed Sibley's supplies at Glorieta Pass. Consequently, the Confederacy abandoned its designs on the Southwest.

The **Anaconda Plan**, the Union plan to blockade and isolate the Confederacy, and its naval blockade did affect Texas. In October 1862, during the **Battle of Galveston**, the Union army occupied the city, at that time the largest city in mostly rural Texas. However the Confederates recaptured Galveston on January 1, 1863; the Union relinquished control and maintained the blockade successfully from New Orleans. The Confederacy continued to export cotton surreptitiously through Mexico and Cuba. But ongoing shortages of medicine, mechanical and farming tools, coffee, clothing, shoes, and other necessities strained the people of Texas and the state's economy.

The Confederacy surrendered at Appomattox on April 9, 1865. Even though the South had surrendered, the final battle of the Civil War took place a month later near Brownsville—the **Battle of Palmito Ranch**, in which Confederate troops fought arriving Union troops.

On June 19, slavery ended in Texas when US General Gordon Granger enforced the Emancipation Proclamation. Despite Lincoln's announcement in 1863, news of emancipation had not reached enslaved Black Texas—slave owners who knew of the decree kept silent. **Juneteenth** is celebrated today in honor of the end of slavery in the state.

Reconstruction

After the war, Texas suffered economically like much of the South. Given the wartime disruption of production and markets, the devaluation of investments, real estate, stocks, bonds, and currency following the collapse of the Confederacy, and economic uncertainty as Reconstruction loomed, the state faced a depression.

At the same time, societal change gripped the state. The end of slavery was a time of uncertainty. President Lincoln's assassination, the limitations of his Ten Percent Plan, and division in Congress between Radical Republicans seeking retribution from the South, and more moderate Republicans and Democrats, muddled the way forward for Reconstruction.

Like most former Confederate states, Texas refused to ratify the **Fourteenth Amendment**, which provided equal protection under the law to American males regardless of race, recognizing Black Americans as US citizens. Consequently, Congress implemented the **Reconstruction Acts** of 1867, which placed the South, including Texas, under military control. Texas was part of **Military District Number Five**, as were Arkansas and Louisiana. At the same time, migration continued into Texas.

While much of the pro-Confederacy Texas establishment bristled under Reconstruction, life began to improve for others. **General Charles Griffin**, who controlled Texas for the Union, ordered elections for delegates to a state constitutional convention. He also appointed former governor Elisha M. Pease to that office again, until a state government could be reestablished.

Because many White supporters of the Confederacy refused to participate, Radical Republicans gathered to write a new state constitution in 1868 (as were ten Black Americans). They ratified the Fourteenth Amendment (as well as the **Thirteenth Amendment**, which abolished slavery). Texas was readmitted into the Union on March 30, 1870.

> **DID YOU KNOW?**
>
> Republicans from the North were scornfully called "carpetbaggers" by supporters of the Confederacy. Southerners who worked with them were derisively referred to as "scalawags."

Meanwhile, the federally supported **Freedmen's Bureau** was established to assist formerly enslaved Black American men and women. Despite the end of slavery, Black men and women faced discrimination and violence, especially from white supremacist groups that formed throughout the South like the Ku Klux Klan. Furthermore, many had little or no possessions, skills, or education. The Freedmen's Bureau offered supplies, schooling, and support in finding homes and paid jobs.

Social and agricultural systems were slow to change. Many of those Black Americans who remained in Texas became **sharecroppers**, frequently on the land they had previously worked and for the same landowners. The landowner lent land and equipment; the sharecropper provided labor and kept about one-quarter of the harvest—part of which had to be repaid in order to cover the debt for renting the equipment and land. Given the inadequacy of their final yield for consumption and profit, sharecroppers became bound to the system in a cycle of debt and dependency.

Some sharecroppers and others managed to become tenant farmers under the **share tenant system**, in which tenants provided their own labor and tools while working the owner's land, and thus were able to keep more of the harvest. However, tenants often required still more capital to invest in better implements or to survive a poor harvest. The **crop-lien system** allowed them to borrow from outside creditors, but forced them to repay the creditor first at harvest, regardless of the yield. This could put them in more debt and still tied them to the land.

Republican **Governor Edmund Davis**, who had been elected in 1869, was opposed by those Texans who had supported the Confederacy. Known as **Redeemers**, they wanted to "redeem" Texas from outside control. In 1873 Davis was voted out of office, replaced by the Democrat **Richard Coke**. Coke reinstated former Texan leaders like Oran Roberts. The former leader of the Secession Convention, Roberts was appointed by Coke as the chief justice of the Texas Supreme Court.

Redeemers had also been outraged by the new, Republican-written constitution, which they believed gave the governor too much power. Coke called for another constitutional convention, this one dominated by Democrats. The resulting **Constitution of 1876**, which replaced the Republican Constitution, decentralized power and limited the power of the state legislature. It remains the state constitution to this day, although over 400 amendments have been added to it. The Democratic Party dominated Texas following Reconstruction until well into the twentieth century.

> **DID YOU KNOW?**
>
> Despite domination of state government by Redeemers, opposition existed. State Senator Matthew Gaines was a Black minister and had himself been enslaved. He served in the legislature from 1870 – 1874 and advocated for Black American rights, including the rights of sharecroppers.

> **DID YOU KNOW?**
>
> Women's voting rights were not even mentioned in the Constitution of 1876. Women would have to continue to fight for the right to vote in Texas as well as in the rest of the United States.

THE FRONTIER

Unlike most of the former Confederacy, Texas was a frontier state in addition to a southern one, and violent clashes with Plains tribes continued. Disorganization in the west triggered by years of political instability at the state and national levels required the attention of law enforcement.

- The **Texas Rangers** focused on managing domestic conflict rather than the threat from Indigenous Americans.
- Union troops stationed in Texas concentrated on carrying out federal policy and Reconstruction away from the Frontier.
- Kiowa and Comanche became stronger and raiding became more profitable thanks to **comancheros**, who provided them with supplies in exchange for goods stolen from raids on settlements.
    - Comancheros then sold these goods on the market farther north or in Mexico.
- In central Texas, Black American military contingents (called **buffalo soldiers** by Native Americans) were assigned to protect roads and outposts.

During the late nineteenth century, the federal government was taking action against Native American tribes in order to capture the Frontier, and Texas was no exception. As it organized the reservation system and continued campaigns against tribes throughout the Great Plains, the federal government came to focus more on Texas following the **Salt Creek Massacre**. Comanche and Kiowa led by **Satanta**, attacked US military near Fort Worth in 1871, triggering an overwhelming response led by **General William T. Sherman**. At the same time, massive buffalo hunts continued, destroying Native American ways of life. US legislation like the **Dawes Act** of 1887 continued to subdue Plains tribes. By the end of the nineteenth century, ongoing violence between settlers and Native Americans ultimately resulted in the destruction of tribal societies in Texas as in other states in the country.

Hunting buffalo was especially impactful in Texas because it allowed the development of the **cattle** industry. Both cattle and buffalo flourished on the same land; the fewer buffalo using resources, the more available for cattle.

> **DID YOU KNOW?**
>
> Resisting movement to reservations, the Comanche leader **Quanah Parker** led an alliance of Comanche, Kiowa, and Cheyenne warriors against buffalo hunters in 1874. Defeated by US forces after a year of conflict known as the Red River War, Quanah Parker became a leader in the reservation system and advocated for the Comanche at the national level.

PRACTICE QUESTION

3) Which of the following describes the Redeemers?
   A. They reinstated several prominent, pro-secession Texans to public office after the war.
   B. They avoided writing a new constitution, preferring the Republican-written one.
   C. They supported Republicans after the Civil War.
   D. They wished to move the capital of Texas to Dallas.

POSTWAR DEVELOPMENT

From 1870 to 1900, Texas politics, economics, and society would change rapidly. Population grew from just over 800,000 Texans in 1870 to over three million Texans in 1900, making Texas the sixth-largest state. More people moved to cities. The population of people of color declined. More White migrants moved to the state. People of color, especially Black Americans, left Texas and the South in search of opportunities elsewhere in the United States as part of the Great Migration. Finally, the number of foreign-born Hispanic Texans—mainly born in Mexico—increased.

Texas' population growth has been possible because of its tremendous wealth. The state is rich in natural resources, which helped attract settlement. The economy has continued to grow over decades as natural resources were (and are) further discovered, developed, and exploited.

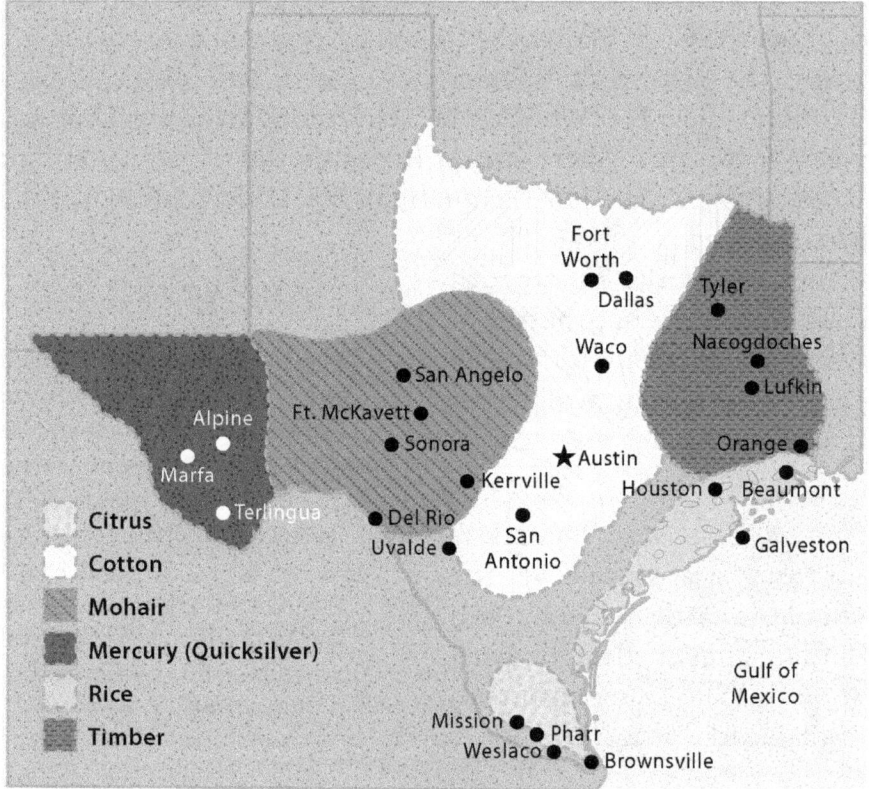

Figure 3.7. Major Texas Products by Region

CATTLE AND RANCHING

Following the Civil War, the Texas economy began to grow—thanks in great part to cattle. A wartime halt to trade had allowed a surplus of Texas cattle to develop. **Joseph G. McCoy** built the first "cow town," Abilene, Kansas, to receive cattle and ship them east to markets via train. This marked the beginning of the cattle trade; cattle were driven north to receiving areas, for railroads had not yet been built farther south or east than Missouri and parts of Kansas.

Cattle drives became an industry dominated and organized by contractors who led organized teams ensuring the security and progress of the animals. The ideal of the frontier cowboy took root in American folklore, but cattle-driving as an industry was short lived.

Cattle originated in southern Texas, but major ranches, or "spreads," appeared throughout the state, some of which still exist. The **King Ranch**, founded in 1853 by Richard King and Mifflin Kennedy, is one of the largest. Still in use today for hunting and tourism, it encompasses more land than the state of Rhode Island. The **Matador Ranch**, based in the Texas Panhandle, historically included parcels of land throughout the Great Plains as far north as the Canadian border, and its remnants exist today as part of a larger corporation.

Ranching continued (and continues) to be a major part of the Texas economy; however, cattle drives only lasted until the end of the nineteenth century. Cattle drives were no longer necessary as meatpacking facilities opened in Texas' growing cities and as railroads extended farther west and into Texas itself. Still, the development of railroads would only add to Texas' own economic growth.

> **HELPFUL HINT**
>
> Some enterprising ranchers also raised goats to make **mohair,** another important Texas product, generated in West Texas. Made from the fleece of the Angora goat, mohair was sold for high prices. Today, the region still boasts more Angora goats than anywhere else in the United States.

RAILROADS

Initially, most railroads centered on Houston and Galveston; the **Houston, East & West Texas Railroad (HE&WT)** connected Houston and Shreveport, Louisiana. Meanwhile, the first major east-west and north-south railroad crossing was built in Dallas. Eventually lines like the Kansas City Southern, Missouri Pacific, Santa Fe Regional, Texas & New Orleans, and Cotton Belt crossed the state. Existing lines like the Kansas City Southern and Union Pacific continue to do so. Crossings and construction sites gave rise to towns like Lufkin.

The construction of transcontinental railroads throughout the United States included development in Texas. Texas' geography made the state key to railroad development, and Grenville Dodge began construction of the **Texas and Pacific Railroad** in 1869 in Marshall, Texas. Jay Gould—a New York City "robber baron"—took over the T&P in Dallas in 1874, completing construction across the state to El Paso. There, the T&P connected with the **Southern Pacific**, which originated in San Diego. The Southern Pacific was able to use track to cross Texas to reach New Orleans. As a result, Texas became integral to continental rail transportation and trade.

TIMBER

Given the size of the state, by 1904 over 10,000 miles of track had been laid. The subsidized industry was growing exponentially like many others. Railroads helped trigger economic development in small and widely dispersed towns: businesses relocated to areas that were easy to access, and population centers that attracted railroad companies grew.

Railroad construction also spurred development of the **timber industry** in East Texas. Rich in pine woods, the 68,000 square mile region north of Beaumont was estimated to contain enough wood to produce 300 million board feet of lumber. Cross ties for track were made out of wood, so demand for timber was linked directly to railroad construction. Furthermore, the HE&WT provided a means for Texas timber to reach the rest of the United States and even the world.

The "lumber baron" John H. Kirby's **Kirby Lumber Company** led the exploitation of most of the old growth forest by 1920. Based in Beaumont, the Kirby Lumber Company functioned by constructing and operating mills and company towns throughout the region, maintaining a grasp on the workforce. Smaller companies emerged as well; later movements experimented with sustainable forestry and management of what forest was left.

AGRICULTURE

Railroads were also key in promoting another important agricultural product. The terrain around Houston and Galveston close to the Gulf Coast was suitable for **rice**, and the Houston Chamber of Commerce, in conjunction with the Southern Pacific railroad, promoted rice growth in the area. Louisiana settlers had already been growing rice in the region, but the Houston Chamber of Commerce invited Saito Saibara, a Japanese scholar studying in the United States, to teach Texas farmers more rice-growing techniques. Japanese immigrants in turn came to the region to take advantage of agricultural opportunities. The region produced 99 percent of the US rice by the twentieth century, and the Southern Pacific profited from transporting the product.

Rice was only one of many profitable agricultural products in Texas. Until the late nineteenth century, **cotton seeds** had been discarded in the cotton harvest. Indeed, the cotton gin had been one of the most important inventions of the Industrial Revolution, for it quickly separated the seeds from the fiber, substantially speeding up the process. However, valuable uses for cotton seeds were discovered, including its high levels of nitrogen. The pulp from crushed cotton seeds supplemented animal feed—especially feed for cattle, one of Texas' most valuable products—and was also a powerful fertilizer. Furthermore, oil for industrial lubrication could be extracted from cotton seeds. Cotton was a cash crop in Central Texas; the sharecropper system in the region was effectively an extension of slavery, allowing maximum exploitation of labor to harvest cotton seeds.

Farther north and west, **wheat** became an important agricultural product. Migrants to Texas—including recent European immigrants—began settling the area after the Civil War, and by the beginning of the twentieth century over 300,000 family farms were established in the plains regions of the state. Irrigation, crop diversification, and farming methods that allowed for maximum absorption of water enabled farmers to coax crops from the rough terrain. Eventually, better farming technology improved agriculture in the region; the discovery of the Ogallala Aquifer improved irrigation. However, the drought and Dust Bowl phenomenon of the 1930s harmed farmers throughout the Great Plains, and Texans were no exception.

Later in the early twentieth century, citrus products would become important in South Texas. While the Rio Grande Valley region seemed unsuitable for agriculture, in 1912 a pharmacist from Iowa, **John Harry Shary** acquired land, irrigated it, and planted citrus trees, successfully growing **grapefruit**. Meanwhile, migrant workers moved in the region with their families, finding work in the fields.

Mercury (Quicksilver)

Toward the end of the nineteenth century, based on rumors, small mines began operating in the desert of West Texas in search of quicksilver, or mercury, in demand for chemical and industrial goods. **Howard Perry** purchased land in the Big Bend region and discovered large amounts of mercury. His mining operations produced mercury throughout the early twentieth century. Texas became the second-largest producer of mercury by the mid-twentieth century.

Oil and Gas

Texas' most famous product, and arguably its lifeblood, is petroleum. In 1901, Patillo Higgins posited that there was oil under a salt hill called **Spindletop** near Beaumont, despite some ongoing production farther north in **Corsicana** since the late nineteenth century. Hiring the Czech engineer Anthony Lucas to drill, Higgins struck oil on January 10. The **Lucas Gusher** would prove to be the largest oil source in the world at that time.

Figure 3.8. Lucas Gusher

Beaumont would become home to the nascent Texas oil industry. New companies like the Guffey Oil Company (later to become Gulf Oil, and then **Chevron**) and the Texas Oil Company (**Texaco**) opened offices in Beaumont and refineries in Port Neches and Port Arthur. Oil, which demanded specialized equipment like pipelines and drills, developed a new economy of its own; it also energized existing industries like the timber industry.

Drilling continued at Spindletop, and in 1926 even more oil was discovered. Investors explored possibilities throughout Texas, and the oil industry developed as wells popped up in Humble, Sour Lake, Batson, and Goose Creek. Eventually exploration in the **Permian Basin**, located on public land in West Texas, yielded considerable revenue, much of which went to support education (including a substantial endowment for the University of Texas).

Early Twentieth Century

Populists and Progressives

The Populist attorney general **James Stephen Hogg** took office in 1886. Popular with the public, Hogg targeted insurance companies, assisting in lawsuits against insurers that did not meet their obligations and saving Texans over a million dollars. Hogg especially targeted the powerful railroads, which were under attack nationally. Prosecuting railroads that sought to limit or halt unprofitable service to small towns, he also forced railroad companies to invest more in safety.

In 1890, Hogg was elected governor, in part due to his plan to create a **Texas Railroad** Commission. This would be the first state agency created for the purpose of regulating the activities of a specific industry. Hogg appointed the Texas congressman John Henninger Reagan as chairman of the commission; Reagan had himself introduced legislation creating the Interstate Commerce Commission in Congress.

> **DID YOU KNOW?**
>
> The Texas Railroad Commission also oversees oil and gas matters because petroleum management was not originally believed to be a major issue, nor oil an important resource. So with no one else willing to handle it, that work was handed off to the Railroad Commission.

Governor Hogg enforced progressive legislation reining in corporate interests. Known as the **Hogg Laws**, they included forcing corporations to either use or return state property subsidies within a certain time period, and requiring insurance companies to utilize Texas banks when depositing insurance premium payments in order to allow Texas courts to access the funds.

Edward M. House, a wealthy cotton magnate, was extremely influential in Texas politics and helped ensure Hogg's reelection. House also supported subsequent Texas governors who shared Hogg's populist and progressive inclinations.

Texas Progressives unexpectedly gained ground in 1900 when Galveston was hit by a devastating hurricane. **The Galveston Storm** on September 8 of that year killed an estimated six thousand people, exposing the city's vulnerability to storm surges and flooding. In responding to the crisis, city officials divided responsibilities in a structured fashion that became the foundation for modern city government and planning; city management became separated from legislation.

In 1914, **James E. Ferguson** ran for governor. His broad efforts throughout rural Texas, despite his roots in banking and lack of political experience, propelled him to office. Ferguson focused on the plight of sharecroppers and proposed a farm tenant rent law (that would later prove unsuccessful), to stabilize the yields sharecroppers paid to landowners.

As governor, Ferguson continued to focus on the rural poor. The Rural High School Law assisted schools to pool and improve educational resources, and the state highway department improved Texas roads in time for the advent of the automobile. The state would be able to standardize construction and continue to improve planning.

Nevertheless, scandals wracked the Ferguson administration, and a dispute between Governor Ferguson and Robert Vinson, president of the University of Texas, eventually resulted in the impeachment of the governor by the Texas House of Representatives. Ferguson was found guilty of several improprieties and was to be forbidden from ever again holding public office in the state; however he resigned a day before the legislature's ruling in order to claim he would still be able to be politically active in the future. Lieutenant Governor **Willian P. Hobby** took over and was reelected in 1918.

Hobby faced a Texas recovering from the First World War, which meant that many working people had returned from fighting overseas, reenergizing the limited labor movement in Texas. Unlike the populist and progressive bent of Ferguson's administration, Hobby acted against labor, including forcing striking dockworkers in Galveston back to work via the Open Ports Law.

A few years later in 1924, another Ferguson would take office: Jim Ferguson's wife **Miriam "Ma" Ferguson**. One feature of the post-war South, including Texas, was a resurgence of the Ku Klux Klan, which advocated not only racism, but also nativism and Christian fundamentalism. Ferguson took steps to fight the Klan, including supporting anti-mask legislation, which curtailed its activities since it depended on anonymity and secrecy to practice its criminal and racist violence. Governor Ferguson also pardoned an estimated 2,000 convicts.

When Ma Ferguson was elected, women had only been able to vote for four years. Activists including Rebecca Henry Hayes, Annette Finnegan, Eleanor Brackenridge, and Minnie Fisher Cunningham worked to get women the right to vote in Texas. Women could not vote in state primaries until 1918, and then they voted a woman into public office: Annie Webb Blanton became state superintendent of public instruction.

Texas activists were also influential in the ratification of the Nineteenth Amendment, giving women the right to vote nationally. **Jane Y. McCallum** was president of the Austin Woman Suffrage Association, actively working for women's right to vote. Texas was the first state in the South to ratify the Nineteenth Amendment, on June 26, 1919.

In 1929, the **League of United Latin American Citizens (LULAC)** was founded in Corpus Christi to support Mexican American civil rights. Originally composed of small business owners and skilled workers, LULAC addressed civil rights legislation and still works today.

International Issues

Texas was key to US foreign policy during the early twentieth century. Sharing a long border and history with Mexico, Texas became enmeshed in political tensions that led to the 1910 Mexican Revolution and its impact on the United States.

Mexican revolutionaries fighting the dictator Porfirio Diaz were based in Texas, and the border region bore the brunt of fighting; furthermore, Mexican refugees fled to Texas. Even following Diaz' overthrow, tensions grew as Mexico became unstable.

During the **Tampico Affair** in 1914, a confusing situation led to the arrest of US soldiers by the Mexican military; in retaliation, the United States occupied Veracruz. Attacks on US interests by **Pancho Villa** resulted in limited US military action, but President Wilson took a conservative approach. Ultimately, the United States became distracted from the situation upon the interception of the **Zimmerman Note**, an invitation from Germany to Mexico to form an alliance in the First World War against the United States. As a result of the publication of the note, the United States entered the war in Europe and the situation with Mexico on the Texas border cooled.

The Great Depression and the New Deal

Texas, like the rest of the country, suffered from the Great Depression. Despite its diversified economy, the state exhibited severe income inequality. Oil, cattle, and cotton "barons" enjoyed great wealth, but most Texans lived paycheck to paycheck, unable to save or invest.

Following the First World War, national demand for consumer goods dropped; factories began laying people off. Furthermore, demand for agricultural goods dropped as wartime demand for food and fibrous substances declined. The collapsing price of cotton devastated that industry; over-farming in the Great Plains, combined with a major drought in the 1930s, resulted in the **Dust Bowl** and crop failures throughout the region, including northern Texas. Farmers were forced to leave their land.

In 1932, Miriam Ferguson was reelected governor of Texas. At the same time, **Franklin Delano Roosevelt** became president of the United States. His **New Deal** legislation was eagerly adopted in Texas and supported by the Ferguson administration.

During FDR's administration, the United States emerged from the Great Depression and entered the **Second World War**. Texas played an important part in the war as home to several military and training bases, as a producer of military ships and aircraft, and as an essential source of petroleum, petroleum products, and synthetic rubber, all necessary for military activity. Texan war leaders included **Col. Oveta Culp Hobby**, who commanded the Women's Army Corps.

PRACTICE QUESTION

4) **Which of the following is an example of the Progressive tradition and movement in Texas?**

    A.   Governor Hobby acting to protect striking Galveston dockworkers

    B.   restrictions on corporate behavior and benefits for the rural poor

    C.   increased job opportunities for migrant workers in south Texas in the citrus industry

    D.   the successful connection of the T&P and Southern Pacific

MODERN TEXAS

POSTWAR TEXAS

As Texas grew, so did its national presence.

The Democrat **Lyndon B. Johnson** was appointed by FDR to run a New Deal program, the National Youth Administration, in Texas in 1935. Two years later, he successfully ran for Congress and represented Texas in Washington. He lost a senatorial campaign in 1941 and served in the military, returning to public office following election to the Senate in 1948 with the defeat of Coke Stevenson in the primaries and Jack Porter in the general election.

A powerful Democrat in Congress and the Senate, LBJ developed a reputation as a "favorite son" and as a legislator who was able to push through legislation working with interests on both sides of the aisle. His sometimes aggressive and controversial style made him a strong voice for Democrats in the Progressive tradition and a strong voice for Texas on the national stage.

Johnson took a strong role in the Civil Rights Act of 1957, foreshadowing civil rights legislation he would preside over in the 1960s as president. He also oversaw the 1950s hearing on the space program in the wake of the Soviet launch of Sputnik. LBJ led the National Aeronautics and Space Act of 1958, and he ensured that **NASA** would be based in Houston. In 1960 he was elected vice president on the ticket with John F. Kennedy, and upon Kennedy's assassination in 1963, became president of the United States.

In the Progressive tradition, Johnson's administration saw the passage of liberal legislation in support of the poor and of civil rights. In 1964, Congress passed the **Civil Rights Act**, which outlawed segregation. While according to the Fifteenth Amendment and the Nineteenth Amendment, all African Americans—men and women—had the right to vote, many Southern states, including Texas, had

> **DID YOU KNOW?**
>
> In 2011, Texas introduced a law forcing voters to show identification in order to cast a ballot, which disproportionately affects the ability of minorities and the poor to exercise their right to vote.

voting restrictions in place, such as literacy tests and poll taxes, which disproportionately affected African Americans. In 1965, led by President Lyndon B. Johnson, Congress passed the **Voting Rights Act**, which forbade restrictions impeding the ability of African Americans to vote, including literacy tests. Separately, the **Twenty-Fourth Amendment** made poll taxes unconstitutional.

Promising a **Great Society**, LBJ embraced **liberalism**, believing that government should fight poverty at home and play an interventionist role abroad (in that era, by fighting communism).

- His administration launched a **War on Poverty**, passing reform legislation to support the poor.
- The **Medicare Act** provided medical care to elderly Americans.
- The creation of the **Department of Housing and Urban Development** increased the federal role in housing and urban issues.
- Johnson's **Head Start** program provided early intervention for disadvantaged children before elementary school (and still does today).
- The **Elementary and Secondary Education Act** increased funding for primary and secondary education.
- The **Immigration Act of 1965** overturned the provisions of the Emergency Quota Act, ending the racist limitations on immigrants to the US.

At the same time, LBJ's overseas agenda was increasingly unpopular. Adhering to containment and Domino Theory—US policy toward communism in an effort to stop its spread—Johnson drew the United States deeper into conflict in Southeast Asia. The **Vietnam War** was extremely unpopular in the US due to high casualties, the unpopular draft (which forced young American males to fight overseas), and what seemed to many to be the purposelessness of the war. Student activists, organizing in the mold of the Civil Rights Movement, engaged in non-violent (and, at times, violent) protest against the Vietnam War.

Deeply unpopular by the end of the 1960s, Johnson announced he would not run for reelection in 1968. He remains a controversial figure in US history, but one of Texas' most important leaders on the national stage.

CIVIL RIGHTS

As Texas continued to grow, so did its diverse populations, including Hispanic and Mexican-American Texans. Hispanics faced discrimination in public life. **Hector P. Garcia**, a veteran of World War Two, established the **American GI Forum** to ensure access for veterans of color to the benefits to which they were entitled.

Furthermore, Texas remained segregated under **Jim Crow** laws. Many Hispanic Texans were oppressed like Black Texans were under Jim Crow. All Texans of color struggled against segregation. Consequently, Texan leaders became important voices in the Civil Rights Movement.

In 1956, **Henry B. Gonzalez** became the first Mexican American elected to the Texas Senate. A community leader, Gonzalez organized the Hispanic community and became known as a crusader against segregation on the San Antonio City Council, supporting legislation to desegregate public parks and other areas. During his time in the state legislature, Gonzalez continued to focus on civil rights and fighting segregation, filibustering state efforts to bypass civil rights legislation and reinstitute segregation in schools. Despite considerable opposition, in 1961 Gonzalez, with the support of President Kennedy and Vice President Johnson, was elected to the House of Representatives—the first Texan Hispanic American in Congress. Gonzalez served until 1997.

Figure 3.9. Rep. Henry B. Gonzalez

In Washington, Gonzalez supported landmark civil rights legislation and LBJ's Great Society programs. Notably, he opposed the Bracero program, which had provided jobs to migrant Mexican workers beginning in WWII, due to the poor conditions faced by workers under the program.

Texas was also a battlefield in the fight for civil rights in the courts:

- In 1950, Herman Sweatt, a Black man, sued the University of Texas when he was denied admission to its law school based on his race.
- Eventually reaching the US Supreme Court, the case **Sweatt v. Painter** forced the desegregation of UT.
- *Sweatt v. Painter* became precedent for *Brown v. Board of Education.*
- Thurgood Marshall argued the case.
- Sweatt was backed by the National Association for the Advancement of Colored People (NAACP), led in Texas at the time by **Lulu Belle Madison White**, one of the first female leaders of the organization in the South.

In 1965, **Barbara Jordan** was elected to the Texas State Senate—the first African American woman in the legislature. Jordan focused on civil rights and equality in employment, lobbying for a minimum wage and the creation of the Fair Employment Practices Commission. Jordan also advocated for anti-discrimination wording in business contracts.

Figure 3.10. Rep. Barbara Jordan

In 1972, for the first time Texans sent a woman and a Black Texan to the House of Representatives when they elected her as a representative. As a member of the House Judiciary Committee, Representative Jordan played an important role during the hearings debating the impeachment of President Richard Nixon due to the Watergate scandal. She also advocated for broader civil rights provisions on the national level. Jordan was only able to serve three terms due to illness; she later took a position at the University of Texas.

From Blue to Red

At the end of the 1960s, Conservatives became more powerful in the United States, and Texas was no exception. Despite giving the country one of its foremost Democrats—LBJ—Texas began to turn from a blue state to a red one.

Conservative working- and middle-class White Texans who had traditionally supported the Democratic Party in the South became disillusioned after the Johnson administration's support of the Civil Rights movement. Democratic strongholds in the South and in Texas began to turn red; Democrats switched parties and became Republicans.

Meanwhile, Texas continued to grow. More conservative Republicans migrated to Texas suburbs, bringing more Republicans to the state. Conservative Democrats declined in Texas, as they did elsewhere in the United States, so Republicans were more likely to defeat liberal Democrats in moderate-to-conservative districts, putting more Republicans in office throughout the state. While many Democrats remained in power throughout the end of the twentieth century, the trend toward a Republican Texas was rooted in the beginning of the conservative movement in the 1970s.

Also during the 1970s and 1980s, fluctuations in the oil market led to economic change in Texas. The **1973 oil crisis** was triggered by oil-producing Arab countries, which imposed an **oil embargo** on the West in retaliation for its support of Israel during the Yom Kippur War that year. OPEC states inflated oil prices. Consequently, oil-producing areas like Texas experienced huge economic growth as the price of oil skyrocketed. Later, in 1979 the Iranian Revolution deposed the Shah of Iran, a major US ally in the Middle East. As Iran was an important source of world petroleum, instability from the revolution increased prices further, causing the **energy crisis.** Finally, the beginning of the Iran-Iraq War in 1980—a conflict between two major oil producers—further destabilized the market and raised prices.

Dizzying growth in the oil industry brought revenue to Texas, especially Houston. However, during the 1980s, slowed manufacturing and conservation measures taken in response to the 1970s crises resulted in an **oil glut**, and oil prices began to fall. The petroleum industry suffered. Eventually, the energy sector would diversify and invest in natural gas resources throughout Texas and Louisiana.

Texas remained central on the political stage throughout the 1980s as well. **Senator Lloyd Bentsen**, a Democrat, was the vice presidential nominee in 1988.

Bentsen was an influential senator and served on the Joint Economic Committee, Finance Committee, and Campaign Committee; he eventually became Secretary of the Treasury under President Clinton. Bentsen was succeeded by **Senator Kay Bailey Hutchison,** Texas' first female senator. Hutchison served on the Commerce, Science, and Transportation Committee throughout her tenure from 1993 – 2013; she focused on deregulating Amtrak, improving security after the attacks of September 11, 2001, and nurturing NASA and research in STEM (science, technology, engineering, and math).

In 1990, **George W. Bush**, son of the Republican national leader and contemporaneous president George H.W. Bush, ran for governor against the popular Democratic incumbent **Ann Richards**. He would serve as governor until his controversial election to the national presidency in 2000. Bush's governorship emphasized criminal justice, capital punishment, tax cuts, and faith-based social service models. Bush also instituted educational reforms. Some of his state policies influenced later change at the national level, another example of Texas' influence on the country.

Following Bush's election as president, Lieutenant Governor **Rick Perry** took over. Perry was elected as governor in 2002 and became the state's longest-serving governor, remaining in office until 2015. State government became solidly Republican under Perry's watch; at the same time, urban and suburban populations increased while rural populations decreased. Hispanic and Black populations grew in the first fifteen years of the twenty-first century. White populations declined. Energy production skyrocketed not only in the oil and gas industry but also in wind power, and Texas became a national leader in job growth. Texas also spent more on education.

Perry's tenure was also controversial nationally. During his term, Texas executed more prisoners than any other state in the nation, carrying on a tradition begun by Governor Bush. Perry also presided over a state increasingly restrictive of personal rights. He obstructed women's health and reproductive rights in Texas, limiting the ability of health care clinics (particularly in rural areas) to provide treatment and offer abortions. Both developments earned Texas widespread criticism across the United States.

Recently, Governor **Greg Abbott**, formerly Perry's lieutenant governor, has stirred controversy by supporting even more restrictive measures on women's health and suggesting that US military presence in Texas threatens state sovereignty.

Texas Today

Texas, with its long border with Mexico, remains a flashpoint in the debates over **immigration reform** in the United States. It is estimated that Texas is home to the second-highest population of undocumented immigrants in the country. Many are from Mexico and Central America, but others come from Asia, South America, Africa, and elsewhere. The state and the country continue to struggle to find a long-term solution for the millions of people who reside in the United States without visas.

Questions about how to monitor and manage the Mexican border, the humanity of immigrant detention centers where people await deportation—sometimes for years—and the harms of deportation on families when members have different residency statuses remain unresolved. Advocates favor a path to citizenship. Legislation proposed by both Democrats and Republicans at the national level (and even jointly sponsored legislation) has failed. Whatever the outcome, Texas will remain at the forefront of the debate.

Texas is a global leader in **medical research**, with several world class hospitals and research facilities throughout the state, notably in Houston at the Texas Medical Center. People from around the country and the world travel to the state for cutting edge treatment, especially in cancer, children's care, and to access the newest medical technology and medical trials at hospitals like M.D. Anderson Cancer Center, Texas Children's Hospital, and other leading institutions.

Texas is also a national leader and major international player in **technological manufacturing and export**. The state surpasses California in technological manufacturing and generates hard currency by exporting to Mexico. Texas Instruments, Verizon, and other companies in Dallas and San Antonio provide manufacturing jobs for thousands of Texans. The business-friendly climate of the state has encouraged tech startups in the fast growing cities of Austin, San Antonio, and Houston, where more tech development is under way.

With five of the fastest-growing cities in the country (Houston, Austin, Dallas, Fort Worth, and San Antonio), Texas continues not only to grow in population size, but to experience rapid **urbanization** and its accompanying problems. Urbanization challenges include:

- overwhelming traffic on freeways built to accommodate far smaller populations
- the immediate environmental impact of an influx of people and automobiles
- long-term concerns about affordable housing and sustainable development

Rapid **suburbanization** as city dwellers and the middle class aspire to home ownership or larger homes beyond urban areas has a negative environmental impact. Suburban sprawl is a feature of the Texas landscape, placing a heavy burden on roads, reservoirs, drainage systems, and other existing infrastructure. The state must find ways to keep up with growth.

Texas remains one of the most economically and politically influential states of the Union; the history of Texas will no doubt continue to have an impact on the history of the United States as a whole in the twenty-first century.

PRACTICE QUESTION

5) **What development has influenced modern Texas?**

   A. Texas has a low population of undocumented immigrants due to border policies.

   B. Suburban areas in Texas are declining in size as people move to other states.

   C. Today Texas is the national leader in tech manufacturing.

   D. Urbanization is limited in Texas, which is primarily a rural state.

Answer Key

1) **D.** From the perspective of the Mexican government, Mexico was losing control of Texas to Anglo interests allied with the United States, and possibly losing Texas to that country. The Law of 1830 was intended to consolidate Mexican control over the region.

2) **B.** Only Tejano and White men were entitled to citizenship of the Republic of Texas. Black men and women, Tejano women, White women, and Native American men and women were all disqualified from citizenship due to their race and/or gender.

3) **A.** The Redeemers reinstated pro-succession Texans to public office after the Civil War. The Democratic Redeemers were so-called because they wanted to "redeem" Texas from outside control. They also replaced the Republican-written constitution with the Constitution of 1876.

4) **B.** Hogg and the Fergusons were politicians in the Progressive tradition. Hogg was especially known for taking action against big business, and the Ferguson administrations acted in favor of the rural poor.

5) **C.** Texas leads the United States in tech manufacturing, thanks to companies like Texas Instruments and Verizon.

4

Foundations, Skills, Research, and Instruction

Historical Perspectives

Understanding Chronological Relationships

Understanding **chronology** is essential to student knowledge of history at the elementary level. Teachers must cover classical civilizations, US history from the country's founding to the twenty-first century, and worldwide developments and transformations in the twentieth century. If it is determined to be developmentally appropriate, teachers may also help students begin to consider historiography. **Historiography** is how history is recorded and describes historians' secondary interpretations of historical topics and the way their views of historical events have changed and evolved.

To help students understand these events, teachers should select a variety of sources to supplement textbooks, including historical maps and photographs, architecture, and political cartoons.

Developing **chronological thinking** is one of the first steps in understanding history. Chronologies help students examine relationships between the past and present and the causes and effects of historical events. Teachers help students identify the temporal structure of a historical narrative (the beginning, middle, and end) so they can construct their own historical narratives. Students should practice explaining the origins of an event and how it developed over time.

Assignments that may help students develop chronological thinking include creating and interpreting **timelines** that illustrate the differences among the past, present, and future. Teachers should select well-written historical narratives such as biographies and historical literature to supplement classwork. These resources enable students to analyze patterns of historical duration (like the legacy of a notable historical document,

> **TEACHING TIP**
>
> Adding pictures to timelines can help students visualize events in history.

such as the US Constitution) and historical succession (such as the evolution of broad systems, like trade and communication networks).

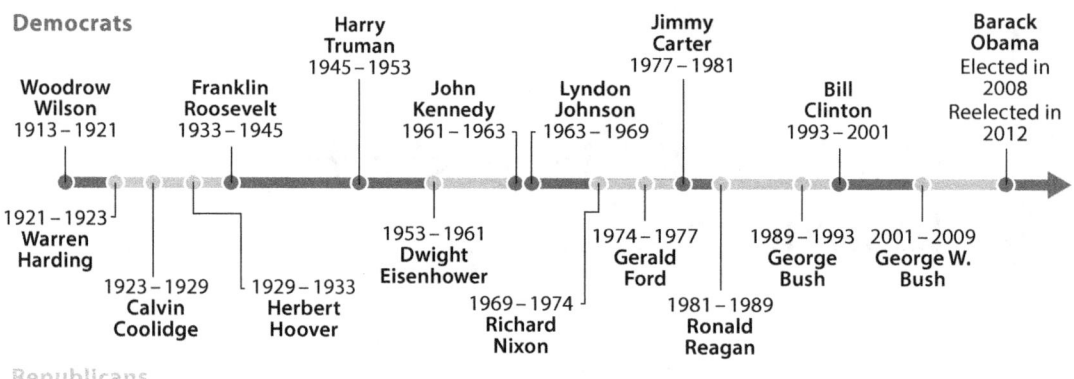

Figure 4.1. Presidential Timeline

PRACTICE QUESTION

1) A social studies teacher wants to help students understand the way time periods impact historiography. Which activity should the teacher choose?

   A. have students create and illustrate a timeline of the periods in which major historians lived

   B. have students read two excerpts covering the same historical event written at different times

   C. have students gather photographs depicting historical events and order them based on time period

   D. have students research a historical event and write a historical narrative with a clear beginning, middle, and end

Instructional Strategies

Social studies teachers must help students understand the skills and processes they need to be informed and engaged with people in the world around them. Students should be aware that their world is continuously changing; the skills they learn in social studies enable them to cope with social change and thrive in society.

Teachers must deliver social studies content in a way that students can understand. Furthermore, teachers should help students develop their written and oral abilities so that they can communicate their interpretations of current and historical events and contribute to broader historical conversations.

By having students evaluate primary and secondary sources, instructional strategies should address

- economic reasoning;
- chronological and spatial thinking;
- historical interpretation.

Students should also be encouraged to **compare and contrast** historical events, such as the French Revolution, the Haitian Revolution, and the American Revolution.

Such comparisons and contrasts should be part of a broader analysis of historical events that goes beyond simply remembering important names and dates. Students should be prompted to consider how historical events reflect change or a break with the past in terms of old governments, social systems, or ways of life. They should also note instances when historical events reflect continuity with the past, which may involve the perpetuation of long-held values or beliefs, such as those upon which a nation or government was founded.

When teaching chronology, dividing major eras into periods, or **periodization**, can be helpful. Students may, for example, note the periods during which major **civilizations**, or societies based on certain shared governmental and social structures, existed in certain regions. As part of understanding chronology, students may trace the evolution of civilizations from their origins in small settlements to **city-states**, which may then turn into large **empires**, such as Rome.

Graphic organizers like diagrams, tables, and graphs help visually impart information, allowing students to identify variables or values affecting relevant data and determine the pros and cons of issues.

Popular types of graphic organizers include the following:

- Venn diagrams, which compare and contrast issues
- semantic webs, which help students brainstorm ideas
- mind maps
- KWL charts, in which students write down what they <u>k</u>now, <u>w</u>ant to know, and what they have <u>l</u>earned about a given topic
- concept circles, in which students categorize words related to a certain topic

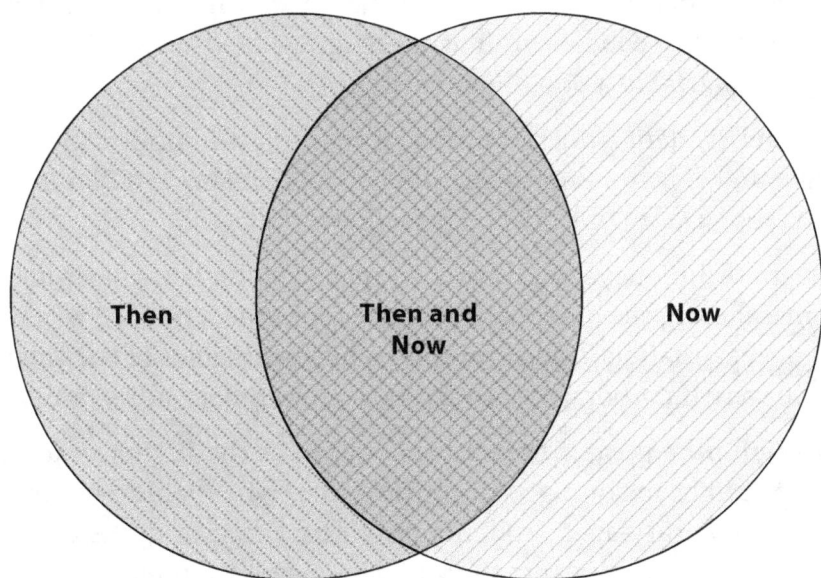

Figure 4.2. Venn Diagram

Graphic organizers also help students develop decision-making skills: They learn to consider values, different courses of action, and potential consequences. As a result, students are guided toward better decision-making in their lives.

Assessment Strategies

Assessment of student understanding of historical topics should be both formative and summative and should make use of multiple modalities. **Formative assessment** techniques include

- class discussions and oral comprehension checks;
- creating summaries, chronologies, or timelines;
- informal writing assignments such as journaling;
- daily exit tickets to review key information.

Summative assessments may take many forms, including

- more traditional selected-response or constructed-response tests;
- essays;
- oral presentations.

Project-based learning (PBL), in which students partake in hands-on, "real-world" projects, is a best practice in social studies classrooms since it helps drive student engagement and interest while encouraging depth of analysis. A history lesson on Rome, for example, might lead to students creating a website or blog chronicling the rise and fall of the empire. Such a project puts students in the role of historians and allows them to contribute to the historiography in a meaningful and relevant way.

Because history is the study of the written word, some instructional and assessment strategies will likely be text-based and may overlap with English language arts skills. Students may be asked, for example, to identify the central claim being made in a primary or secondary source or recognize how a historical actor's point of view shapes material in a document of import.

In assessing student understanding of history, it is important to consider cognitive rigor and depth of knowledge, as described in Howard Bloom's taxonomy or Norman Webb's Depth of Knowledge framework.

Assessment techniques should cover a range of skills, from basic identification or recall (remembering the date the Declaration of Independence was written, for example) to deeper analysis (understanding which principles of the Declaration of Independence were incorporated into the new government, for example).

Analysis will have greater breadth and depth at the higher grades, but even young students can be encouraged to consider the "why" behind historical events. For example, elementary-aged students might be asked to make connections to their lives with discussion starters such as "How would you feel if you were in the same position as [historical actor]? What would you have done?"

Professional Standards

State standards will often guide much of the curriculum and instruction in the classroom. The National Council for the Social Studies (NCSS) also publishes a framework for social studies education, the *College, Career, and Civic Life Framework for Social Studies Standards*, colloquially known as the **C3 Standards**. These standards outline components of rigorous social studies instruction aligned with related English language and literacy standards reflected in the Common Core State Standards (CCSS).

The C3 framework outlines key skills to be developed across grade levels in the domains of civics, economics, geography, and history. These standards focus on core skills, but they are not necessarily content focused. These skills were developed to inform the creation of new state social studies standards rather than to replace them. They can, however, still prove useful to teachers of various social studies disciplines in planning rigorous and appropriate activities aligned with specific state standards.

Teachers should also consider the professional standards established by the **American Historical Association** in terms of teaching history. This organization advocates for an accurate, rigorous, and honest presentation of the past.

Technology

When teaching history, educators can—and should—leverage the power of technology as appropriate. Technology provides students with a broader perspective and can scaffold learning in myriad ways. Digital textbooks or other educational technology products may offer texts at various reading levels to make content more accessible to all. They may also offer definitions of key terms with the simple hovering of a mouse.

Technology brings historical artifacts, once tucked away in libraries and archives, into the hands of students. Sites like the Library of Congress and the National Archives offer primary-source materials related to a variety of events. Other sites offer multimedia elements, including video reenactments, that may help students better visualize what life was like in a given era.

PRACTICE QUESTION

2) Which of the following would be the MOST appropriate graphic organizer for a student who is organizing a series of significant events?

   A. KWL chart
   B. timelines
   C. Venn diagram
   D. semantic web

Historical Sources of Information and Perspectives

Primary and Secondary Sources

Teachers should help students determine the credibility of sources. For example, the internet provides a wealth of information, but not everything a student finds online is relevant or true. Students should understand that determining the credibility of online resources requires knowledge of the author and the author's reputation, whether the domain name is linked to a reputable organization, and whether other references are cited (peer-reviewed articles and other appropriate authoritative sources, for example).

The next step is learning to organize research to ensure it is relevant. Students should be exposed to different kinds of social science resources and learn how to interpret and understand various types of information. For example, if students are studying deforestation, they might gather **maps**, **datasets**, or **images** that show how many trees have been cut down over a certain amount of time. Such projects can be used in lessons to illustrate the value of specific resources and how to find them.

Teachers should also help students understand **information analysis:** students consider an issue and gather information to help them approach it. Lessons should address how students can find information, including appropriate source materials, **text resources**, and technology to use in the inquiry process.

Students should also learn the difference between primary and secondary resources, the advantages and disadvantages of each, and when it is appropriate to use them. For example, students should understand that **photographs** are considered a primary resource since they depict an original perspective on an event. Other important primary sources include

- **newspaper articles** that report on historical events immediately after their occurrence;
- **diary entries** of people who lived during a particular era or who experienced a significant historical event;
- **personal correspondence** between political leaders or everyday people;
- **oral histories**, either previously recorded or conducted in the present;
- **census data** that show the population of a given location during a time of interest;
- **tax lists** that allow for inferences about a community's employment rates and income;
- **physical archaeological artifacts** that provide information about a culture beyond or in addition to the written record.

The advantage of **primary sources** is that they represent the time period of study. They can give student historians important information about people and events of the past. However, like any source, they are products of the cultural and social norms of the time and are therefore subject to bias.

For example, articles, letters, diaries, and oral histories are heavily impacted by the perspective of the individual writer or speaker. Students should recognize that a letter written by the owner of an early American factory, for example, will likely reflect a different perspective than a letter written by a worker in that factory.

Primary sources like census data and tax lists are less impacted by subjectivity, but even official records may not be accurate. Censuses are not 100 percent accurate even today and were likely even less accurate hundreds of years ago. Even physical artifacts are not completely reliable as sources because the way they were used often has to be inferred. Researchers can conclude that small figurines found from excavations of ancient civilizations, for example, were used for worship or decorative purposes, but this is just an educated guess if there are no written records describing the explicit use of such objects.

Secondary sources are those composed with greater distance from the historical event, typically by modern historians. Common secondary sources include

- **encyclopedias** that give broad overviews of historical topics or actors;
- **biographical dictionaries** that provide information about the lives of historical actors;
- **periodical guides** that categorize and list historical articles by topic;
- **bibliographies** that list books or articles pertinent to a topic of interest;
- **books, articles, and websites** written by modern historians.

Some types of sources do not fit neatly into a primary or secondary source framework. For example, **almanacs**, which give detailed information about history or weather for a given year, may be either modern or historical. **Maps** may also be from a particular period or modern-day creations.

The key to helping students conduct historical research and use sources is to match the type of source with the purpose. When beginning historical research, students may consult encyclopedias or biographical dictionaries to gain background information on a topic and consider subtopics to explore further. Then, materials like periodical guides and bibliographies may be used to find other resources, such as books and articles written by experts on a given topic.

Overall, students need a variety of sources to understand the topic being discussed. Reliance on only one source, or type of source, should be discouraged, as it will likely lead to biased research. Students should consider the most appropriate type of resource to answer their research questions. If students want to know what childhood was like during the Great Depression, for example, they might combine diaries and oral histories of this era with relevant secondary sources like books, articles, and websites written by modern historians.

> **PRACTICE QUESTION**
>
> 3) After reading a letter written by a military leader, a student concludes that most people in that time and society supported military expansion. How can the teacher help the student recognize a possible problem with this conclusion?
>
>   A. encourage the student to identify the difference between primary and secondary sources
>
>   B. ask the student to consider the particular point of view from which the source was written
>
>   C. encourage the student to prioritize the use of secondary sources over primary sources
>
>   D. ask the student to consider whether this conclusion can also be confirmed through physical artifacts

INTERPRETING INFORMATION

After finding information, students should learn how to organize and **synthesize** it. Social science students must process and interact with information rather than just regurgitate it. Strong reading comprehension skills are essential. Furthermore, students should learn to closely examine data for repeating patterns and trends. Teachers help students apply new knowledge to gain new insights.

As part of the synthesis and analysis of historical information, students must recognize that any historical event will produce multiple interpretations. Students should be prompted to recognize that there is no single lens through which the past can be examined with total objectivity. Instead, they should be exposed to the major theories and interpretive frameworks that underscore the study of the past, while recognizing the benefits and limitations of each. Some of the more common approaches to the study of history follow.

Narrative history is one of the more common approaches to historical inquiry, especially when writing for a younger audience. As its central goal, narrative history tells the story of the past from beginning to end, chronicling the major events and figures involved. This type of history helps the reader follow events, although critics note that it may focus on only the most dominant voices and leave out others. It may also focus more on major events rather than people's everyday experiences.

Social history focuses more on lived experiences and the way individuals experienced the society in which they lived. Common topics in social history are the family, education, gender, and ethnicity. Social historians tend to take a broader view than narrative historians and may capture the voices of those in a society who were not involved in major events as political or military leaders. However, social history may also be narrowly focused. For example, studying family dynamics during the Han dynasty in China would give valuable insights into social dynamics but not important military and political events.

Cultural history may or may not be seen as a separate field from social history. It is primarily concerned with the specific elements of culture in a given civilization, such as art, religion, or legal or cultural frameworks that undergird the society. Many texts for young readers include elements of cultural history, which can help them understand a civilization. One limitation of some cultural histories is that they may focus more heavily on the dominant culture within a society, as that is the culture that tends to leave the most records.

There are also other, more specific, **thematic approaches** to history, such as military, economic, diplomatic, political, and even the newer field of environmental history. Some historians may focus on a particular region, such as Europe or North America. Others may use an interdisciplinary approach combining historical research with sociology, psychology, anthropology, economics, or other social science fields. These fields are frequently listed in academia under terms like *American Studies* or *Asian Studies*.

Approaches to recording history have changed with time. **Great man history**, which attributes progress to the work of key leaders, has largely been abandoned for more modern approaches, and new theories that impact historical inquiry abound. For example, **colonialism** and post-colonialism, which examine how much of the world's history is tied together with colonies of great empires that created subject peoples, are common themes in the history of certain regions, such as Latin America and Africa.

One approach to colonialism in historical study is termed **subaltern history**, or subaltern studies. This methodology seeks to uncover the historical experiences of the people in a subordinate position in the colonial enterprise.

These various historical approaches have numerous advocates and critics. Critics of any framework often call out the bias that a specific method produces. Bias comes not only through the historian's interpretation of events but also from what that historian chooses to include and exclude in a text.

Texts that discuss diplomatic history, for example, may feature global leaders, which help students recognize important historical figures and their contributions. However, this focus might neglect the "everyday" people who lived at that time. Conversely, a social history on marriage patterns in early-modern Spain may provide an in-depth analysis of young people's experiences but may exclude other, broader political or economic issues that were relevant at the time.

One notable bias applicable to any historical study is that those in positions of power or wealth tend to leave behind more evidence of their lives due to their prominent status, which causes more to be written about them during their lifetime. This bias is present in almost all studies. As with the example of marriage patterns in early-modern Spain, historians typically had far more access to the records of wealthy, literate Spaniards than their impoverished, illiterate compatriots, so the experiences of the wealthy and powerful tend to dominate the history.

Nonetheless, historians employ innovative methods to uncover the history of civilizations and people typically underrepresented in the historiography due to a lack of written records. Historians use tools from disciplines like anthropology, archaeology, and **ethnohistory**, an interdisciplinary subfield that focuses on Indigenous civilizations in the Americas.

Even within a more traditional historical framework, there are other approaches to bringing certain groups to the center of the historical conversation:

- Historians may focus on the intersection of gender and history, viewing the historical experience through the lens of how experiences differed between men and women.
- They may examine the way race and/or ethnicity intersect with the historical experience and how these identities have led people to experience events in different ways.
- Other historians focus on social class and its intersection with lived experiences.

As mentioned, historical inquiry may also focus on a specific **region** or take an **interregional** approach in examining the way certain areas have interacted in terms of trade, military actions, or cultural diffusion.

The study of US foreign policy is a good example of an approach that spans regions. In an American history class, for example, a teacher may use this topic to encourage students to learn US history and the history of other nations with which the United States has interacted.

Within a single region, historians may focus on the **local history** of a city, town, or neighborhood. Or, they may take a broader approach and focus on a state or nation. Others may focus on world or global history, though they usually divide their research by topic.

The multiplicity of historical fields and perspectives means teachers should expose students to different types of history, different historical theories, and history written for diverse audiences. They should encourage students to recognize not only what a certain historical framework *brings into* the narrative but also what it invariably *leaves out*.

Students should recognize that, as consumers of history, they must read texts for both their explicit and implicit meanings, recognizing biases and forming their own interpretations based on analysis from multiple perspectives. Teachers should consider developmental appropriateness and should not overemphasize historical theory before students can comprehend it.

However, even very young students can be prompted to recognize that people of varied genders, races, ethnicities, religions, and beliefs have existed throughout history, and that while we cannot learn about them all from a single text, we must strive to obtain as balanced a perspective as possible.

PRACTICE QUESTION

4) A student finds a biography of Alexander the Great written in the late nineteenth century that credits him with "furthering the progress of humanity." Which type of history BEST describes this text?

   A. subaltern history

   B. social history

   C. ethnohistory

   D. great man history

SOCIAL SCIENCE INQUIRY AND INTERDISCIPLINARY PERSPECTIVES

SOCIAL SCIENCE RESEARCH METHODS

Social science research takes many forms. Students may write papers, create presentations, compose artistic representations, or record videos; however, there are some basic steps upon which they should base their research to ensure it is sound.

1. **Formulating research questions.** Students should be encouraged to brainstorm topics of interest and then narrow them down to one specific, manageable topic. Then students should formulate a few specific research questions that can be answered via the project. Depending on the type and scope of social sciences research being conducted, some questions to guide topic selection and formulate research questions include:
   - Is the topic broad/narrow enough to compose a paper/presentation of ____length/duration?
   - Is there sufficient information from sources to answer these research questions?
   - Are the research questions open-ended enough to compose a paper or presentation of sufficient length or duration?
   - Is this topic of enough interest to keep me motivated in my work?

2. After formulating research questions, students should **select a research design or methodology**. This design will likely be informed by the social sciences discipline to some degree.
   - For example, administering surveys would be highly relevant and appropriate for certain sociological research questions but would likely not be appropriate for historical research.
   - Similarly, while consulting records from the Federal Reserve Bank might be a reasonable approach for a research project in economics, it would yield little useful data for a psychology project.

Social sciences research is described as being either quantitative, focused on describing mathematical relationships, or qualitative, focused on describing the nature of a phenomenon or event.

Most K–12 students will not use complex statistical procedures, a hallmark of most quantitative research. Still, they can and should be encouraged to represent data in multiple forms, including charts, graphs, and infographics as appropriate to the research focus.

3. **Data collection** in social sciences research is also dependent on the discipline, but certain best practices apply to virtually all subjects. Students should be encouraged to
    ▷ gain informed voluntary consent from all people who will be surveyed, interviewed, or observed;
    ▷ keep data organized and confidential;
    ▷ collect data in a systematic and regimented way;
    ▷ gather enough and the right kind of data to answer the research questions.

Students should consider that unexpected problems may occur during any research project and that they may have to be flexible and adaptable. Surveys often have very low response rates, interviewees may not have the type of information needed, and primary sources may fail to present enough data to answer the research questions. Students must be willing to adjust their research questions, research design, and data collection methods as the situation requires.

4. **Communicating results** clearly and effectively is the cornerstone of high-quality social sciences research. Students should present their data in a way that is both developmentally appropriate and subject-matter appropriate. Depending on age and discipline, this may include posters, oral reports, papers, or multimedia presentations.

If students are conducting historical research in particular, their data collection process may follow certain additional important steps:

1. **Gather relevant source material**. This may include consulting both print and digital primary and secondary sources, watching archived film or video, examining photographs, or listening to oral history interviews.
2. **Take notes from the source material**. Students should be encouraged to find a note-taking system that works best for them. This may include the use of note cards, digital tools, or traditional notebooks.
    ▷ As students take notes, they should be reminded of the difference between **paraphrasing**, or rewording content from the text in a way that maintains its central meaning, and **direct quotation**, or quoting the author's words directly.
    ▷ Keeping paraphrases and direct quotations separate during the note-taking process will aid students as they communicate their results.

- ▷ Teachers should encourage students to avoid overreliance on direct quotations, even if properly cited, as they make a text hard to read and limit the degree of analysis on the part of the student.
- ▷ Students should also be encouraged to keep their notes and source material well-organized so that they can easily access and use the information.
- ▷ Color-coding schemes, accordion files, and digital tools can all be helpful for this purpose.

3. Write the paper or **compose the paper or presentation**.
    - ▷ At this stage, students should use their research notes and a standard method of documentation such as Chicago Style (popular in history) or American Psychological Association (APA) Style (popular in other social sciences disciplines) to cite sources as appropriate.
    - ▷ There are several digital tools, such as RefWorks, Citation Machine, or Scribbr, that may make this process easier and more organized. Students should also revise and polish their paper or project before submission.

4. **Compose the bibliography or references page**.
    - ▷ Again, students may use both an online tool and/or a hard-copy style manual.

Social sciences research may also be part of curriculum integration whereby students complete a research project across multiple classes.

For example, students may use surveys to gather public opinion about a planned school bond initiative in their social studies class, create graphs and charts to communicate the results in their math class, and present their research in their speech or language arts class.

PRACTICE QUESTION

5) As part of a project on local history, students must create a multimedia presentation. Which step should they take first?
    - A. find source materials
    - B. create a bibliography or reference page
    - C. input information into a file management system
    - D. identify research questions

SOCIAL SCIENCE ANALYSIS

For students to understand history, they cannot simply view it as a series of facts. Students must develop an understanding of **historical analysis**, the interpretation of historical processes, documents, and events. The goal is for students to understand not only *what* happened but *how* and *why* it did.

Historical analysis requires evaluating sources and developing reasonable conclusions based on the evidence. Students need to address multiple perspectives so they can assess whether a source is credible. Teaching students to use primary and secondary sources is integral to their deeper understanding of the topic.

Students who successfully grasp historical analysis will be able to **analyze** the causes and effects of events by looking at both immediate and underlying causes. Immediate causes are what trigger the main event. For example, Japan's surrender in the Second World War was an immediate cause for the war's end. Underlying causes are more likely to be trends that existed long before the event in question. For instance, sectionalism was an underlying cause of the US Civil War.

Students must also learn to compare events from different times and regions and hypothesize how the past influences the present. These comparisons can be as simple as, for example, comparing and contrasting Greek inventions with Roman ones, or discussing the ways Egyptian papyrus influenced how people communicate today.

Students should receive explicit instruction in the analysis of historical information from a variety of sources. Some of these tasks will overlap with English/language arts skills, but the two subjects can inform and complement each other.

When reading a historical text or analyzing a historical resource, students must first identify the author's or creator's **purpose**. Is it to inform, as in a newspaper article or historical textbook? Is it to entertain, as in a magazine article or popular literature? Is it to argue for or against a position, as in an editorial or political cartoon? These types of questions can help students consider the background of a resource, which informs not only *what* it communicates but also *why* it communicates.

The **point of view**, or perspective, of the author or creator is also worth considering. Students should ask how that individual's perspective influences the source. For example, a photograph can be taken from multiple points of view, both literally and figuratively. A parent photographing a child has a different perspective than a journalist photographing a political demonstration. Because point of view is entwined with the content itself, students must recognize the "who" behind the source, which may require additional research.

When examining the source, students should be guided with **central questions** to aid in their understanding. Such questions can help them make **inferences**, or reasonable conclusions, based on the evidence in the text. These questions might include the following:

- What does this explain about people who____?
- What can be concluded about_____?
- What does the author see as the most important reason that_____?

Even the most factual interpretations of history are not free from opinions. Students should practice distinguishing between **facts and opinions** in historical texts and should recognize that one sentence may include both facts and opinions. Younger students can be instructed to look for clues that suggest an opinion is being offered (a shift to the first-person point of view, loaded language, qualifiers like *best* or *most*, for example). Older students can be prompted to identify more implicit opinions revealed by subtler shifts in word choice, mood, or tone.

Students should also try to glean meaning from the text and make necessary connections in order to make inferences and draw conclusions. Identifying specific parts of a text that support a given inference or conclusion is another important skill that students should practice.

Of course, not all texts or sources are created equally, and students should consider the information they are presented with. Just as they must use valid and reliable evidence and source material in their research, they must look for it in others' work.

As noted previously, part of **bias** in social sciences sources comes from what information is included and excluded, so students may benefit from considering the "voices" left out of a source versus those which are included. Certain underlying assumptions may also be part of an author's bias toward or against a subject. For example, individualist cultures, like the United States, tend to value autonomy and independence, which might be a common bias in a secondary source written by an American. Conversely, collectivist cultures, like many Asian cultures, may see certain acts of autonomy or independence as selfish or too inward-focused. Students must recognize that neither perspective is intrinsically right or wrong but rather serves as an important lens through which a text may have been conceived.

Research suggests that many students benefit from learning information that is presented in varied formats.

Graphic sources are extremely useful in the social sciences. **Charts**, **graphs**, and **diagrams** can show, for example, population growth or change, mean earnings, and political perspectives. Maps may show political boundaries, natural resources, geographic features, and weather patterns. Age-appropriate **political cartoons** are a relevant graphic resource for the study of the social sciences, as they typically provide a nuanced critique of government or society.

In training students to use graphic sources, teachers should first clarify key terms and tools, such as scale, compass rose, legend, units, and so on. Teachers can then help students evaluate from a macro- and micro-level perspective.

For a graph of crop production during the Dust Bowl in Kansas, for example, teachers might ask students to look at the trends in Kansas wheat production over the given years. Then students can consider more general information about the Dust Bowl, such as how it impacted American farmers and the American Midwest environment.

PRACTICE QUESTION

6) A teacher asks students to compare different songs and poems about the War of 1812. In small groups, they must explain how these sources help people understand significant historical events and others' perspectives on them. This assignment is an example of what?

   A. questioning
   B. chronology
   C. interpreting timelines
   D. historical analysis

INTERDISCIPLINARY PERSPECTIVES

As the C3 standards attest, there is an interrelationship between many social studies concepts, particularly those that are political, economic, and geographic.

Geography impacts the physical landscape and natural resource availability, which in turn impacts the local economy and the political structure. For example, an area with rich farmland may develop an economic system centered around grain production and trade. Thus, governmental policies are likely to encourage farming and trade activities.

The earliest sedentary agrarian human populations likely lived in a subsistence or **bartering economy**, whereby they farmed to meet their immediate needs, trading items of equal value when necessary. As civilizations became more centralized into a state with a single government entity, more advanced economies developed because more resources—both human and financial—could be invested into wide-scale projects, such as irrigation systems, roads, and markets.

As agricultural surplus grew, people began to specialize, and a merchant class emerged. Still, economic activities tended to benefit the already wealthy and powerful and do little to improve the social status of those farming the land. In some places, like Europe, a system of **feudalism emerged**, in which farmers were granted use of the land owned by the nobility in exchange for military or other service.

After the discovery of the New World in North America and South America in the fifteenth century, feudalism eventually gave way to **mercantilism**, a highly regulated system whereby wealth was funneled to European empires by maximizing exports and minimizing imports. During the heyday of mercantilism, from the sixteenth to the eighteenth centuries, raw materials were extracted from colonies, often through the labor of the enslaved, for the sole benefit of the mother country. Tight trade regulations and partnerships with a few select private companies established and enforced by European governments kept wealth flowing from the colonies to Europe. Military force was a hallmark of the mercantilist system, with governments building overseas empires through the conquest of Native populations.

Economic protectionism gradually began to shift into what is most commonly referred to as **capitalism**, or free enterprise. Unlike mercantilism, which emphasizes the channeling of wealth toward the government via regulation, capitalism emphasizes the channeling of wealth into the hands of private individuals without government intervention. The capitalist enterprise was furthered by a groundbreaking book published in 1776 titled *The Wealth of Nations*, written by Scottish economist and philosopher Adam Smith. The book argues that economic progress depends on

- people pursuing their own self-interest;
- the division of labor;
- freedom of trade without government regulation.

These principles became key components of modern capitalist systems. The role of many governments changed from a very "hands-on" economic approach to a "hands-off" approach, whereby "natural forces" like supply and demand were left to dictate markets.

Of course, even in a capitalist system, government is not completely inactive in the economy. For people to hold on to the resources they gain from participating in capitalism, governments must support and protect **property rights**, or the right to hold something to the exclusion of others.

National governments also control the supply of money and set interest rates. While the role of local government may be less pronounced in a capitalist economy, it is still present. States pass legislation and regulations permitting or prohibiting certain economic activities or discouraging them through oversight or high taxation. Even county or city governments have a hand in the economy by funding or preventing infrastructure development, like roads and ports, which are essential for certain economic activities. Further, restrictions like zoning or even property tax rates or cuts in a certain municipality may promote or discourage certain economic activities.

Most economies do not operate in isolation but rather on a global scale where things are far from equal. The **dependency theory**, developed in the 1960s, posited that the globe can be partitioned into the periphery, or the underdeveloped nations, and the core, or the wealthy "first world" nations. Wealth flows to the core from the periphery via the extraction of raw materials, use of cheap labor, and sale of marked-up manufactured goods. Dependency theory maintains that peripheral nations will continue in a state of chronic underdevelopment as long as they are exploited by the core nations.

Although dependency theory is not as popular now as it was in the 1960s and 1970s, **globalization**, or the reality of global interaction among all peoples, has made clear that economic activities do not happen in isolation and that many economic, governmental, and social realities are interconnected.

Refugees, or people fleeing one country for another to escape natural disaster, war, or violence, present both an economic opportunity and a problem. While they represent a new potential labor force to help drive the market economy, they may not be paid a living wage and may be subject to harsh working conditions in their new nation. Refugee populations also represent lost human capital in their home nations, which may further underdevelopment. In some cases, human migrations, both by refugees and people simply looking for a better life, may be viewed by a nation's existing population as a threat for scarce jobs or resources.

The movement of people from war and oppression markedly impacts global stability, as does the use and control of natural resources like fossil fuels, food, and water. Wars, coups, and governmental collapse are all possible consequences of fights over control of natural resources. Even in places rich in natural resources, those resources may be controlled by foreign governments or investors who extract them with little or no benefit to the local population.

Many areas have tried to better manage their natural resources and to use the resources in a manner that limits environmental degradation. Unfortunately, the less developed nations typically lack modern methods of natural resource extraction and management. They may also have fewer environmental regulations that encourage private companies from foreign nations to use environmentally sustainable methods. Such a reality contributes to global instability in myriad ways. Refugee populations may increase as a direct result of destroyed land or natural disaster. Governments of underdeveloped nations may also struggle to address such realities without the funds to invest in environmental sustainability.

Another global problem is **systemic oppression**, or the oppression of certain cultural, religious, ethnic, racial, gender, or other groups by a dominant culture. Such oppression is often deeply rooted within a society or civilization and may make it hard for the dominant group to recognize and address.

> **HELPFUL HINT**
>
> Identifying and addressing systemic oppression in the United States has become controversial in many state educational systems. Some people believe that to make society more equitable, systemic barriers must be identified and addressed. Others see such efforts as divisive or unnecessary. Educators should be aware of this and of the laws in their state that govern the way such topics are handled.

PRACTICE QUESTION

7) A teacher assigns students an excerpt from *The Wealth of Nations* and asks them to identify its central points. What economic system would most likely be the focus of the discussion?

   A. mercantilism

   B. feudalism

   C. capitalism

   D. bartering

Public Discourse and Democratic Values

Public Discourse

Civics education is an important component of social studies education. Central to partaking in the civic life of the nation is respectful and productive participation in **public discourse**. Students should be taught the steps to responsible citizenship through a productive response to issues of public concern.

Before any meaningful discourse can occur, the issue or issues at hand must be clarified. What may at first seem like one problem may actually be another.

For example, business owners in a strip mall may express concern about parents of students at a nearby middle school using the parking lot, making it hard for customers to find parking. Though this might be the *effect* of an issue, the real issue may be that the middle school lacks enough parking or an effective student pick-up or drop-off procedure.

Once finite issues or problems have been identified, the next step is to consider multiple viewpoints. The parents may see the parking lot as a public space and feel that using it for ten or fifteen minutes poses little disruption to the businesses. The school officials may feel that there is an adequate pick-up procedure that parents are simply not following. Or, the school may lack funding to expand its existing parking lot and pick-up facilities.

In engaging in public discourse, **democratic values** should be referenced as common ground whenever possible. One value might be freedom, which may be translated as the freedom to park wherever one wishes. However, another value might be private property, which suggests there should be limits to how a particular space can be used. Another, and likely shared, value of all involved is the safety and protection of children, which could help guide the discourse in a direction in which all parties are working toward a shared goal.

When considering such a matter, those involved must also anticipate any consequences resulting from a proposed course of action. Would changing the traffic flow to and from the school back up traffic on the street, causing even more problems for the strip mall merchants? Would allocating a third of the parking lot for parent use between the times of 3:45 p.m. and 4:00 p.m. on weekdays meet the school's needs with minimal disruption to the businesses?

As stakeholders present their perspectives and suggestions for a path forward, the goal should be **consensus**, or general agreement among the parties that although no solution is perfect, the solution presented is the best for all involved. It may not be possible to achieve consensus among all participants, depending on the scale of the issue and the number of people involved. Voting or some form of compromise may be useful tools in such cases.

In situations where citizens are to vote or make a reasonable and informed decision about a public issue in some other manner, they must follow a similar process by first identifying the nature of the issue in clear terms. For example, if people are deciding on a school bond issue, they must identify how much taxes would increase and what the bond money would be used for. The origins of the issue should also be addressed, if pertinent. Has the school been underfunded for years? Are buildings deteriorating? Has the number of students increased?

There will always be multiple perspectives on any issue, big or small. Some people may believe that tax rates are already too high or that the schools do not use funds appropriately. Others may have a personal reason for supporting the bond, such as a child who attends one of the schools to be funded. These various perspectives must be considered before any decision is made.

Multiple solutions should be considered and evaluated for their efficacy. Perhaps a large school bond is not needed if a building can be repurposed or renovated, or if there are other sources of funding. All possibilities should be considered systematically and not be immediately dismissed simply because they do not align with one's viewpoint.

Processing information from any type of public discourse, whether by speaking, writing, or some multimedia format, requires great care. Arguments must contain **logical validity**, the condition in which a true premise means a true conclusion can be drawn from it. For example:

- If the premise is that all human beings are multicellular organisms and Susan is a human, then she must be multicellular.

If the premise is false, then the conclusion cannot be true, even if it is correctly tied to the premise:

- If the premise is that all human beings are unicellular organisms and Susan is a human, we might conclude that Susan is unicellular, which is based on the premise.
  - Since the premise is false, the conclusion must also be false.

Arguments or claims should also be analyzed for factual accuracy. For example, in the school bond issue, if one argument is that "the school bond issue will improve student test scores," this must be supported with reasonable evidence. If the school bond is intended to fund a building project, then it is unlikely to directly impact test scores. Part of accuracy is including all the facts and not omitting those that might offer a reasonable **counterclaim**.

For example, if the school bond is the third such bond in the last ten years, then that fact can be debated and considered and should therefore not be **omitted** from a presentation to the public.

Emotions are a part of human decision-making and are often used to make appeals to an audience. In rhetoric, this is sometimes referred to as **pathos**. Pathos contrasts with an appeal to ethics, or **ethos**, and an appeal to logic, or **logos**. Perhaps someone advocating for the school bond issue shows a video with sad children standing outside a dilapidated building in the hopes of garnering sympathy for the cause. This would be a pathos appeal, which is far less sound than a logos, or logical, appeal.

Credibility of evidence is another important consideration in evaluating arguments.

> **HELPFUL HINT**
>
> A pathos appeal should not be considered to be of the same weight and validity as a logos appeal.

Some people, and thus some sources, are widely considered to be more credible than others. In assessing credibility, formal expertise from a profession or schooling might be part of the evaluation, as might familiarity with the issue or problem. Assessment of credibility may be subjective. In the school bond example, an expert on school bonds who lives in a different state may be considered credible by some for his expertise on the subject. Others may consider him to lack credibility because he is unfamiliar with the particular school district or the local population.

Otherwise solid arguments may also be hampered by **unstated assumptions**, or points that a writer or speaker believes are "givens" that do not require explicit discussion.

Oftentimes, unstated assumptions are implied cause-effect relationships. In the school board example, a speaker at a public forum might say, "The hallways at the school are narrow. Our kids will get hurt if we don't pass this bond issue." An unstated assumption is that narrow hallways lead to injury. The speaker didn't mention this connection because she thought the audience would or should make it on their own. Unstated assumptions can be very dangerous because they are omissions, and anything omitted from an argument may not be thoroughly considered or debated.

Arguments should also be evaluated for common logical fallacies, or reasoning errors.

Table 4.1. Logical Fallacies

Fallacy	Definition	Example
Hasty Generalization	a conclusion without enough evidence	We must pass the school bond immediately, because if we do not, student performance will suffer.
Ad Hominem	an argument based on an individual rather than a position	People opposed to the school bond are selfish and do not care about children.
Bandwagon	an argument based on popularity or appeal to others	Everyone in our neighborhood is supporting the school bond issue, so you should too.

continued on next page

Table 4.1. Logical Fallacies (continued)

Fallacy	Definition	Example
Red Herring	a technique of drawing attention away from the real issue	The school bond is only a minor issue; the real problem is the district superintendent's job performance.
Straw Man	an oversimplification of a counterclaim	Supporting the school bond issue comes down to common sense in that taxes must fund schools.

Beyond these common logical fallacies, speakers or writers may attempt to persuade others through complete distortions or exaggerations. ("The school bond will bankrupt our community.") Appeals to existing bias or prejudice may also be used. ("Expanding our schools may attract more people to our community, and we will lose our small-town feel.")

The key to identifying reasonable arguments with sound evidence is to separate the rhetoric, or how a point is conveyed, from the logic behind it. Some speakers and writers are very skilled at their craft and may rouse audiences or readers with persuasive rhetoric without logical points based on factual evidence.

PRACTICE QUESTION

8) A teacher asks students to identify an ad hominem argument in an early twentieth-century magazine article. Which sentence should students identify?

    A. People from all over the country and the world are aggrieved by the way farmers are being treated by their government.

    B. Those opposed to the new bill granting subsidies to farmers are clearly bad Americans with little sense of patriotic duty.

    C. The issue is really more than whether farmers have the help they need to feed the nation; the issue is whether they are appreciated.

    D. If the new farming assistance bill is not passed by the end of the year, many Americans will go hungry for lack of food production.

DEMOCRATIC VALUES, RIGHTS, AND RESPONSIBILITIES

In social studies classes, especially when studying government and civics, students learn about **politics** and the rights and responsibilities that accompany citizenship. Learning about government systems helps students understand their duties and rights as citizens. It also helps them become active, engaged, and informed citizens.

Teachers should develop these concepts by helping students deepen their understanding of **democracy**. Lessons should emphasize the choices and opportunities that allow US citizens and residents to improve both their country and their lives. To effectively teach these principles, teachers should model democracy in the classroom. For example, teachers can have students vote on class issues (like what to name a class pet) to show how democracy works.

Citizens must select people to fill positions of authority, like local and state representatives. To choose someone who best represents the interests of the people, citizens must be informed. Teachers should emphasize that voting occurs at the federal, state, and local levels and that it is the voter's responsibility to learn about electoral candidates.

Students should also understand the role of the US Constitution in the federal government. To help them understand how and why the Constitution was formed, lessons may address the separation of powers. Students should understand that the federal legislative, judicial, and executive branches all check each other's powers to maintain a balance and that similar processes occur at the state and local levels throughout the country. Examples include studying the roles and actions of political entities, departments, or administrators in the local community.

Teaching **citizenship** is another integral part of civics education. Students should learn how a person becomes a citizen and the attitudes and actions that reflect responsible citizenship:

- The Bill of Rights is a strong discussion point in explaining how US citizens are granted certain freedoms.
- Well-known national symbols like the flag, the Statue of Liberty, and the Liberty Bell are some examples that can be used as discussion points to teach students about US values.
- Exploring themes like responsibility, compassion, respect, and courage teaches students the value of participating in their communities to maintain a strong democracy and protect their civil rights.

Lessons can present students with situations that contrast responsible citizenship with poor citizenship, conflict resolution, and the importance of democratic participation. Holidays like Presidents' Day, Veterans Day, and Independence Day are a few examples of traditions students can study to explore themes like governance, civil liberties, and military and civil service.

PRACTICE QUESTION

9) Which of the following activities would be the BEST way for a teacher to address the theme of courage in a civics class?
    A. taking a class trip to help clean up the local park
    B. discussing the activism of Dr. Martin Luther King Jr.
    C. establishing a classroom lost-and-found area
    D. holding a mock trial to explain the concept of jury duty

Answer Key

1) **B.** Historiography is the way history is recorded, which varies with the times. This activity will help students compare and contrast the historiography of different time periods.

2) **B.** Timelines allow students to sequence events, which helps them organize their thoughts.

3) **B.** Students should consider that primary sources, like letters and diaries, will be affected by the author's personal bias.

4) **D.** Great man history is rooted in the belief that certain key individuals are responsible for most historical achievements.

5) **D.** Students should first create specific research questions to help them focus their research and conduct it effectively.

6) **D.** This assignment requires students to understand the events of the War of 1812, analyze primary resources, and develop their own conclusions.

7) **C.** Adam Smith's book promotes a free enterprise, or capitalist, system based on the division of labor and free trade.

8) **B.** Ad hominem arguments focus on a person or group of people instead of the position they are arguing for or against.

9) **B.** Dr. Martin Luther King Jr. fought for the civil rights of people of color even though it was dangerous to do so. His story is a clear example of courageously doing the right thing, even when it might be unpopular or dangerous.

Practice Test 1

1

In the nineteenth century, Britain occupied parts of Somalia, Kenya, and Egypt, and negotiated boundaries and treaties with other colonial powers and local governments. Which of the following best explains why the British prioritized organizing this area?

A. Britain wished to safeguard shipping routes through the Red Sea and into the Indian Ocean.

B. Britain wished to control the valuable and popular routes in the Red Sea to Mecca and Medina.

C. Britain was concerned about instability in Somalia.

D. Britain was unable to consolidate control further inland into Africa.

2

How did the colonies in New England differ from southern ones like Virginia, the Carolinas, and Georgia?

A. Farms tended to be larger in the southern colonies and produce cash crops; in the north, smaller family farms and early urbanization were more widespread.

B. Northern farms produced cash crops like tobacco and cotton, using the labor of enslaved people.

C. The southern colonies were wealthier than the northern colonies, with a more educated population.

D. There were no major differences between the northern and southern colonies before independence.

3

Who were the first Texans to make contact with Europeans?

A. the Apache
B. the Karankawa
C. the Caddo
D. the Comanche

4

A kindergarten social studies teacher wants to help students understand chronology. Which activity is MOST appropriate?

A. having students put picture cards in a sequential order
B. asking students what they do each afternoon after school
C. teaching students major figures in the founding of the United States
D. encouraging students to trace a holiday back to the event it commemorates

5

How did the views of the Federalists and the Anti-Federalists differ during the Constitutional Convention?

A. The views of the Federalists and Anti-Federalists did not significantly differ at the Constitutional Convention.
B. The Anti-Federalists did not believe in a Constitution at all, while the Federalists insisted on including the Bill of Rights.
C. The Anti-Federalists favored a stronger Constitution and federal government, while Federalists were concerned that states would risk losing their autonomy.
D. The Federalists favored a stronger Constitution and federal government, while Anti-Federalists were concerned that states would risk losing their autonomy.

6

Many scholars argue that modern banking began in Venice in the fifteenth century. Which of the following strengthens this argument?

A. Venice was the first major colonial power and developed mercantilism.
B. Venice was a center of intellectual and cultural development.
C. Venice was a commercial center, ideally situated to profit from goods imported on the Silk Road and from Africa.
D. Venice was not badly affected by the plague.

7

A third-grade teacher wants to help students brainstorm different types of natural resources. Which resource would be MOST appropriate?

A. KWL chart

B. Venn diagram

C. line graph

D. semantic web

8

Which of the following best explains why the Spanish were threatened by French exploration southwest into Texas?

A. France had allied with the Karankawa in order to drive the Spanish from Texas.

B. French exploration southwest from the Great Lakes and Quebec into the Mississippi region threatened Spain's dominance of the North American continent.

C. French exploration southwest from the Great Lakes and Quebec toward Texas was a potential threat to the Spanish empire in the Americas.

D. France showed interest in taking control over Texas' considerable gold and silver resources.

9

Which of the following best describes the conditions faced by Latinos and Latinas who had remained in western territories won by the US in the Mexican-American War?

A. They were treated with derision; many lost land and wealth they had held under Mexico and did not enjoy the same rights under the law as citizens, even though they had been promised American citizenship in the Treaty of Guadalupe Hidalgo.

B. While many had lost land and wealth they had held under Mexico, they were entitled to and received restitution from the government of the United States.

C. They were treated equally in social and political situations under the United States.

D. Most Latinos and Latinas left the western territories for Mexico following the Mexican-American War due to discriminatory conditions they faced under the US government.

10

Which of the following statements best describes the Qur'an?

A. It contains the legal teachings of Islam.

B. It contains the legal teachings of Judaism.

C. It is believed to have been transmitted from Allah and is the holy book of Islam.

D. It was written by Muhammad and is the holy book of Islam.

11

The early Democratic Party (the Democratic-Republicans) was mainly concerned with which of the following?

A. agrarian issues, small landowners, and maintaining a weaker federal government

B. fiscal policy in support of urban areas and big businesses

C. limitations on federal oversight of business and banks

D. maintaining a strong federal government

12

Why was early resistance disorganized in the Texas Revolution?

A. Even though Sam Houston was chosen to lead an army, James Bowie and James Fannin were already leading uprisings, making it difficult to consolidate military power against Mexico.

B. Texans were reluctant to unite under Sam Houston's leadership because he had been governor of Tennessee.

C. Infighting between Sam Houston and Stephen F. Austin threatened unity among Texas' leaders.

D. Sam Houston and David Crockett, both formerly of Tennessee, were unable to win the loyalty of people born in Texas who were needed to serve in a military capacity.

13

Despite the period of relative stability enjoyed by Europe during the High Middle Ages, the Black Death resulted in which of the following outcomes?

A. European powers were made vulnerable to attacks by the Magyars, who toppled the disorganized Holy Roman Empire.

B. Instability in Europe led to military conflict, division within the Catholic Church, and weakening of the Holy Roman Empire.

C. The Mongols were able to expand their empire into Eastern Europe.

D. Islamic powers were able to completely conquer the Iberian Peninsula as a result of instability there.

14

A teacher wants to assign a social studies exercise that allows students to devise and implement solutions to a real-world problem. What is the BEST description of this type of activity?

A. direct instruction

B. collaborative learning

C. project-based learning

D. scaffolding

15

What did the Compromise of 1850 accomplish?

A. It admitted California and Maine as free states and strengthened the Fugitive Slave Act.

B. It admitted California as a free state, Utah and New Mexico with slavery to be decided by popular sovereignty, and strengthened the Fugitive Slave Act.

C. It strengthened the Fugitive Slave Act and admitted California, Utah, and New Mexico as free states.

D. It admitted California, Utah, and New Mexico as states with slavery to be decided by popular sovereignty, and strengthened the Fugitive Slave Act.

16

At the Convention of 1833, Texans drew up a resolution demanding what?

A. an end to slavery in Texas

B. separation from Coahuila

C. more trade with the Apache and Comanche

D. to join the United States

17

What was a consequence of the Kansas-Nebraska Act?

A. the Fugitive Slave Act

B. the Compromise of 1850

C. "Bleeding Kansas"

D. the Missouri Compromise

18

What happened during the Peloponnesian War?

A. Persia defeated the Roman Empire in Anatolia.

B. Rome defeated Carthage for the second time.

C. Greece fought against Persia and the Ionian Greeks.

D. The dominant Hellenic powers, Athens and Sparta, went to war with each other.

19

What did the Missouri Compromise accomplish?

A. It admitted Missouri as a free state.

B. It admitted California as a free state.

C. It allowed slavery in New Mexico and Utah to be decided by popular sovereignty.

D. It banned slavery north of the thirty-sixth parallel, so that new states formed in northern territories would be free.

20

An early-elementary teacher wants to design an activity to encourage students to develop spatial thinking skills. Which activity should he choose?

A. writing and editing a class newspaper

B. creating a map of the school building

C. developing a list of rules to place in a common area

D. comparing past and present building construction

21

How did the Lincoln-Douglas debates impact the nation before the 1860 presidential election?

A. They reflected the national mood: the country was deeply divided over the question of slavery and whether states had the right to determine its legality.

B. They enabled Douglas win the presidential election of 1860 on a platform of states' rights.

C. They reinvigorated the debate over slavery, which had been overshadowed by debate over states' rights.

D. They reinvigorated the debate over states' rights, which had been overshadowed by debate over slavery.

22

How might a teacher BEST integrate technology into the classroom to help students understand an economics concept?

A. using an online interactive supply-and-demand chart that updates in real time to illustrate the relationship between the two

B. using a clicker to help students count and keep track of the number of different food and beverage options available in the school cafeteria

C. encouraging students to go online to research the prices of various computer models and write down their findings

D. having students use collaboration software to communicate with students in another country using skills they have gained in another language

23

Which of the following explains Governor James Ferguson's popularity?

A. his promises to subsidize cotton farmers

B. his support for Texas financial interests thanks to his roots in banking

C. his support for the rural poor and improvements in infrastructure and education

D. his vows to abolish the Texas Railroad Commission

24

The Qin dynasty was able to consolidate its power in China due to which of the following?

A. The Qin enforced Confucianism throughout China as a means to consolidate its power.

B. The Qin developed a common written language, allowing them to unite the disparate Chinese-speaking groups of people throughout China.

C. Emerging dominant following the Warring States period, the Qin developed standardized weights and measures and a unified bureaucracy.

D. The Qin dynasty established a democracy where everyone was unified and equal.

25

During periods of high tension between the United States and the Soviet Union in the 1950s, how was the US affected?

A. Fear of communism was pervasive; during the McCarthy era, accusations were made against public figures.

B. Fearing Soviet communism, the United States supported Maoism in China as a counterweight to Leninism.

C. During the McCarthy hearings, several members of Congress were found to be communist and were removed from office.

D. During the McCarthy hearings, several members of Congress were found to be Soviet spies and were removed from office.

26

Which of the following best explains the decline of the cattle drive?

A. Violence in northern Texas from Great Plains tribes prevented ranchers from driving cattle north to Kansas for transport on railroads to population centers in the east.

B. The development of north-south railroads in Texas made it unnecessary to drive cattle north to meet intercontinental railroad lines.

C. Ranching declined in Texas as settlement increased in Montana and Wyoming, where developments like the Matador Ranch proved the practice was more profitable.

D. Laborers left jobs as cowboys for work in the growing urban areas of Dallas and Houston.

27

What of the following best describes one result of the Iranian hostage crisis?

A. It resulted in the establishment of an anti-American theocracy in Iran.

B. It contributed to the election of Ronald Reagan to the presidency, which led to the escalation of weapons production and the arms race.

C. It resulted in regional instability and forced the Soviet invasion of Afghanistan.

D. It contributed to the election of Jimmy Carter to the presidency, which led to a period of détente with the Soviet Union.

28

Which of the following best describes the Russian strategy of empire-building?

A. Russia focused on colonizing overseas, strengthening its navy to build a transoceanic empire.

B. Russia focused on overland expansion, moving eastward into northern Asia across Siberia and westward into Eastern Europe.

C. Russia remained isolated and avoided expansion, focusing on industrialization instead.

D. Russia lacked the resources to build an empire and struggled to maintain its agrarian-based society.

29

Which of the following were included in Johnson's vision of a Great Society?

A. programs to stabilize the economy and promote civil rights, such as Social Security

B. programs as part of the War on Poverty to support the disadvantaged, like Medicare, Head Start, and the Department of Housing and Urban Development

C. programs to strengthen society in the face of communism, like the CIA and the Department of Homeland Security

D. a plan to end the war in Vietnam

30

Which of the following describes one reason the Muslim Arabs were able to take over Byzantine- and Persian-controlled areas?

A. The Greek Orthodox Byzantines and Zoroastrian Persians preferred Arab-Muslim rule to more oppressive power structures.

B. Arabic-speaking people in the region were more responsive toward Arabic-speaking rulers.

C. Muslims already living in the Byzantine and Persian empires welcomed Islamic rule.

D. A and B only

31

What were the goals of Cesar Chavez and the United Farm Workers?

A. to support Mexicans who wanted to join the Bracero program and become guest workers in the United States

B. to support Mexican-American agricultural workers in California and the Southwest and provide a foundation for later advocacy groups supporting the rights of Hispanic Americans

C. to work on behalf of Texas farmers to coordinate agreements with agricultural workers from Mexico

D. to overthrow a farm labor system and treat farmers as human beings

32

In the early twenty-first century, how has Texas' population changed?

A. Hispanic and African American populations are growing.

B. Hispanic and African American populations are shrinking.

C. More people are moving to rural areas.

D. More people are leaving Texas than ever before.

33

Why did the Silk Road eventually fall out of use?

A. The length of time it took for caravans to reach Europe from Asia interrupted trade within Europe, and demand for Asian goods there declined as a result.

B. Continuing attacks on caravans along the Silk Road eventually made it too dangerous to use and not worth the potential profit.

C. Thanks to new technology developed in the Umayyad Empire, better and safer roads were being used for transcontinental trade.

D. Sea travel was faster and more practical; improvements in navigation and ship construction had made it a more feasible alternative.

34

In which of the following international conflicts of the 1990s did the United States play a major role in peacemaking?

I. the war in Bosnia

II. the Rwandan Civil War

III. the conflict in Northern Ireland

A. I only

B. I and II

C. I and III

D. I, II, and III

35

How should a teacher express to students that data from physical artifacts from a civilization may be limited or unreliable?

A. Inferences must sometimes be made about how the artifact was used.

B. Guesses must sometimes be made about where the artifact was first discovered.

C. Determinations must sometimes be made about what civilization the artifact represents.

D. Analysis must sometimes be undertaken to date the artifact within a certain time period.

36

How did the protectorates established after WWI in the Middle East effect the Middle East in the twentieth and twenty-first centuries?

A. The Middle East has not been greatly affected.

B. Illegitimate national borders and rulers have led to instability in the region.

C. Improved governance, thanks to the protectorates, improved stability following the decline of the Ottoman Empire in the region.

D. European investment in strategic resources supported long-term political stability in the Middle East.

37

What led to the US invasion and occupation of Iraq in 2003?

A. The US believed (incorrectly) that Saddam Hussein held weapons of mass destruction and was linked to al Qaeda, which had recently attacked the US.

B. The US wanted to capture Osama bin Laden, who was under the protection of Saddam Hussein.

C. It was proven that Iraq provided al Qaeda with the weapons it used to attack the United States on 9/11.

D. Iraq attacked the United States on September 11, 2001.

38

Which of the following best describes the consequences of the Opium Wars?

A. British occupation of China

B. Chinese victory over Britain

C. unequal trade treaties favoring China

D. unequal trade treaties favoring Britain

39

What was one reason for the election of Andrew Jackson?

A. Jackson was able to find a solution to the first Nullification Crisis.

B. Allowing White men who did not own property to vote was a boon to Jackson, who was popular with the "common man."

C. Jackson's popularity with landowners in Northern states guaranteed him the funds he needed to win the presidency.

D. Jackson and his vice president, John C. Calhoun, were a strong and popular team when running for election.

40

The Babylonians are known for having developed an early form of

A. irrigation, increasing agricultural production in the fertile areas near the Tigris and Euphrates Rivers.

B. Cuneiform, the first known example of writing in which characters were connected to form words.

C. rule of law: the Code of Hammurabi.

D. iron weaponry and chariots, enabling them to control large areas of land.

41

Which of the following is NOT a reason that nineteenth century workers organized labor unions?

A. they were not paid fairly for their work

B. their shifts were frequently twelve to fourteen hours a day

C. to overthrow capitalists like Carnegie and Rockefeller

D. dangerous work conditions

42

A teacher invites a historian from a local university to speak to the class. A student asks, "How has history changed over your career?" What type of discussion is likely to follow this question?

A. one centered around chronology

B. one centered on cause-and-effect relationships

C. one focused on historiography

D. one focused on narrative history

43

By signing the Atlantic Charter, the United States and Great Britain

A. agreed to divide the world into democratic capitalist and communist regions.

B. decided to jointly occupy Europe indefinitely.

C. established the Atlantic Ocean as a neutral area.

D. agreed on a postwar world characterized by free trade and self-determination.

44

What was the driving force behind Spanish exploration and settlement of Texas?

A. to convert native Texans to Christianity

B. to capture land to raise cattle, a profitable good to satisfy demand for beef in Europe

C. to create a buffer zone to prevent French incursions into Mexico

D. to pursue rumors of gold farther inland in Texas

45

Which of the following Cold War events is an example of the US foreign policy of containment, in the spirit of the Truman Doctrine, put into effect?

A. the Cuban Missile Crisis

B. the Korean War

C. glasnost and perestroika

D. the Non-Aligned Movement

46

Which of the following describes the political leader Henry B. Gonzalez?

A. He was the first Hispanic governor of Texas.

B. He fought to overturn Sweatt v. Painter.

C. He filibustered state efforts to circumvent federal civil rights legislation.

D. He played an important role in the Watergate hearings, representing Texas nationally.

47

Which of the following is a hallmark of conservative ideology?

A. open borders to facilitate international trade

B. low taxes

C. labor rights

D. a small, efficient military

48

Following the collapse of the Western Roman Empire and the subsequent, disorganized "Dark Ages" in Europe,

- A. The Catholic Church based in Rome lost power in Western Europe to the rising Greek Orthodox Church based in Constantinople.
- B. The Byzantine Empire was able to conquer unorganized European land in what is today Germany.
- C. Charlemagne united parts of Western and Central Europe—what would become the Holy Roman Empire—leading to a period of stability.
- D. Charlemagne united parts of Western and Central Europe (including what would become France) under his rule, leading to a period of stability.

49

What was a consequence of Operation Desert Storm, or the Gulf War of 1991?

- A. the occupation of Iraq by the United States
- B. the occupation of Kuwait by Iraq
- C. the de facto establishment of the United States as the world's sole superpower in the wake of the fall of the Soviet Union
- D. improved cooperation in the United Nations between the United States and the former Soviet Union, now represented by the Russian Federation

50

A social studies teacher wants to help students find primary-source materials on the topic of Manifest Destiny. Which resource should he recommend?

- A. encyclopedia articles
- B. peer-reviewed journal articles
- C. Wikipedia
- D. the National Archives website

51

Which of the following describes an important tenet of Judaism?

- A. There is only one God and Muhammad is God's Prophet.
- B. A harmonious society is the ideal society.
- C. The moral codes provided by God in the Ten Commandments apply to all, even slaves.
- D. The son of God is both human and divine.

52

What advantage did the colonists have in the American Revolution?

A. vast financial wealth

B. superior weaponry

C. strong leadership and knowledge of the terrain

D. a professional military and access to mercenaries

53

Which of the following best describes the Caste system in India?

A. It is a defined, unchangeable social and religious hierarchy that is determined by birth.

B. It is a changeable social hierarchy.

C. It is a hierarchy determined by skills and education wherein one's position can be changed.

D. It is a defined, unchangeable social hierarchy, determined by birth.

54

Which of the following best describes filibuster settlers?

A. They were settlers from Mexico who sought to prevent Anglo settlement in Texas.

B. They legally came from the United States in search of land and economic opportunity.

C. They were Anglos who illegally immigrated to Texas seeking land and economic opportunity.

D. They were invited by Galvez and Bouligny to settle in Texas.

55

Why was the Mayflower Compact an important contribution to the foundation of American government?

A. It provided for equal treatment of all Christians under the law.

B. It was the first treaty between European settlers (the Pilgrims) and Native Americans.

C. It laid out terms for government with the consent of the governed.

D. It allowed people of all faiths to practice their religions freely under the law.

56

How did the Neolithic Era mark a major development in human evolution?

A. the development of agriculture and beginning of settled societies

B. the early use of the wheel

C. the use of bronze to develop basic tools

D. early medical treatment

57

Which of the following would a high school teacher use as an example of historical continuity?

A. victory gardens
B. the assembly line
C. the Treaty of Versailles
D. the Declaration of Independence

58

What was the purpose of The New Deal?

A. to provide immediate economic relief to those suffering from the Great Depression
B. to stimulate short-term economic and social recovery for US society through various targeted programs
C. to implement temporary reforms in banking and finance
D. to re-energize the public

59

How did the Republic of Texas raise income?

A. printing money
B. selling the rights to Galveston
C. attracting settlers with land and land scrip
D. investing in infrastructure

60

Which of the following best describes the motivation for Protestant reformers?

A. Protestants, including Martin Luther, originally sought to develop a new form of Christianity separate from the Catholic Church.
B. Protestants like Martin Luther originally sought reform and were unhappy with corruption and the teachings of the Catholic Church, including Papal indulgences.
C. Protestants were initially influenced by European political leaders, who used them to limit the power of the church.
D. Protestants, including Martin Luther, originally sought to topple the Catholic Church, believing it had become too corrupt.

61

Following the Civil War, the United States ratified the Thirteenth, Fourteenth and Fifteenth Amendments to the Constitution. What did these amendments guarantee?

A. an end to slavery, equal rights for all Americans, and voting rights for all Americans, respectively

B. an end to slavery, equal rights for all Americans, and voting rights for all African Americans, respectively

C. an end to slavery, equal rights for all American men, and voting rights for all African American men, respectively

D. an end to slavery, equal rights for Americans, and voting rights for African American men, respectively

62

Which of the following BEST describes the Treaty of Westphalia?

A. It marked the end of the Seven Years' War.

B. It put an end to nationalism in Europe and promoted unity.

C. It strengthened the power of religious leaders like the pope.

D. It remains the model for international politics around the world.

63

What was the ultimate result of the Cuban Missile Crisis?

A. the installation of the Castro regime

B. the fall of the Castro regime

C. a new opening of dialogue between the United States and the Soviet Union

D. the end of a period of détente between the United States and the Soviet Union.

64

How was Europe affected by the Civil War in the United States?

A. European powers were inspired to make slavery illegal following the American Civil War.

B. Industrialized European powers that relied on Southern cotton were encouraged not to trade with the Confederacy in order to prevent support for slavery, which had already been abolished in Europe and most European empires.

C. Industrializing European powers relied on Southern cotton and traded with the Confederacy, supplying them with needed income during the Civil War.

D. European countries lost significant access to food and supplies.

65

What did the Civil Rights Act of 1964 accomplish?

A. It struck down restrictions on voting rights for African Americans.

B. It guaranteed equal rights for all Americans, regardless of their race, gender, religion, or sexual orientation.

C. It ended segregation.

D. It guaranteed equal access to public and private education.

66

Which of the following best explains the economic impact on Germany following the First World War?

A. Overspeculation on German farmland caused the market to crash.

B. Wartime reparations mandated by the Treaty of Versailles and the worldwide Great Depression caused inflation to skyrocket, plunging the German economy into crisis.

C. Germans were forced to pay extra taxes to cover reparations; due to high prices, many could not afford to do so.

D. The Reichsmark was removed from circulation and replaced with the dollar as a means of punishment, forcing many Germans into poverty.

67

In 1861, the Secession Convention wrote a new constitution. What was one of its stipulations?

A. special protection for minorities of Czech and German descent

B. the legality of slavery

C. special protection for Tejanos under the Confederacy

D. Texan independence

68

The Boer War is an example of which of the following?

A. British imperialism in Africa

B. Dutch imperialism in the East Indies

C. South African repression of minority groups under Apartheid

D. Dutch imperialism in Africa

69

In the Emancipation Proclamation, President Lincoln declared an end to slavery

A. in Kentucky and Missouri.

B. in the Union only.

C. in slave states that had not seceded from the Union.

D. in the rebel states.

70

Enslaved African people were originally brought to the Americas as part of the triangular trade to do what?

A. work in factories and on assembly lines

B. own sugar plantations

C. work in Africans' homes

D. work in agriculture, mining, and domestic service

71

A teacher wants to include a question on a history unit test that requires students to analyze. Which question should she use?

A. When was the United Nations founded?

B. What nations comprised the Axis powers?

C. How did some colonists benefit by staying loyal to Great Britain?

D. How many years passed between the end of WWI and the beginning of WWII?

72

Which of the following is true about the Neolithic Era?

A. Homo sapiens was the only species of human in existence.

B. multiple species of human existed.

C. Homo sapiens likely eliminated all competition for resources.

D. humans had not yet evolved.

73

During FDR's terms in office, which of the following was created?

A. Medicare

B. Social Security

C. the Federal Reserve

D. welfare

74

How were Texas' current borders finalized?

A. Texas claimed land won by the US in the Mexican-American War.

B. Texas retained the same borders it had been assigned when it was part of Mexico.

C. Texas accepted its present-day borders as part of the Compromise of 1850.

D. Texas' borders were drawn following the Civil War and the dissolution of the Confederacy.

75

Which of the following BEST describes the Mediterranean region during the Pax Romana?

A. It was a period of anxiety and civil unrest under Roman rule.

B. It was the center of farming activity.

C. It was a time of stability under Augustus Caesar.

D. It was a time of artistic advancement.

76

Women did not receive full suffrage in the United States until which of the following?

A. The Seneca Falls Convention was held.

B. The Nineteenth Amendment was ratified.

C. The Equal Rights Amendment was ratified.

D. The Voting Rights Act of 1965 was passed.

77

Which of the following best describes the Constitution of 1868?

A. It was written by Democrats who wanted to undo the changes made by Republicans, many of whom came from outside Texas, to Texan law.

B. It decentralized government, weakening the state legislature.

C. It is still Texas' constitution today.

D. It was written by Republicans during Reconstruction, strengthening state government.

78

What was the Meiji Restoration?

A. a Japanese attempt to restore and reinvigorate the country and its culture as it had been before Western incursions into the country

B. a period of modernization and westernization in Japan

C. the early stage of Japanese imperialism in Asia when it invaded Korea

D. a cultural movement in Japan to restore Shintoism and traditional poetry

79

Which of the following contributed to the destruction of Native American populations in North America?

A. intentional transfer of smallpox from Europeans to Native Americans

B. unintentional transfer of smallpox from Europeans to Native Americans

C. peace agreements over land and resources between Europeans and Native Americans

D. geographical isolationism by colonists

80

In the nineteenth century, one of Texas' major products was cotton. What was the impact of the cotton industry in Texas on African Americans following the Civil War?

A. Many African Americans began their own cotton plantations in Central Texas, thanks to the support provided by the Freedmen's Bureau.

B. Enslaved African Americans who had worked on Texas plantations were granted special protection under the Constitution of 1876 and given parcels of land to farm.

C. Formerly enslaved African Americans were expelled from Central Texas to prevent them from becoming successful cotton farmers.

D. Many formerly enslaved African Americans became sharecroppers—often on the same land where they had been enslaved—remaining trapped in an exploitative system.

81

Which of the following helped lead to the Sino-Soviet split?

A. the Chinese alliance with the United States

B. the Soviet alliance with the United States

C. the absence of the People's Republic of China from the United Nations

D. division between the communist philosophies of Maoist China and the Marxist-Leninist USSR

82

Which is the BEST example of a formative assessment technique in a social studies classroom?

A. unit test

B. multimedia presentation

C. term paper

D. exit ticket

83

State Attorney General and Governor Jim Hogg was popular due to which of the following actions?

A. He introduced legislation in Congress creating the Interstate Commerce Commission.

B. He prosecuted railroads that wanted to limit or halt service to small, isolated towns.

C. He empowered insurance companies to do business in the state.

D. He advocated for equal rights for Black Texans.

84

Which of the following statements BEST describes the cause of the Spanish-American War?

A. The United States was eager to control territories in Africa and New Zealand run by Spain.

B. It was triggered in part by public support generated by propaganda and yellow journalism.

C. It served as a precursor to the Roosevelt Corollary which led to the Monroe Doctrine.

D. Cuba held economic power over the United States.

85

Why were the Hittites able to expand from Anatolia?

A. They had superior seafaring technology, which allowed expansion into the Mediterranean.

B. Their superior military technology included chariots and weaponry.

C. They had advanced technology imported from Greece.

D. They developed bronze metallurgy.

86

Which of the following best describes the changing relationships between Anglos and Tejanos in the Republic of Texas?

A. Anglos and Tejanos were able to work together as equals in the Republic of Texas, since they enjoyed equal rights under the law.

B. Tejanos were forced out of Texas to Mexico by Anglo-American immigrants.

C. Tejanos maintained strong economic ties to Mexico, while Anglos had stronger trading links with the United States; the two groups did not interact economically in Texas.

D. Even though Tejano men were Texas citizens, increasing numbers of Anglo-American immigrants saw them as Mexican agents and they lived as second-class citizens, increasing ethnic tensions in Texas.

87

What was the relevance of the Gulf of Tonkin Resolution?

A. It gave Congress the power to declare war against the North Vietnamese forces.

B. It authorized the president to take military action against North Vietnamese forces.

C. It authorized the military to take action against North Vietnamese forces.

D. It authorized the president to take military action against South Vietnamese forces.

88

Which of the following best describes the Hundred Years' War?

A. It is an example of European unity against an outside, non-European invading force.

B. It showed the technological dominance of powers aligned with the Catholic Church, whose resources were massive.

C. It indicated a shift in European politics from allegiance to one's ethnicity or nation to allegiance to the empire.

D. It described ongoing ethnic conflict in Europe.

89

What is a topic addressed by the C3 standards?

A. sociology

B. civics

C. psychology

D. literature

90

What was a major consequence of the Civil War?

A. the rise of the Federalist Party

B. the destruction of the South's economy and the growth of the North's economy

C. the emergence of the Republican Party

D. the growth of the South's economy and the destruction of the North's economy

91

Which of the following was a consequence of nationalism in nineteenth-century Europe?

A. Italian unification

B. the Congress of Vienna

C. American unification

D. the French Revolution

92

What was the impact of the Middle East oil embargo on Texas during the 1970s?

A. The Texas economy suffered as those in the oil industry lost their jobs.

B. The Texas petroleum industry grew rapidly to meet the demand for oil in the United States, which could not obtain it from the Middle East.

C. Drop in demand for oil led to diversification into natural gas.

D. Wind power became an important energy source in Texas thanks to its open plains and empty spaces.

93

What contributed to the continued suffering of African Americans in the rural South, even after the end of slavery?

A. sharecropping, which kept slaves in heavy debt, often to their former "masters"

B. the Colored Farmers' Alliance, which was organized to limit slaves' efforts to become independent farmers

C. the Reconstruction Acts, which specifically punished Southern Blacks who did not join the Union army

D. labor unions, which advocated for White workers' rights in factories in urban areas and ignored rural issues

94

A student is researching the Dust Bowl and wants to find out how many Oklahomans left the state for California. Which is the BEST source for her to use?

A. census data

B. personal letters

C. newspaper articles

D. physical artifacts

95

Which of the following is true about Barbara Jordan?

A. She worked in the State Senate for the creation of the Fair Employment Practices Commission.

B. She became the first Black woman governor of Texas.

C. She represented Texas in the United States Senate for several terms.

D. She supported eliminating the minimum wage.

96

How were European empires affected by nationalism in the eighteenth and nineteenth centuries?

A. European empires like the Austro-Hungarian Empire benefitted from nationalism, as Austrians and Hungarians were more loyal to the imperial government.

B. The Austro-Hungarian Empire lost its Balkan territories to the Ottoman Empire, which was perceived to be more tolerant of Muslim minorities.

C. Ethnic groups, driven by nationalism, began to advocate for representation in imperial government.

D. Nationalism threatened empires as ethnic groups began to advocate for their own independent states.

97

Why did the United States invade Afghanistan following the terrorist attacks of September 11, 2001?

A. to defeat the Taliban, who had attacked the United States

B. to defeat Osama bin Laden and al Qaeda, who had attacked the United States

C. to defeat al Qaeda, the government of Afghanistan

D. to defeat Saddam Hussein, who had weapons of mass destruction in Afghanistan

98

Which of the following best describes the Redeemers?

A. They had supported the Confederacy.

B. They supported Radical Republican intervention in Texas.

C. They had left the Democratic Party.

D. They were recent transplants to Texas.

99

A student wants to determine if the newspaper article she is reading is a primary or secondary source. What question should the teacher encourage her to ask?

A. Who wrote it?

B. When was it written?

C. Where is it from?

D. What is it about?

100

NAFTA accomplished which of the following?

A. It opened borders between the US, Canada, and Mexico, allowing for free movement of goods and people between these three countries.

B. It initiated free trade between the US, Mexico, and Canada, facilitating and strengthening trade between these three countries.

C. It created a union similar to the European Union in North America, in which Canada, Mexico, and the US shared similar policy goals and consulted each other on matters of mutual concern.

D. It established common immigration procedures between Mexico, the US, and Canada

Answer Key

1

A. The valuable routes into and through the Red Sea were essential for the British economy and Britain's connections to its colonies in India, East Africa, South Africa, and Australia. The security of those routes was of paramount importance.

2

A. Southern geography and climate lent itself to labor-intensive plantation agriculture, for which the colonists exploited slave labor. Natural harbors in the north fostered urban development, while the land was more appropriate for smaller farms.

3

B. Cabeza de Vaca encountered the Karankawa on the Gulf Coast in the early sixteenth century; the Karankawa were fishers and hunter-gatherers along the coastline.

4

A. Chronology is about the sequence of events, and this activity is developmentally appropriate for kindergarten students.

5

D. The Federalists were the driving force behind a stronger Constitution that would empower the United States federal government. The Anti-Federalists worked to protect state sovereignty and ensured the passage of the Bill of Rights to protect certain rights not explicitly guaranteed in the Constitution itself.

6

C. As a commercial center and well-situated to handle goods arriving in Europe from both the Silk Road and Africa, Venice developed banking institutions that influenced modern banking.

7

D. A semantic web can help students brainstorm ideas. Students could draw a web with "natural resources" in the middle and then different categories of resources and examples in the outer parts of the web.

8

C. Texas was a useful buffer zone, protecting Mexico and the rest of the Spanish empire in the Americas from French and British interests in North America. A threat to Texas represented a potential threat to the empire.

9

A. Hispanic residents of the land the United States gained in the Treaty of Guadalupe Hidalgo did not obtain all they were promised; in fact, many lost their property and were not treated equally under the law or in society.

10

C. The Qur'an is the holy book of Islam; it is believed that the book was transmitted directly from God to Muhammad.

11

A. The Democratic-Republicans, descended from the Anti-Federalists, focused on agrarian issues and opposed a strong federal government and urban business interests.

12

A. Widespread uprisings made it difficult for Houston to consolidate one army.

13

B. The continental—indeed, global—impact of the Black Death destabilized much of Europe.

14

C. Project-based learning (PBL) engages students in projects with a real-world application.

ANSWER KEY 273

15

B. The Compromise of 1850 admitted California as a free state; however, it strengthened the Fugitive Slave Act. The legalization of slavery in Utah and New Mexico would be decided by the voters.

16

A. The representatives called for separation from Coahuila, an end to restrictions on slavery in Texas, and more protection from the Apache and Comanche.

17

C. Violence broke out over the question of legalizing slavery in Kansas, where it had previously been prohibited.

18

D. The Peloponnesian War was between the major Greek powers.

19

D. The Missouri Compromise prohibited slavery north of the thirty-sixth parallel in new US territories, permitting slavery in Missouri.

20

B. Maps promote spatial thinking skills by showing places in relation to each other.

21

A. The Lincoln-Douglas debates showed how divided the country was over slavery.

22

A. This illustrates an economics concept (supply and demand) and leverages technology to help students visualize the information.

23

C. Ferguson campaigned in rural areas and presided over improvements in infrastructure and education (in addition to scandal).

24

C. Under the Qin Dynasty, the emperor centralized Chinese bureaucracy and standardized weights and measures in order to centralize and consolidate imperial power.

25

A. Public paranoia over communism was widespread, and many public figures were accused of being communist.

26

B. The first major north-south railroad was built through Dallas; there was no need to drive cattle north as they could be transported by rail.

27

B. President Carter's inability to resolve the crisis helped propel Ronald Reagan to victory in the 1980 presidential election; Reagan took an aggressive stance against the Soviet Union and escalated the arms race, intensifying the Cold War throughout the 1980s.

28

B. Russia expanded to the east, taking control of Siberia. Russia also extended westward to an extent, controlling part of Eastern Europe.

29

B. The Great Society was rooted in both Johnson's War on Poverty and liberalism—the belief that government programs should support those in need (and that the US should be active in fighting communism overseas).

30

D. Even though the peoples living under Byzantine and Persian rule were not Muslim or Arab, the Islamic tradition of tolerance toward the "People of the Book" and, to an extent, Zoroastrians, made them more acceptable rulers than the oppressive and disorganized collapsing regimes; furthermore, many people in the region spoke Arabic, which made it easier to accept Arab rule.

31

D. Cesar Chavez and the United Farm Workers (UFW) advocated for the rights of Mexican and Mexican-American farmworkers in the US, who were often disadvantaged and treated poorly; moreover, the activism of the UFW set a precedent for later advocacy in support of Hispanic Americans.

32

A. Since the 1990s, Hispanic and African American populations in Texas have been growing.

33

D. Improvements in navigation and shipping allowed speedier transport of goods from Asia to Europe.

Answer Key 275

34

C. The United States led peace talks to resolve conflict in Bosnia and the former Yugoslavia as well as in Northern Ireland.

35

A. One limitation of physical artifacts is that the researcher may not be able to determine with certainty how an object was used by a civilization.

36

B. Borders did not take into account history or ethnic groups; installed rulers did not necessarily have legitimacy in the eyes of the people, leading to political instability and violence.

37

A. The invasion and occupation of Iraq was part of the War on Terror and in accordance with President Bush's doctrine of preemption—that the US should preempt terrorist attacks by attacking threats first. Erroneous beliefs that Saddam Hussein had weapons of mass destruction and was linked to al Qaeda were reasons for the invasion.

38

D. Britain gained economic and commercial privileges in China it didn't previously have, including gaining Hong Kong, freedom of movement in China, and access to ports.

39

B. Jackson was extremely popular among the lower classes and rural farmers of the South. Changing voting laws to allow dispossessed white males to vote expanded the electorate, giving him a huge advantage.

40

C. King Hammurabi's code meted out justice on an equal basis ("an eye for an eye, a tooth for a tooth").

41

C. Labor unions sought improved working conditions, not the overthrow of capitalism.

42

C. Historiography reflects how historians have recorded history and how this has evolved.

43

D. The Atlantic Charter embodied the shared vision of the United States and Great Britain for the postwar world.

44

D. Early Spanish expeditions in Texas were driven by the search for gold.

45

B. The United States fought North Korean, Soviet- and Chinese-supported communists in Korea, preventing them from establishing an entirely communist Korea and establishing a capitalist, western-allied South Korea.

46

C. Henry Gonzalez filibustered state efforts to circumvent federal civil rights legislation. He supported desegregation. Barbara Jordan was famous for her role in the Watergate hearings, not Henry Gonzalez. Gonzales was never governor.

47

B. Conservatives believe in low taxes to boost business.

48

D. Charlemagne was Frankish and stabilized parts of Western and Central Europe; most of the Carolingian Empire eventually became France.

49

C. Having led the coalition that defeated Iraq in the 1991 Gulf War, the United States proved its position as the sole superpower following the end of the Cold War with the collapse of the Soviet Union.

50

D. The National Archives contain primary-source materials such as advertisements, letters, photographs, and texts of the period.

51

C. The teaching that the moral codes provided by God in the Ten Commandments apply to all, including slaves, is an important tent of Judaism.

52

C. The colonial military did have strong leaders, and an intimate knowledge of the terrain, with many having been born there.

Answer Key

53

A. The caste system is a social hierarchy rooted in religious tradition. It is not possible to change the caste into which one is born.

54

C. Filibuster settlers were Anglo settlers who illegally came to Texas in search of opportunity.

55

C. As a governing document, the Mayflower Compact was notable in that it provided for governance with the consent of the governed, a departure from British rule.

56

A. Developing agricultural practices in the Neolithic Era allowed humans to establish settled societies sustained by reliable food sources.

57

A. Americans maintained victory gardens during WWI and WWII to help the war effort by producing their own food.

58

A. The New Deal encompassed programs providing immediate relief for impoverished Americans, long-term (not short-term) development projects, and permanent (not temporary) financial reforms to prevent a repeat of the Great Depression.

59

C. Rich in land, Texas attracted settlers who would contribute to economic development.

60

B. Martin Luther and his followers opposed corruption in the Catholic Church and wanted changes.

61

D. The Thirteenth Amendment abolished slavery; the Fourteenth Amendment promised equal protection under the law to all US citizens; the Fifteenth Amendment ensured that (male) African Americans and former slaves could vote.

62

D. The Treaty of Westphalia marked the end of the Thirty Years' War. It is considered the foundation of modern international relations and created the model for international politics worldwide.

63

C. Following the extreme tensions between the two countries, the United States and the Soviet Union improved dialogue in the early 1960s, leading to a period of détente.

64

B. Abolitionist European powers were unwilling to support the South economically due to the Confederacy's stance on slavery.

65

C. The Civil Rights Act of 1964 made segregation illegal.

66

B. The main factors in post-WWI German economic collapse are all addressed here.

67

B. The new constitution specifically affirmed the legality of slavery in Texas.

68

A. The British fought the Boer War to maintain control of South Africa from the Boers, or Afrikaners, the descendants of Dutch settlers in the region (who themselves had taken control of territory from Africans already living there).

69

D. The Emancipation Proclamation freed the slaves in the Confederacy.

70

D. Enslaved people were forced to do work on cotton and sugar plantations; they did not run or own them independently. The transatlantic slave trade began long before industrialization.

71

C. This question requires an analysis beyond merely recalling facts or solving a math problem. Students are analyzing the possible benefits behind the choices of historical actors.

Answer Key 279

72

A. By the Neolithic Era, other hominids had died out.

73

B. The Social Security Act was part of the New Deal.

74

C. In exchange for giving up claims to land that would become New Mexico and for $10 million, Texas accepted its present-day borders as part of the Compromise of 1850.

75

C. Augustus Caesar was the ruler during this time of stability.

76

B. The Nineteenth Amendment allowed women to vote; it was ratified in 1920.

77

D. The Constitution of 1868 was written by Republicans during Reconstruction. It strengthened state government; it also represented what Democrats felt to be interference and overreach by "carpetbaggers" and Radical Republicans.

78

B. The Meiji Restoration was a period of industrialization and westernization in Japan.

79

B. In early exploration of North America, European colonists were interested in spreading Christianity, extracting tribute and labor from Native Americans, and establishing trade agreements; however, they did not intentionally spread disease.

80

D. Central Texas cotton production relied on sharecropping.

81

D. The Soviet establishment became increasingly alarmed at Maoist interpretations of communism, which differed from Marxism-Leninism.

82

D. An exit ticket is a formative assessment, or an intermediate check on student understanding, before the summative assessment.

83

B. Hogg prosecuted railroads that limited unprofitable service. He also sued insurance companies on behalf of the state. As governor, Hogg would support Jim Crow laws.

84

B. While there were many causes of the war, two main causes were the explosion of a US ship and yellow journalism.

85

B. The Hittites were skilled charioteers and early pioneers of iron weaponry.

86

D. Tejanos were viewed with suspicion by Anglos, particularly Anglo-American immigrants. Despite their legal standing, Tejanos lived as second-class citizens.

87

B. The Gulf of Tonkin Resolution gave the president power to commit military troops in Vietnam without Congressional authorization.

88

D. The Hundred Years' War was really an ongoing conflict between different European ethnic groups (mainly, the French and the English).

89

B. The C3 standards cover the domains of civics, economics, geography, and history.

90

B. The Civil War devastated the South's economy due to infrastructural damage and international isolation.

91

A. The Congress of Vienna followed the Napoleonic Wars; it was a meeting of European powers to determine how to manage Europe. American unification is unrelated. The French Revolution happened in 1789. Italy wanted unification.

Answer Key

92

B. Texas became a major source for petroleum, boosting the state's economy and enriching many Texans in the energy industry.

93

A. Sharecropping perpetuated racial inequality in the South.

94

A. Census data would show how many people lived in each state during the Dust Bowl era.

95

A. As state senator, Barbara Jordan lobbied for the creation of the Fair Employment Practices Commission. She supported a minimum wage, and eventually represented Texas in the House of Representatives.

96

D. Nationalism triggered independence movements and advocacy.

97

B. Neutralizing Osama bin Laden and his network—al Qaeda—was the stated objective for the invasion of Afghanistan.

98

A. The Redeemers were generally former supporters of the Confederacy. Largely Democrats, the Redeemers wanted to "redeem" Texas from outside (generally Radical Republican) intervention.

99

B. A newspaper article may be a primary source if it reports on events or opinions of the time, but it may also be a secondary source if it presents information about a historical event through the lens of the present.

100

B. The North American Free Trade Agreement (NAFTA) is a free trade agreement among the US, Mexico, and Canada.

Access additional materials at:
www.cirrustestprep.com/texes-history-online-resources

www.ingramcontent.com/pod-product-compliance
Lightning Source LLC
Chambersburg PA
CBHW081150290426
44108CB00018B/2504